KEN PRICE

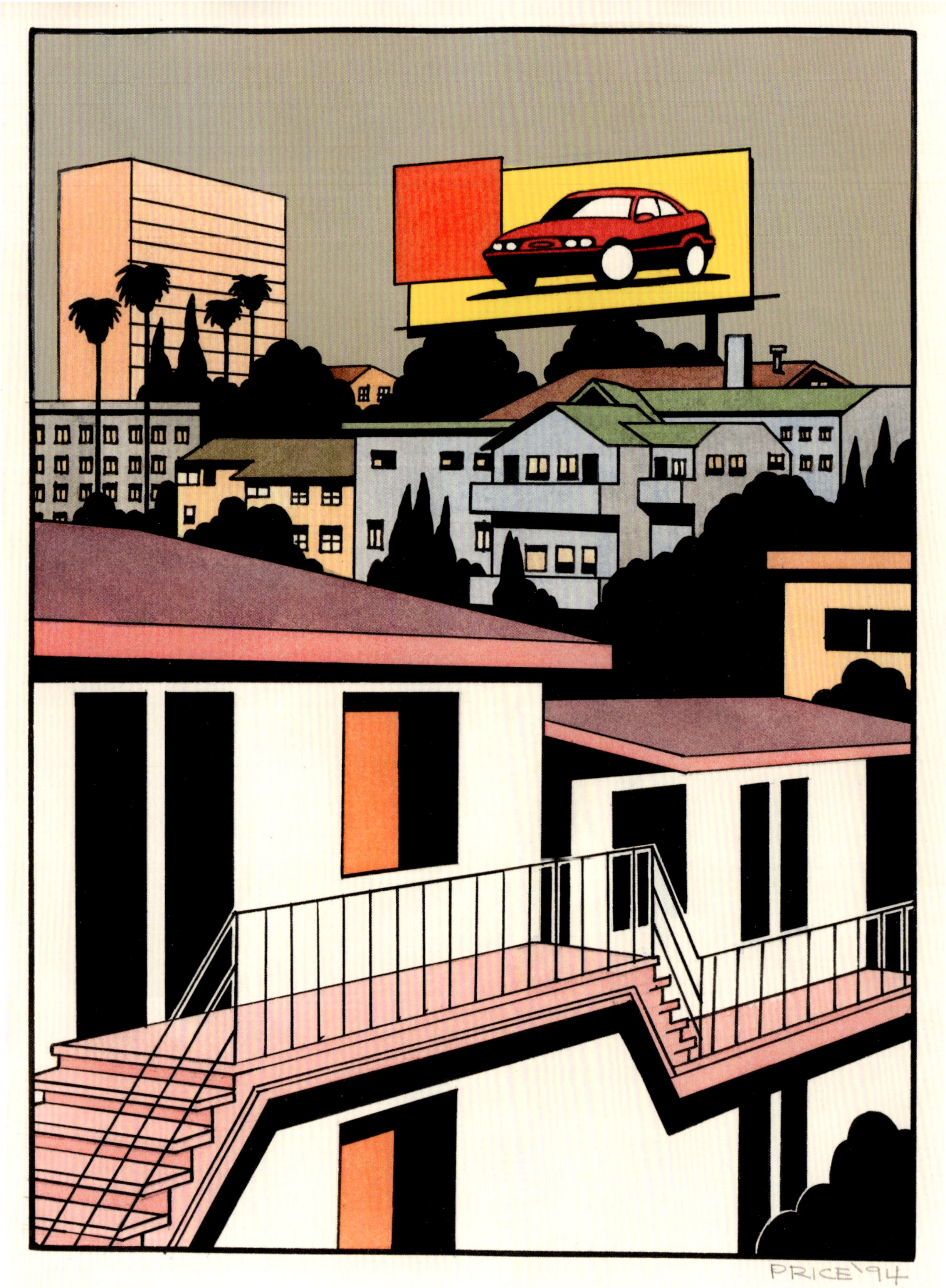

The Capri Apartments, 1994

HEAT WAVE

Charles Bukowski

another one.
this night the people sit drunk or drugged or some of them
sit in front of their tv sets
slapped silly.
some few have air-conditioning.

the neighborhood dogs and cats flop about
waiting for a better time.

and I remember the cars along the freeway today
some of them stalled in the fast lane,
hoods up.

there are more murders in the heat
more domestic arguments.

Los Angeles has been burning for
weeks.

even the desperately lonely have not phoned
and that alone
makes all this almost
worthwhile:

those little mewling voices cooked into
silence
as I listen to the music of a long dead man
written in the 19th
century.

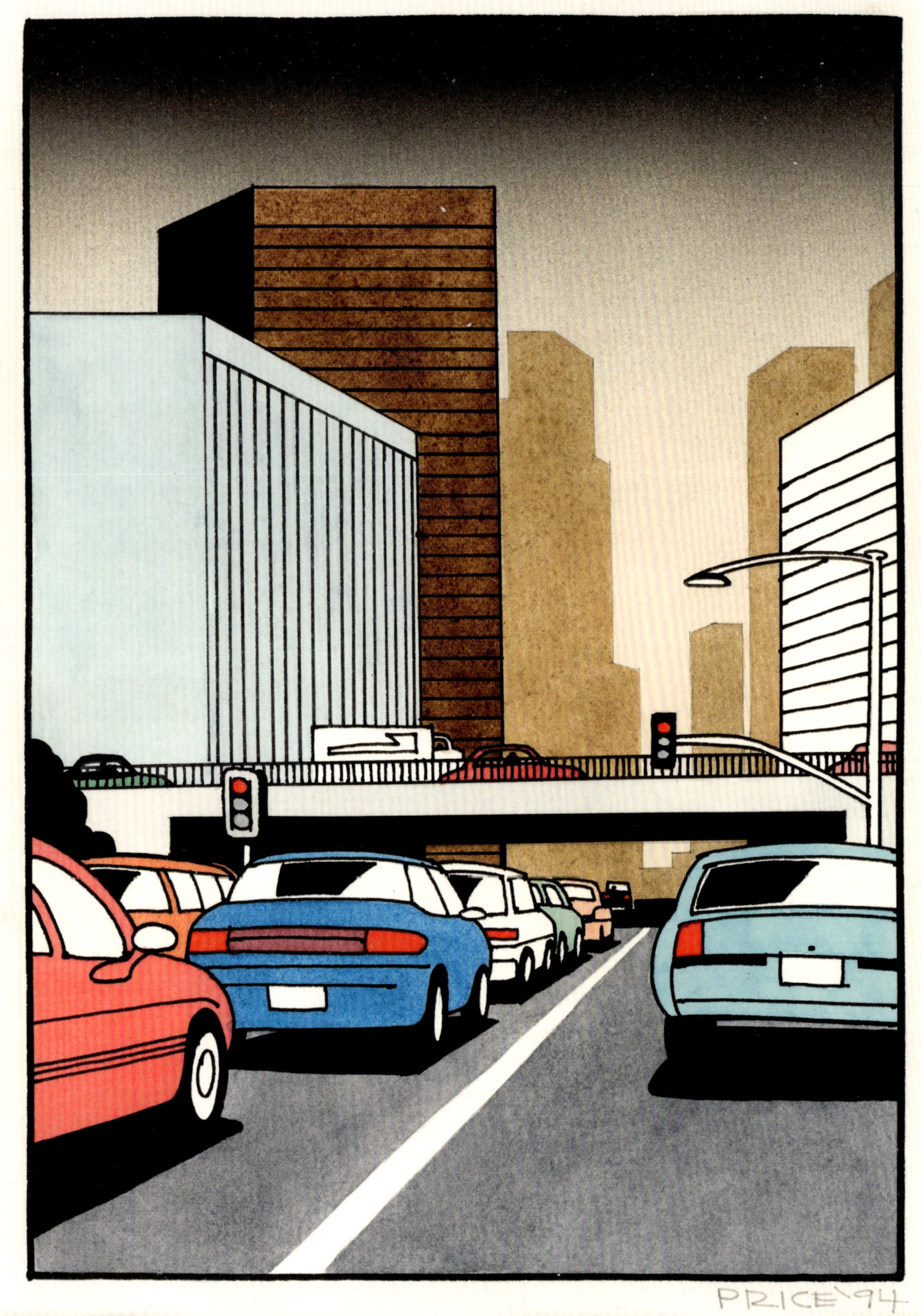

Downtown, 1994

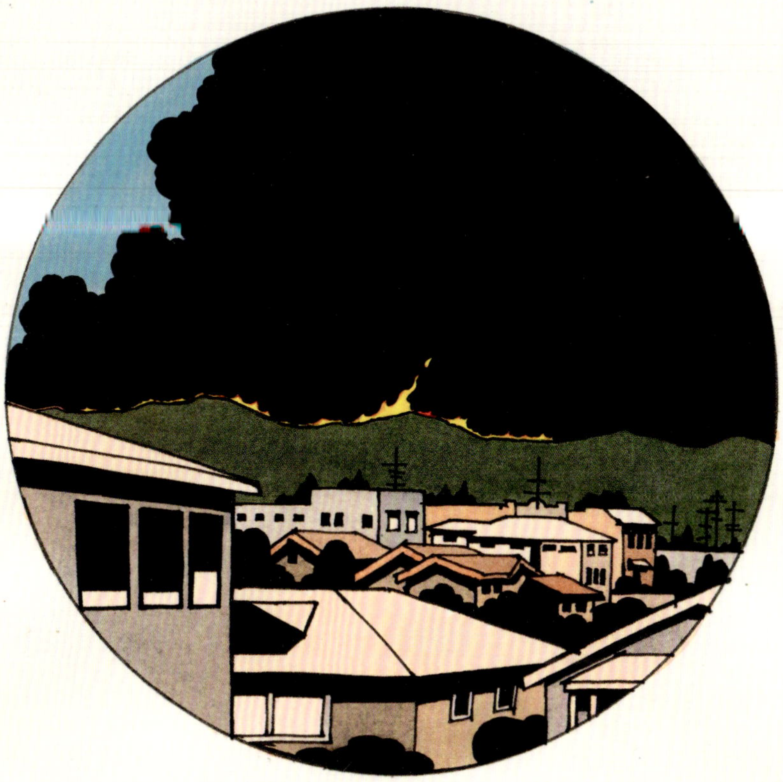

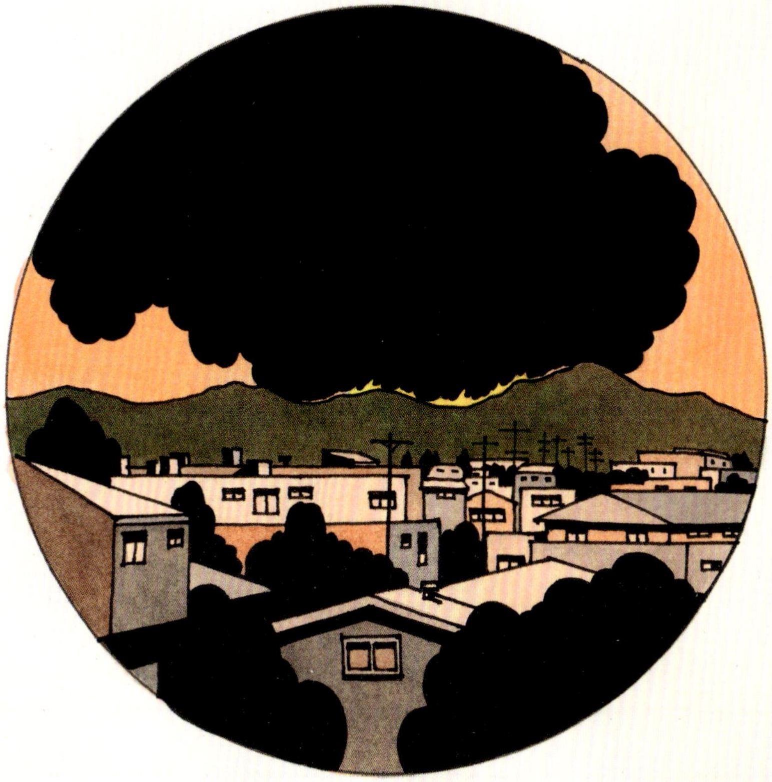

Before the Earthquake, 1994
L.A. Sky, 1994

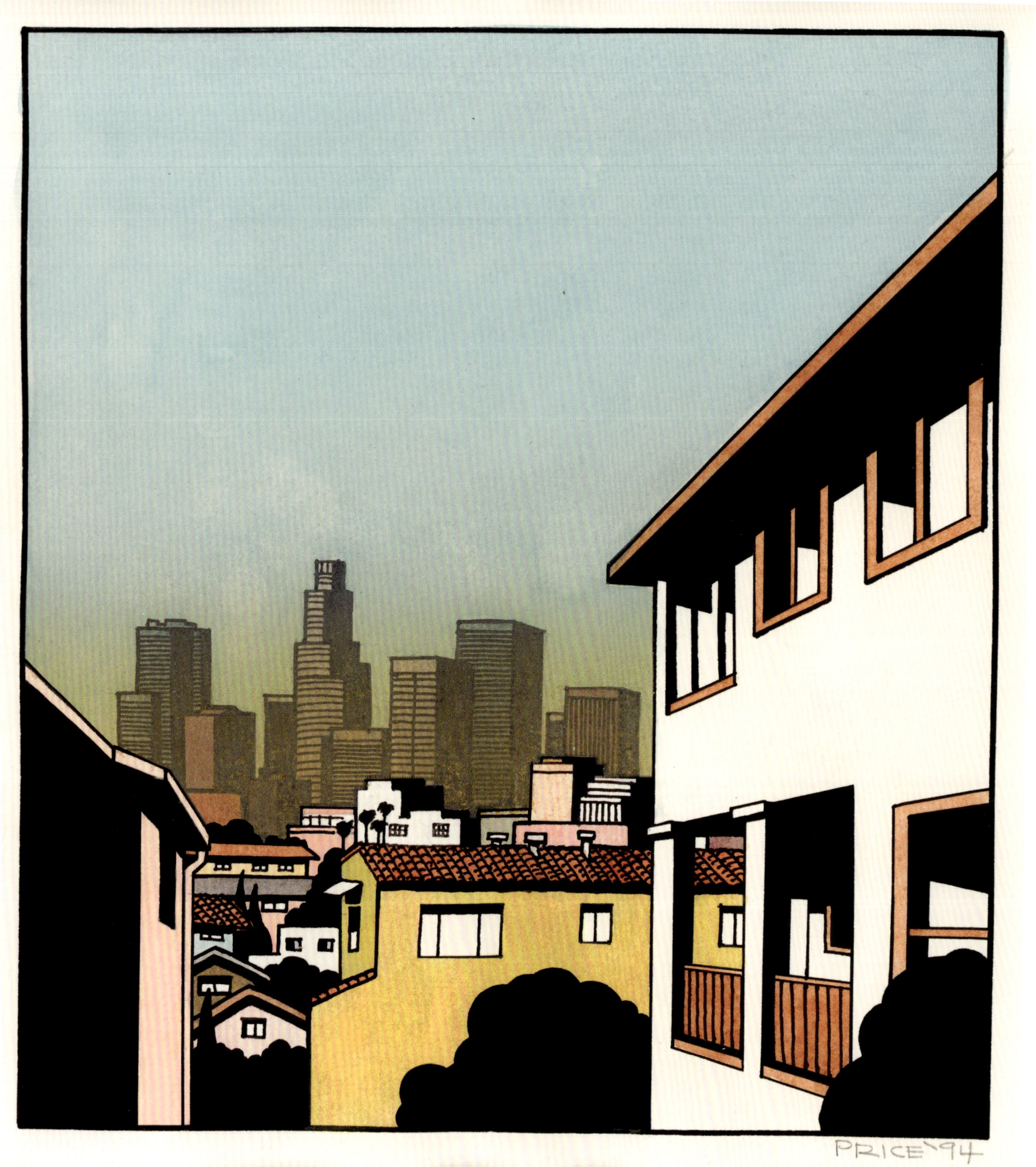

Looking East, 1994

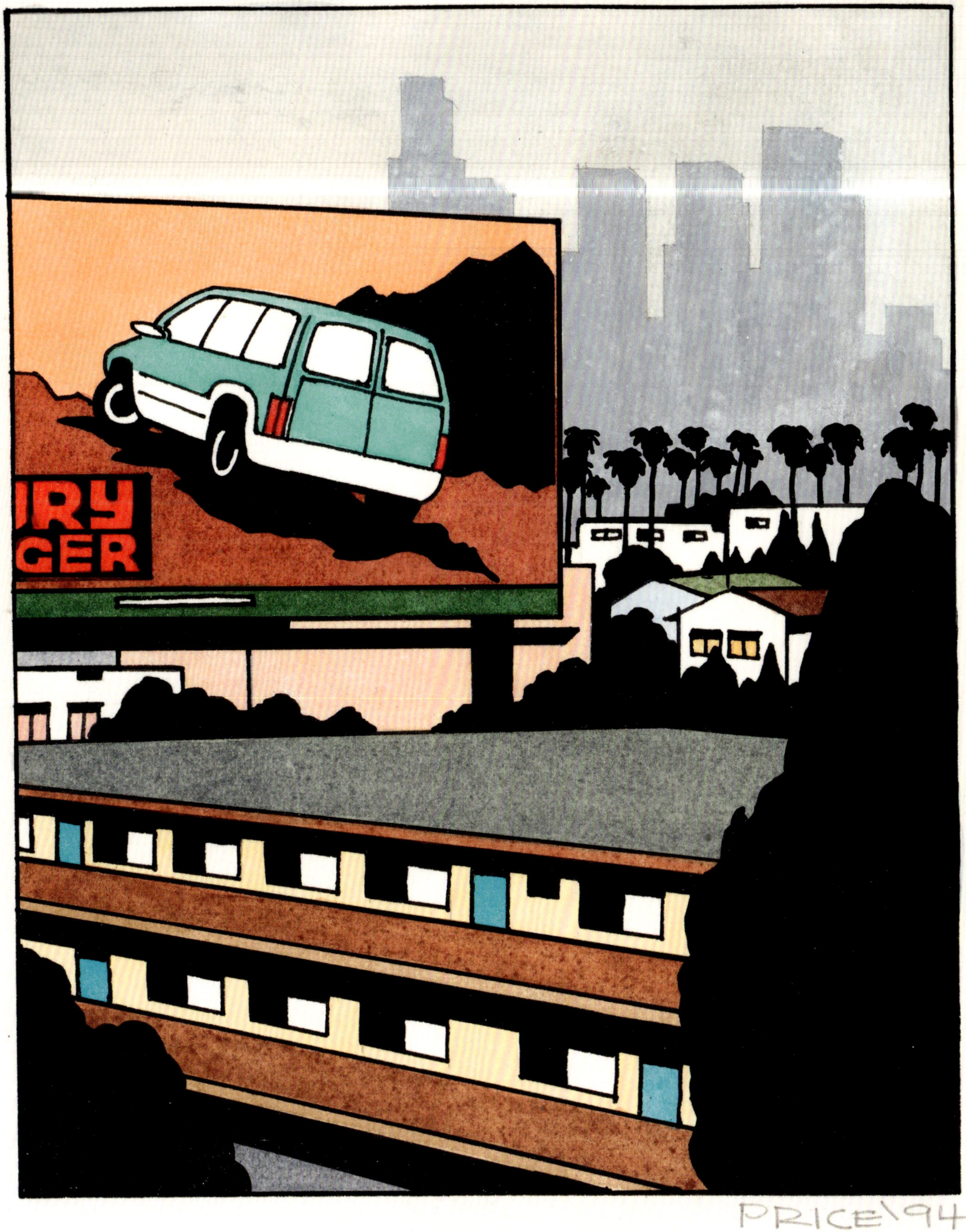

Made in L.A., 1994

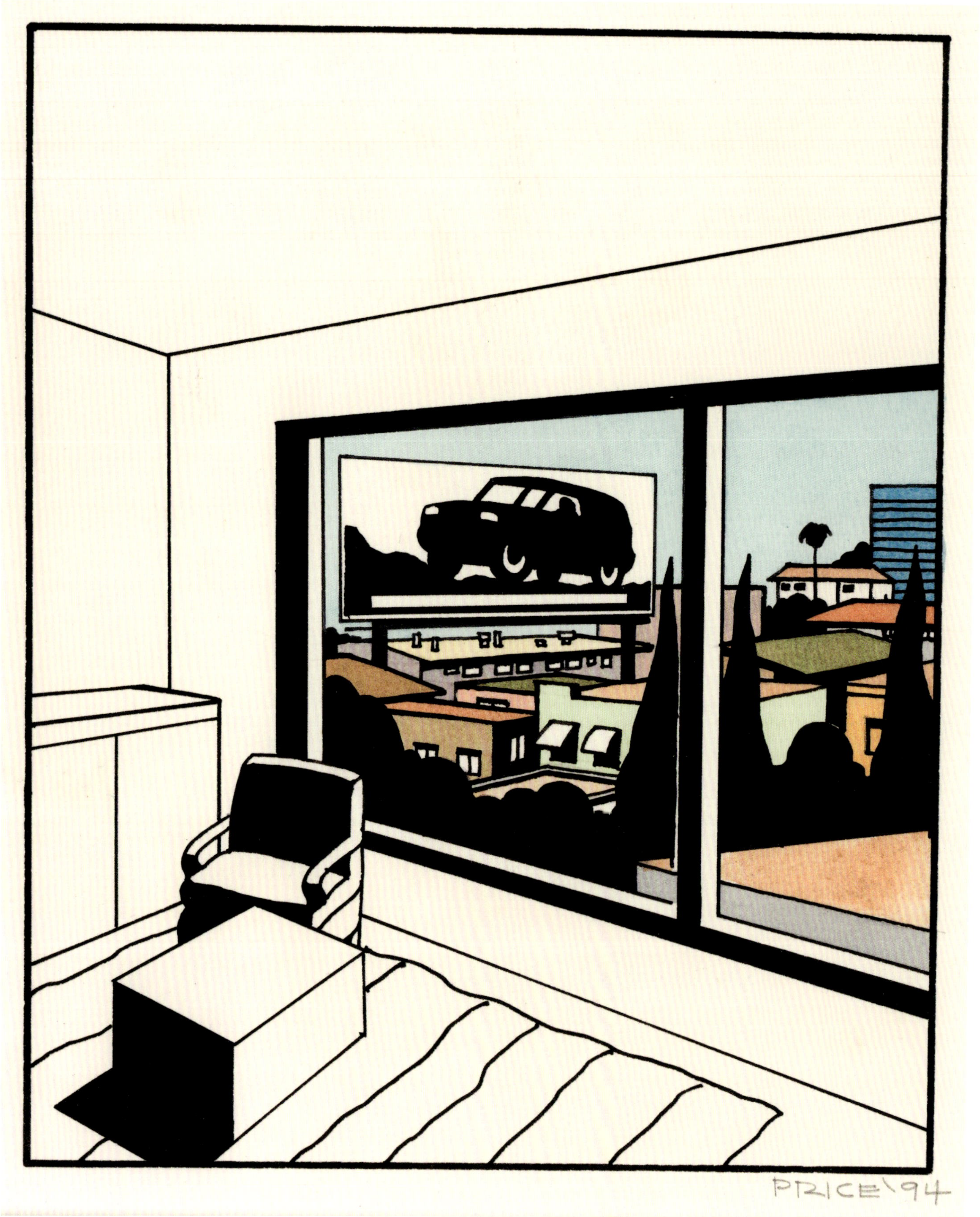

Picture Window, 1994

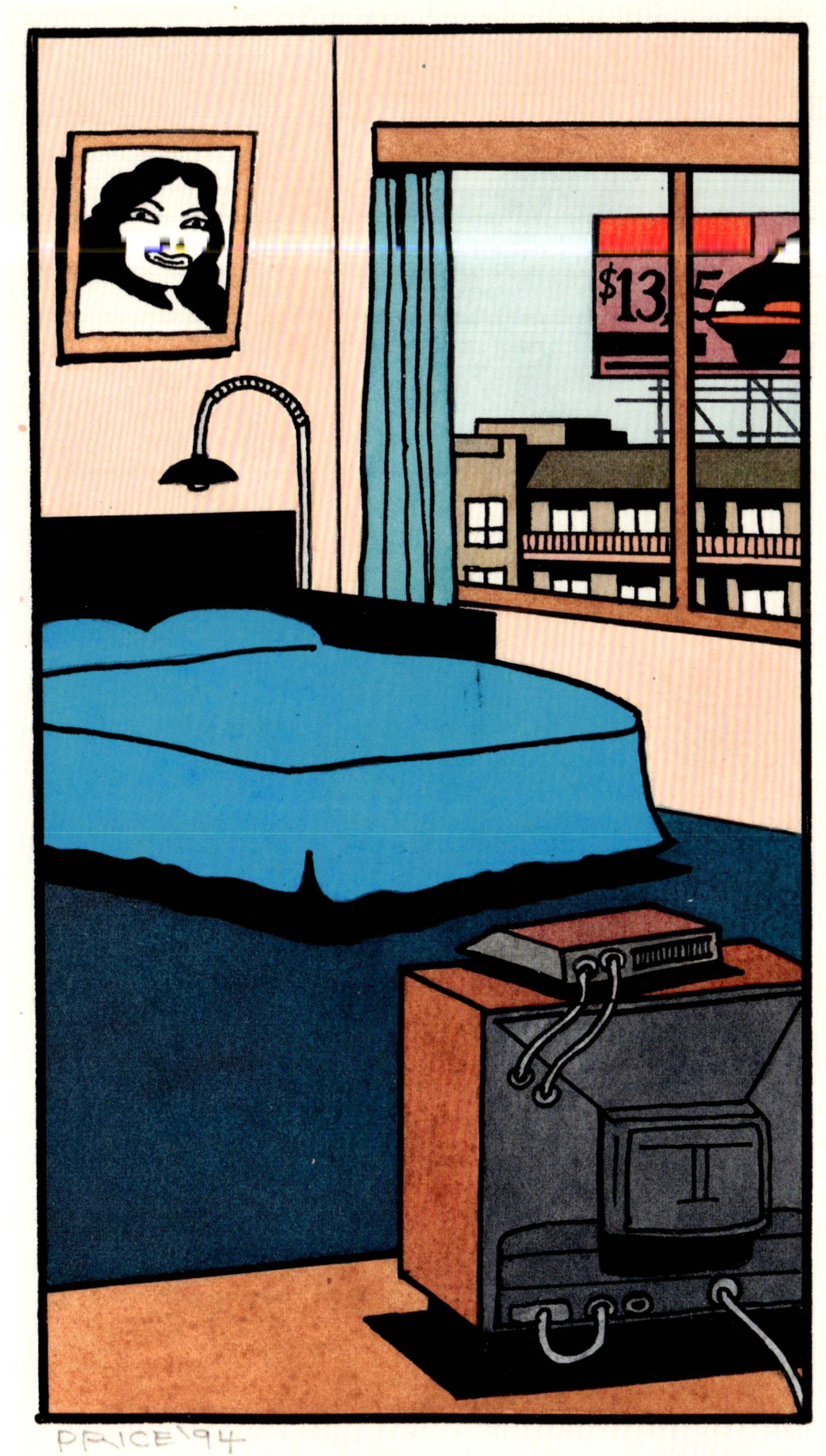

Room 308, 1994

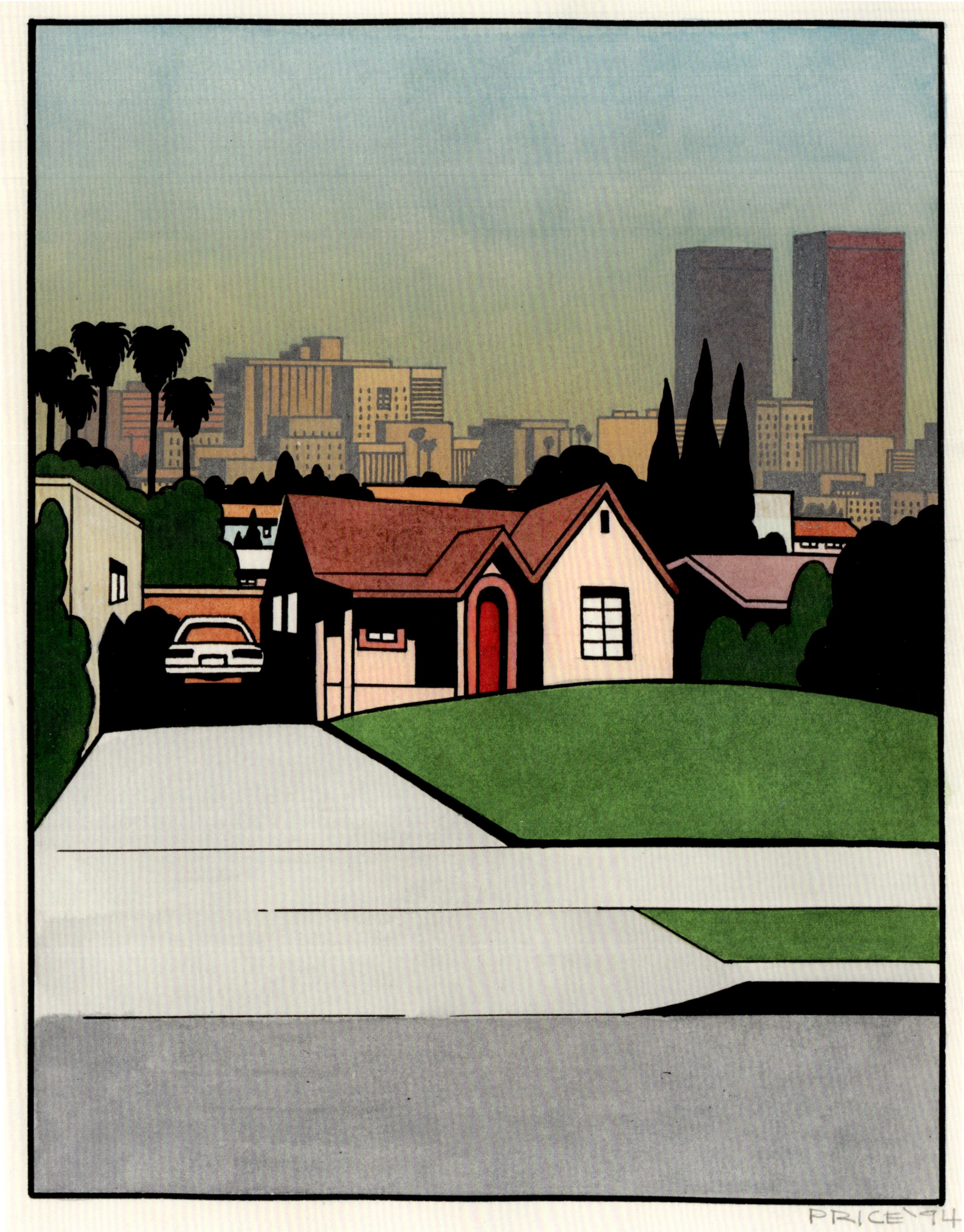

Security, Domesticality, Leisure, 1994

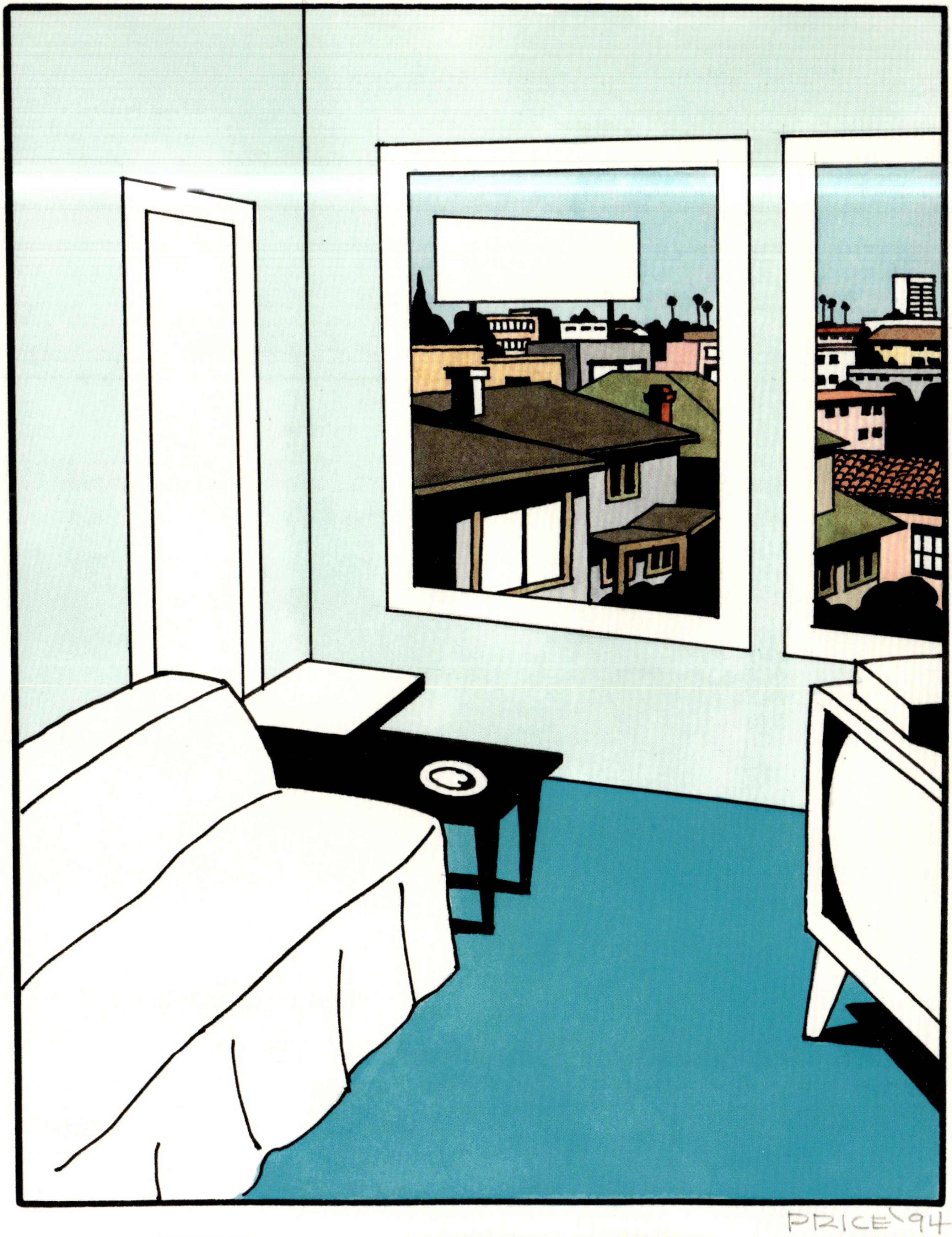

With Everything Turned Off, 1994

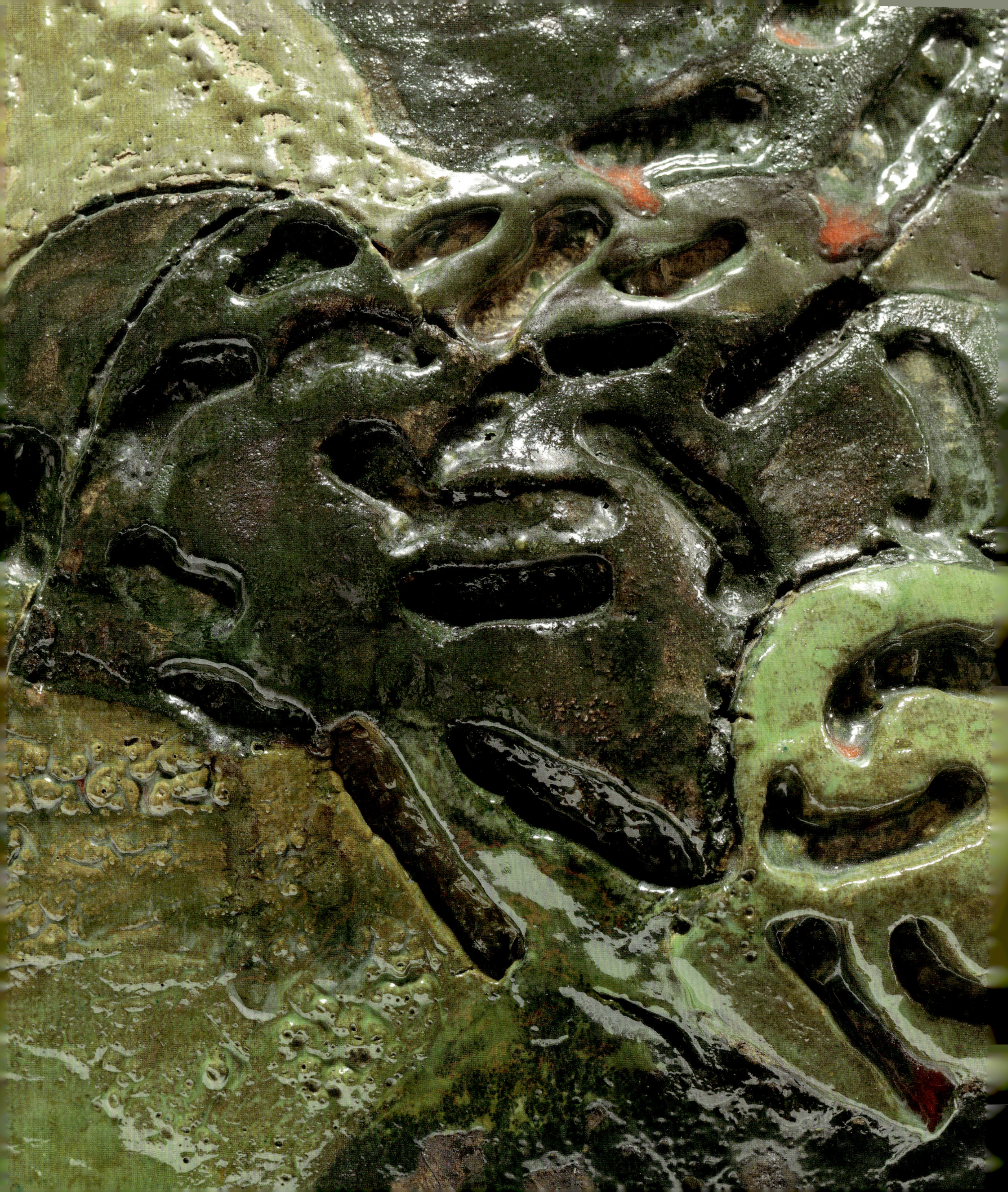

KEN PRICE

A SURVEY OF SCULPTURES AND DRAWINGS

EDITED BY PAUL SCHIMMEL
ESSAY BY SAM THORNE
PHOTOGRAPHY BY FREDRIK NILSEN

DELMONICO BOOKS · PRESTEL
MUNICH · LONDON · NEW YORK

HAUSER & WIRTH PUBLISHERS

WITH THANKS TO JAMES CORCORAN

CONTENTS

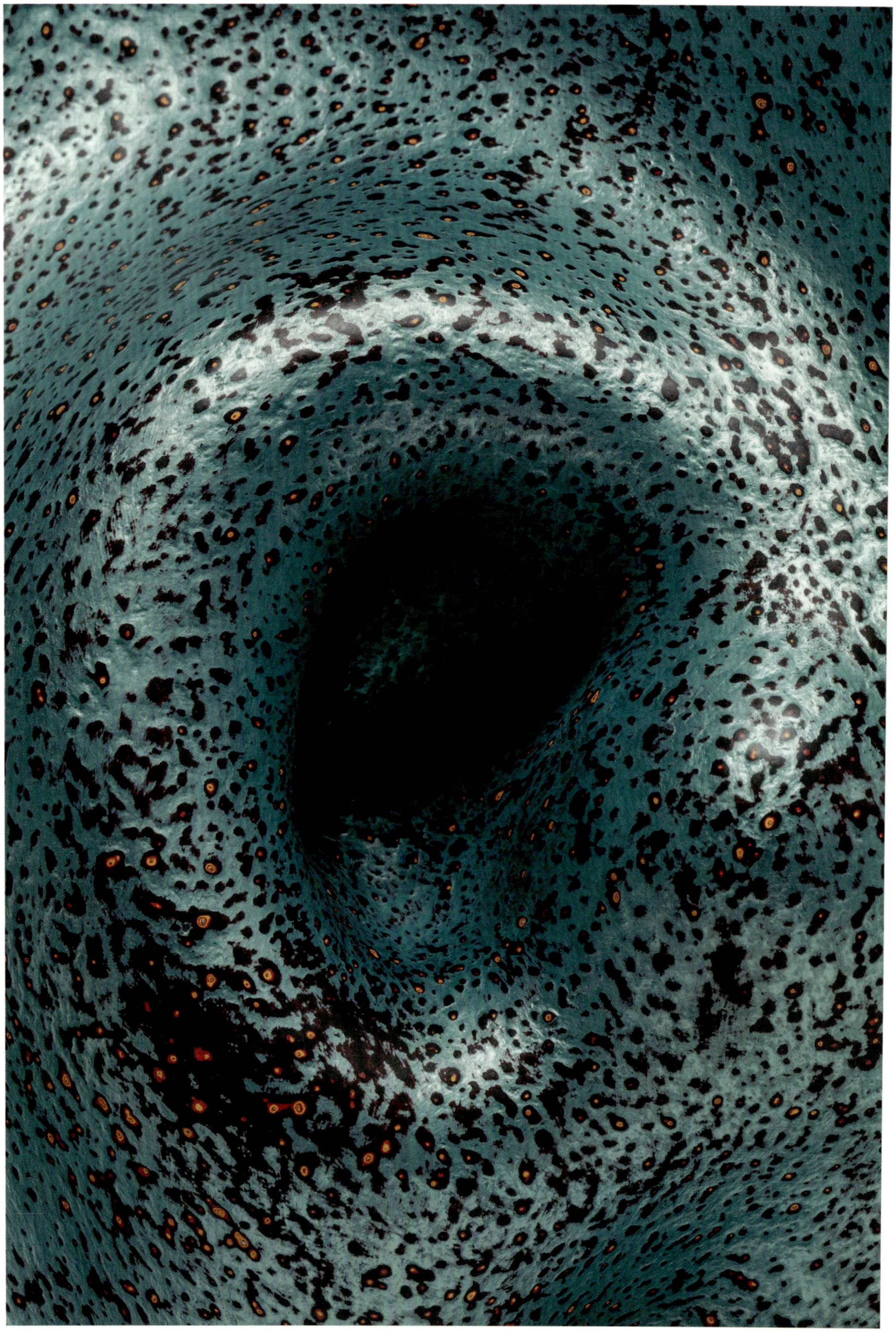

EROTIC BIOMORPHISM
THE WORKS OF KEN PRICE

Paul Schimmel

For over fifty years, the American artist Ken Price (1935–2012) opened up previously unforeseen possibilities for ceramics as sculptural objects. His works simultaneously explore and embody materiality, intimacy, and carnality through their wholly original forms. In addition to his innovative glazing and painting techniques, Price's constantly evolving formats—from traditional cups and vessels to the biomorphic *Eggs* and *Mounds*, from geometric constructions to curvy, lumpy abstractions—prompted a renewed interest in ceramics as a contemporary art form.

Central to Price's development and maturation as an artist was his relationship with the city of Los Angeles as a creative center. It was certainly fortuitous that Los Angeles had so many art schools for Price, who grew up as a surfer and beach bum in Santa Monica and Pacific Palisades, to take advantage of; at various times, he attended the Chouinard Art Institute, the Otis Art Institute, and Santa Monica City College. Also formative for his work were his close friendships with painters and sculptors such as Ed Ruscha, Joe Goode, Edward Kienholz, John Altoon, Wallace Berman, and Billy Al Bengston. His conversations with these artist peers about politics, sexuality, and revolutionary materials in art, as well as the privileged connection they afforded him to the West Coast idioms of assemblage, Pop, figuration, and abstraction, propelled his practice from an early age. While still in his twenties, he exhibited at Kienholz's Ferus Gallery; by 1963, Price's work had been featured on the cover of *Artforum*, and he was being championed in a burgeoning art scene that included the Pasadena Art Museum, the Los Angeles County Museum of Art, and, most significantly, the activities and exhibitions generated by the aforementioned artists, who remained central to both his work and his life.

At the same time, in his artistic concerns, Price operated in a world apart from his peers. As he understood his work, "its purpose is strictly for pleasure."[1] Indeed, the pleasurableness of his objects—their sensuous forms and smooth, colorful surfaces—is their through line, from the early 1960s until the artist's death in 2012. His ceramics embody the sacred and the profane; the earliest works, the *Eggs* and *Mounds* (see p. 53), are handheld, biomorphic forms that reference the moment of conception and creation, birth, and regeneration. Later works feature

FIG. 1. *Ghosted* (detail; see p. 107), 1998. Fired and painted clay, 44.5 × 41.9 × 25.4 cm (17½ × 16½ × 10 in.)

orifices of various sizes, reminiscent of female genitalia, and finger-like tendrils that evolve into bulbous, globular shapes resembling penises or breasts. Intimate, soft, and geometric, the works have a psychological intensity that is erotic but not explicitly sexual. As the curator Douglas Dreishpoon observed, "Price never shied away from drawing overtly erotic images or from making abstract sculpture with robust sensuality. 'I think my work is fairly erotic, all of it, but never intentionally except in the erotic drawings.'"[2]

Sex and procreation were an important source of inspiration for Price. Much has been said about the influence of traditional Japanese ceramics on his work, including by Price himself, who referred to the Momoyama period (1573–1615) as "the ultimate achievement in the history of pottery . . . [which] influenced my sense of scale and my sense of what I want from a piece of pottery."[3] It is worth remembering that eroticism, too, has a long history in Japanese art. Price's interest in European modernism also drove various aspects of his oeuvre, from the biomorphic abstractions of Constantin Brancusi and Jean Arp, which he would have seen in the Norton Simon Museum collection, to Joan Miró and the long history of Surrealist and Abstract Surrealist exhibitions presented at the Pasadena Art Museum. The work of the American proto-Abstract Expressionist Arshile Gorky, whom Price greatly admired, exposed him to the extraordinary iconography and symbolism of birth and renewal, as did the sculptures of Alberto Giacometti, Louise Bourgeois, and, most notably, the German artist Hans Bellmer, with his fetishistic representations of the nude female body.

Price's relationship to the erotic in his own work was complex. Along with many of his Los Angeles artist peers, he advocated for the individual's right to free expression and remonstrated against censorship, although his own confrontations with the Los Angeles Police Department were few—the LAPD was hard pressed to charge him with obscenity, given the predominantly abstract nature of what he exhibited. But Price also declined two opportunities that would have focused, overtly and in public, on eroticism in his work. His 1978 solo show at the Los Angeles County Museum of Art, built around the project *Happy's Curios*, which had occupied his mental, emotional, and financial resources for the previous six years, was meant to have a pointedly erotic centerpiece, but the artist chose not to include it at the last minute. It is unclear whether this reversal came out of a sense of modesty, a concern about staging a repeat of his buddy Ed Kienholz's run-in with the Los Angeles County Board of Supervisors over *Back Seat Dodge '38* (1964) in 1966, or a fear that the centerpiece might cause a sensation that would detract from the overall exhibition. Much later, just before the artist's death, as he was preparing for a retrospective of his works on paper organized by the Albright-Knox Art Gallery in Buffalo, he declined to include a selection of his erotic drawings, preferring to reserve them for a future exhibition—one that might situate them in the broader context of his work as a sculptor and a painter. "I've only shown the [erotic drawings] a couple of times," he told Joan Simon in a 1980 interview for *Art in America*. "I pretty much make them for my own amusement. In my erotic drawings, I'm trying to celebrate a part of life that I really enjoy. They're private drawings and I don't care whether or not they're accepted. They represent a great freedom to me."[4]

The few times I visited Price's studio, I was struck by the palpable gratification he derived from the activity of making art. It was thrilling to watch him add, by hand, layer upon layer of clay or paint to bring to life his fleshy, organic miniature monuments. The technical challenges of making ceramics—the shaping, the firing, and, especially, the glazing—were outweighed by the joy he took in the material itself and in the act of reconciling subject with form. Through his work, he explored the intimacy of touch, the pleasure of shaping forms to their paths of least resistance, and the transformative potential of color. As both a painter and a ceramicist, Price, with his nuanced understanding of the properties of paint and glaze, of their layering and application, was able to produce works that bridge the Color Field paintings of Altoon and Larry Poons with Gerhard Richter's abstractions of the 1980s. Indeed, Price's legacy belongs less with the Ferus generation of artists and his closest friends than with a younger generation of artists, such as Liz Larner and Sterling Ruby. In an age of fabricators, studio assistants, and digital reproductions, there is nothing that provokes a greater erotic pleasure than the evidence of touch itself—something you feel every time you see a sculpture by Ken Price.

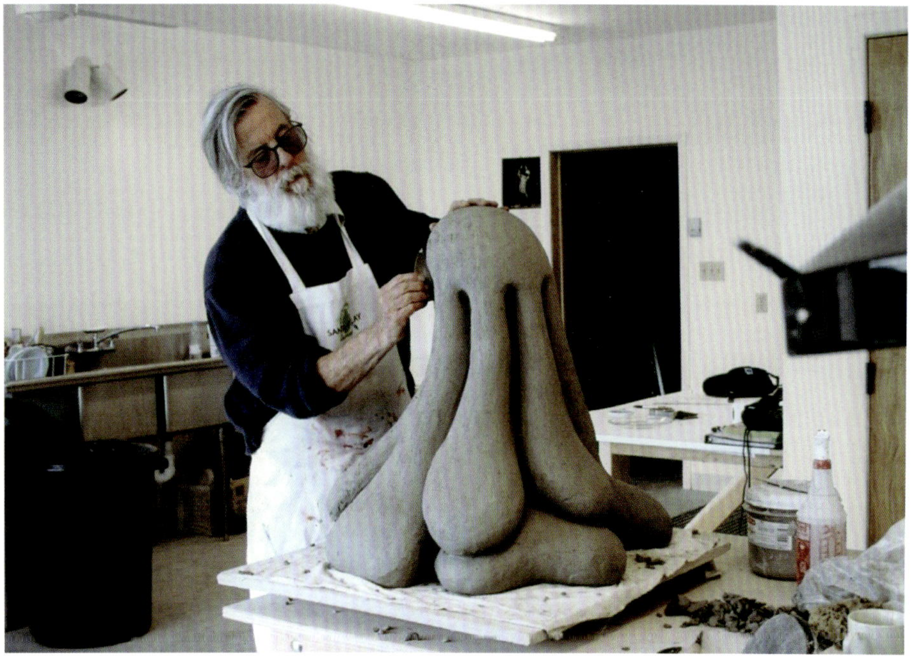

LIVES OF THEIR OWN
KEN PRICE'S SCULPTURES AND WORKS ON PAPER

Sam Thorne

When Peter Voulkos relocated from Montana to Los Angeles in 1954, "clay as an art medium was dead and buried," his student Ken Price noted more than fifty years later.[1] Yet, by the end of the decade, a seismic shift had occurred. This would constitute, as John Coplans, one of the founders of *Artforum*, was quick to realize, "the beginnings of a solid core of development that was to lead to the most adventurous painting and sculpture in California."[2]

Only thirty years old, Voulkos had already taught at Black Mountain College in North Carolina and had crossed paths with the master potters Bernard Leach and Shōji Hamada in Montana, even kicking the wheel for the latter. After moving to Los Angeles, he quickly established the hugely influential ceramics department at the Los Angeles County Art Institute (renamed the Otis Art Institute in 1961). Voulkos and his cohort of Otis students—among them, Price, his close friend Billy Al Bengston, and John Mason, Michael Frimkess, Paul Soldner, and Henry Takemoto—rerouted the "craft" of ceramics, forcibly dislodging it from the potter's wheel. In so doing, they produced a new kind of ceramic sculpture in which slab building, denting, and cracking usurped wheel throwing and careful glazing.[3] Otis became synonymous with the California ceramics revolution.

Although this period and this cohort were important for Price, he was already embarking on his own route, making his own way. While his mentor's towering sculptures were frequently regarded as a West Coast retort to Abstract Expressionism, Price's works were jewel-like and intimate, polymorphic and polychromatic. (He sometimes joked that he couldn't compete with Voulkos's enormous hands, so he relied instead on delicate gestures.) It is also important to recognize Price's evolution directly before and after his time at Otis. Earlier in the decade, as an undergraduate at the University of Southern California, in Los Angeles, he had been introduced to the zoological laboratory, where he became fixated on primary life forms and made a number of ultraprecise drawings (earlier still, he had been a cartoonist for his high school newspaper). Price's sculptures, particularly those of the 1960s and 1970s, exhibit a special affinity for small creatures; taken together, they are a menagerie of turtles, snails, frogs, and lizards (see p. 60). This joy-filled liveliness, this feeling for sculptural forms with lives of their own, was noted early

FIG. 2. Ken Price in 2004 at his studio in Taos, New Mexico

on. In a short *Artforum* profile published in 1963, before the magazine had even moved to Los Angeles from San Francisco, one critic concluded, "Perhaps like the geometric redness of the Black Widow's belly or the burning rings of the Coral Snake, these objects announce their intent to survive."[4]

After a brief stint in the army, having left Otis without a degree, Price enrolled in the highly technical graduate program of the New York State College of Ceramics at Alfred University, in western New York State. There, he hoped to develop brightly colored glazes at a considerable distance from the potent influence of Voulkos, who had little time for such technicalities. On finishing at Alfred with a master's degree in 1959, Price returned to Los Angeles. He was not yet twenty-five years old but already possessed a wealth of experience and tutelage from a number of different schools. Reflecting on this period over three decades later, Price wrote, "We've been cited as the people who broke away from the crafts hierarchy and substituted so-called freedom! Actually, we were a group of people who were committed to clay as a material and wanted to use it in ways that had something to do with our time and place."[5]

Demanding of the Eye

In March 1957, Ferus Gallery, established by the artist Edward Kienholz and the ambitious young curator Walter Hopps, opened at 735a North La Cienega Boulevard in West Hollywood. (Hopps apparently arrived unannounced at Ken Price's studio at three in the morning for their first meeting, and six years later, when Hopps was organizing Marcel Duchamp's first-ever retrospective, at the Pasadena Art Museum, he introduced the septuagenarian Frenchman to the young sculptor; this made for an intriguing rendezvous between the ironic debunker of the "retinal" realm in art and Price, his own generation's foremost advocate of visual pleasure.) Ferus Gallery's inaugural exhibition, *Objects on the New Landscape Demanding of the Eye*, was a curious admixture of painterly fields of color (Richard Diebenkorn, Clyfford Still) and assemblage (Kienholz himself), along with examples of what would come to be identified as the "Finish Fetish" (Craig Kauffman). The title of the exhibition, although a little leaden, is compelling: What kind of

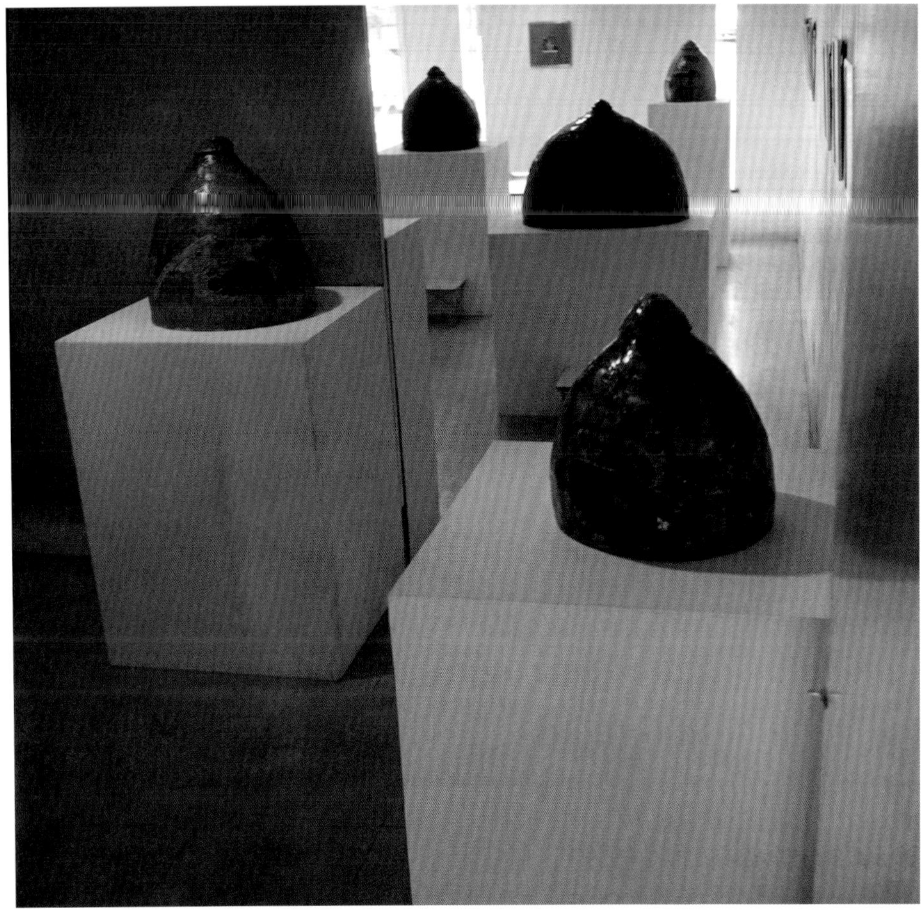

demands do Price's sculptures make on us? How do his works relate to this "new" landscape, in particular, and to the genre of landscape in general? That initial exhibition was soon followed by a more focused show called *Clay Forms*, featuring works by Mason, Soldner, and Jerry Rothman, which demonstrated the gallery's ongoing commitment to ceramic sculpture.

Price had his first exhibition at Ferus, a solo one, in the spring of 1960, when he showed works from two series, *Cups* and *Mounds* (see fig. 3). That debut was followed by two more solo shows—one a year later, when he first showed his *Eggs*, and another in 1964, which introduced his experiments in combining glazes and lacquer with acrylic paint. In these pieces, forms ooze and color seems to erupt from within, then drip down the exterior surface; all the works are titled for the outer rather than the inner colors, as though the antic splurges were completely unplanned.

The early Ferus exhibitions established Price's liking for working serially. Groupings were loose, informal, and affectionate: *Lumps*, *Eggs*, *Bumps*, *Specimens*. As Price would tell the artist Vija Celmins almost fifty years later, "This way an artist can bring a group of pieces through the process together where they inform each other in various ways. By working in series you get a lot more feedback."[6]

FIG. 3. Installation view, Ken Price's solo exhibition at Ferus Gallery, 1960

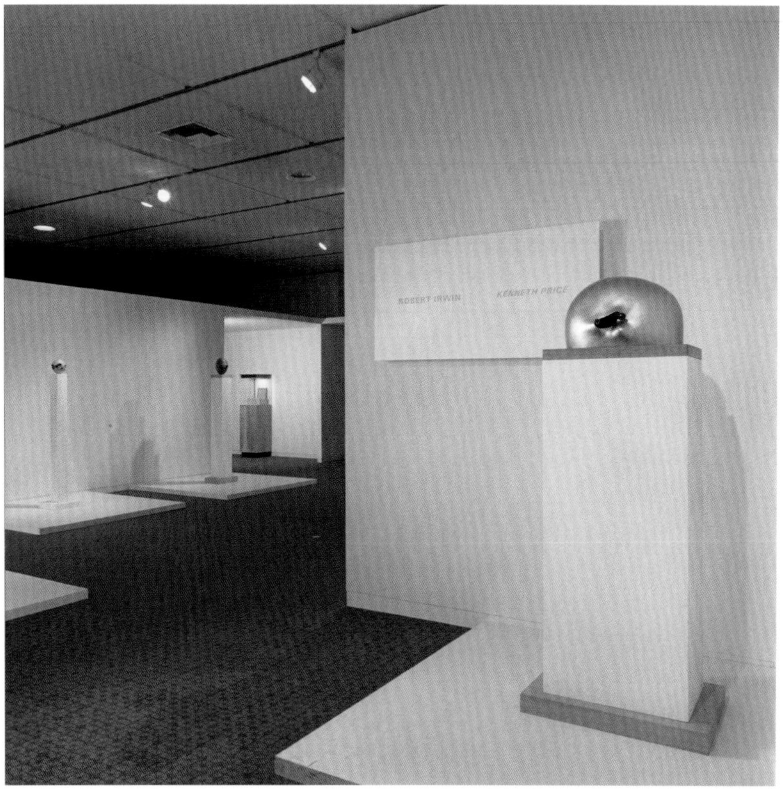

Beach Boy Dadaist

Although Price, a native Angeleno, is today most closely associated with Southern California and New Mexico, in his first decade of exhibiting, his works were more often understood in relation to the European sculptural tradition. To a *Los Angeles Times* critic writing about the artist's 1966 exhibition at the Los Angeles County Museum of Art (LACMA; see fig. 4), Price's works brought to mind "the purist sculpture of Brancusi, the biomorphic shapes and fevered colors of Miró, the neurotic subjectivity of the surrealists."[7] This European flavor was also noted by a peer of Price's, Edward Lebow, who pegged him as "something of a Beach Boy Dadaist."[8] Yet, while Price's work has become synonymous with smooth and precise surface effects, his earliest sculptures—such as *Avocado Mountain* (1959; fig. 5)—are roughly pitted and scarred. The dull greens and browns he used that year are suggestive of an interest in Art Brut, and, indeed, Price remembered clearly how he had been affected by the 1955–56 exhibition *The New Decade: 22 European Painters and Sculptors* when it toured to Los Angeles from the Museum of Modern Art, New York; the show included works by Jean Dubuffet as well as Pierre Soulages, Karel Appel, and Francis Bacon. As he later reflected, "That was my first exposure to the real thing."[9]

FIG. 4. Installation view, *Robert Irwin/Kenneth Price*, Los Angeles County Museum of Art, 1966

Price's palette rapidly brightened, however, as he began to experiment with, then quickly master, a combination of ceramic glazes and automobile paints. In this regard, he was inspired by Bengston, whom he had met surfing and with

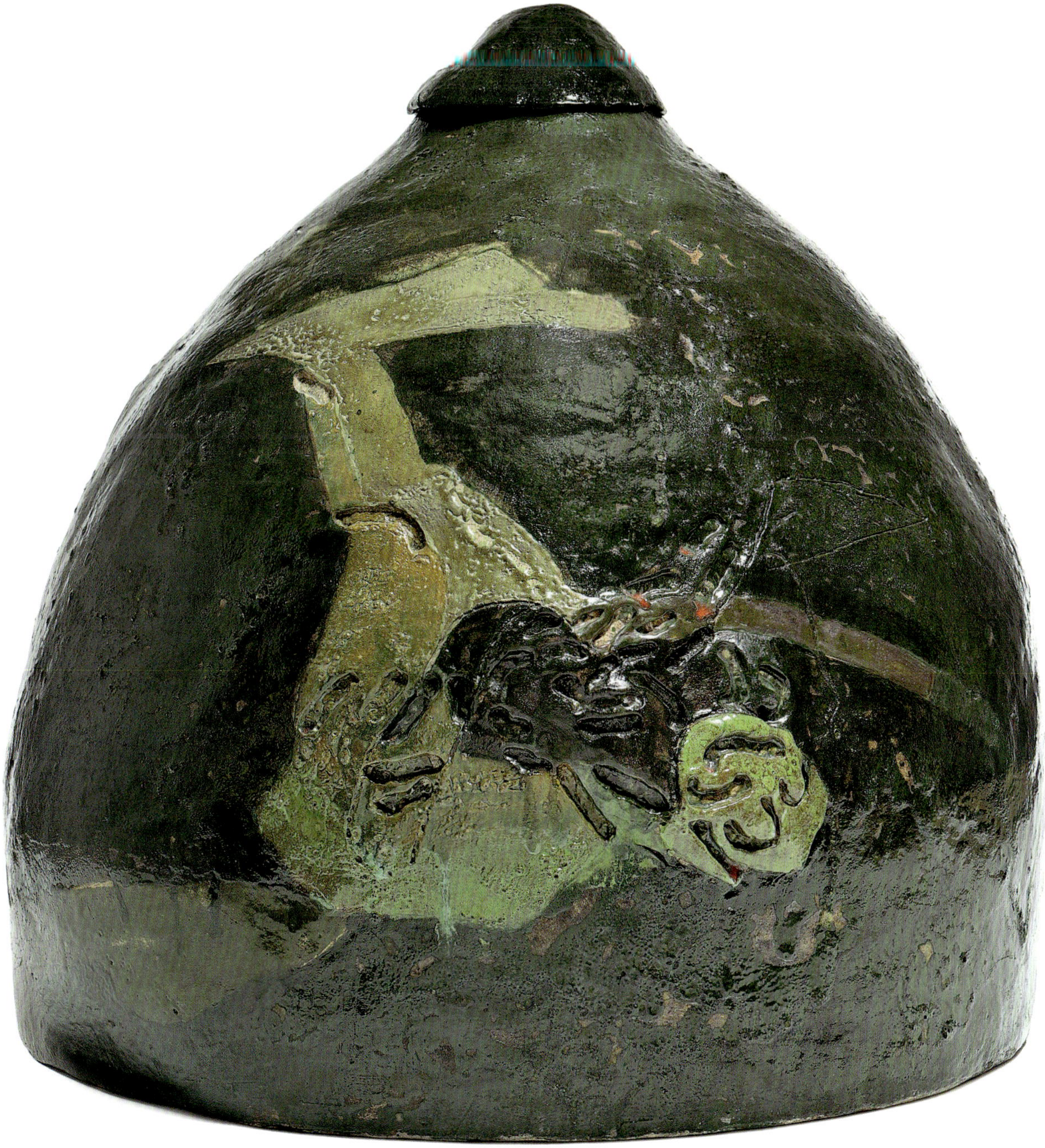

FIG. 5. *Avocado Mountain*, 1959. Glazed ceramic, 61 × 53.3 × 53.3 cm (24 × 21 × 21 in.)

OPPOSITE, CLOCKWISE FROM TOP LEFT:

FIG. 6. *Chevrolet Brothers*, 1960. Fired and painted clay, enclosed in wood box construction; box 17.8 × 25.4 × 13.3 cm (7 × 10 × 5¼ in.), cup 7.5 × 12.7 × 7.5 cm (3 × 5 × 3 in.). Collection of Joan and Jack Quinn, Beverly Hills

FIG. 7. *Astronauts in the Ocean*, 1960–61. Fired and painted clay, enclosed in wood box construction; box 27.3 × 14 × 10 cm (10¾ × 5½ × 4 in.), ceramic 12.7 × 9.5 × 9.5 cm (5 × 3¾ × 3¾ in.). Laura-Lee W. Woods

FIG. 8. *Specimen*, 1963. Glazed clay, acrylic, wood, velvet, and string; pedestal 20.3 × 35 × 35 cm (8 × 13¾ × 10¾ in.), ceramic 8.3 × 4.5 × 5 cm (3¼ × 1¾ × 2 in.). Smithsonian American Art Museum, Washington, D.C., Gift of an anonymous donor and museum purchase through the MCI Fund

whom he shared a studio in Ocean Park around 1960. In the mid-1960s, Price introduced Murano paint, which is intended for custom cars and motorcycles, into his repertoire, playing with its translucent reflectiveness. Price was friendly with other artists who were classified under the reductive term "Finish Fetish," such as Kauffman and Larry Bell, and, like most of his peers, he rejected the label. Still, to Price, integration of surface was undoubtedly key. The artist said of his works of the 1960s that he "wanted them to look like they were sort of made out of color."[10] Coplans, a co-curator of the 1963 Oakland Museum exhibition *California Sculpture Today*, captured this early phase of Price's oeuvre:

> Price developed an orificed pod-like form with several fingers either enclosed within or thrusting out, but saturated with a dramatic range of the most intense and expressive color, either glazed or painted with coat after hard coat of industrial oil lacquers, the latter technique in response to his need for instant control. . . . He attempts to integrate his color and form at a scale that has never been either considered or visualized in sculpture. . . . Price's sculptures look newborn and freshly made; they establish their own "now" moment. They have a curious, timeless quality as though freshly born like a flower, an egg or a chrysalis.[11]

To the East

An imagined Orient played a foundational role in the evolution of twentieth-century studio pottery in the West. As noted by Sōetsu Yanagi, the first director of the Japan Folk Crafts Museum in Tokyo, the British artist-potter Bernard Leach, who had been born in Hong Kong and was "enchanted with the memories of his childhood in the East," arrived in Japan "at the age of twenty-one, full of dreams and wonder."[12] Japan was also crucial to Price. While studying at the University of Southern California in 1954, he had discovered the work of the ceramicist Rosanjin, a contemporary of Leach's who took inspiration from ancient and classical Japanese wares and calligraphy. In 1962, Price spent six months traveling in Japan, an experience he documented that same year in the ten-foot-long ink-on-paper scroll

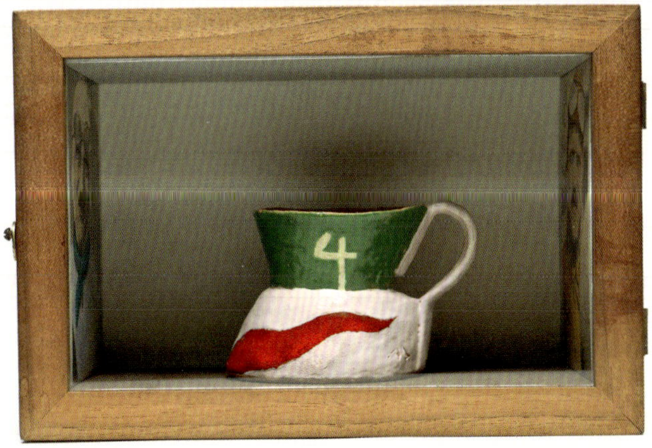

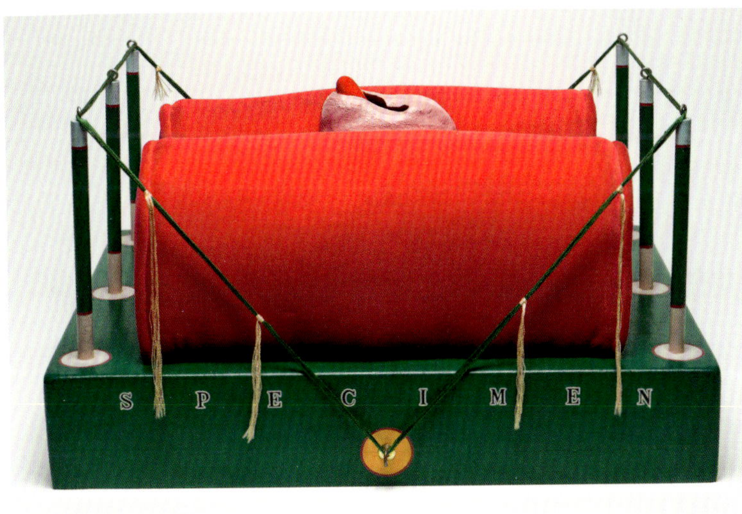

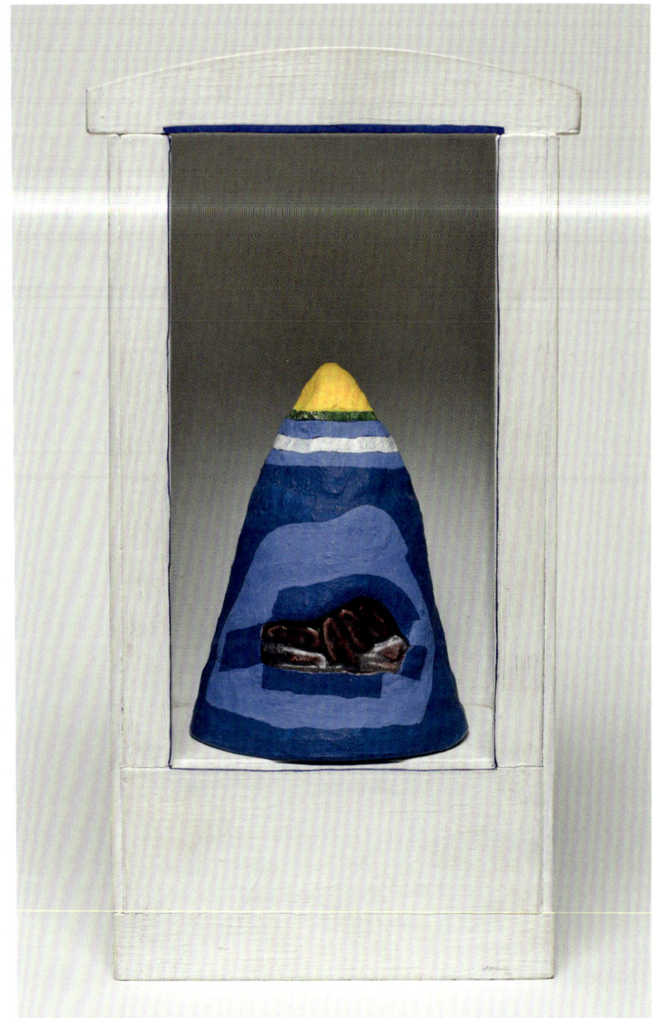

K.P.'s Journey to the East. Following the long trek of "Price-san," this tongue-in-cheek *Künstlerroman* is a litany of encounters with a knowingly essentialized vision of Japan: rock gardens, Zen koans, Bashō haikus, geishas, karate masters.

What did Price learn from his travels? He must surely have been struck by the meticulous display systems—of lacquered shelves, small pots holding bonsai trees, and so on—that he would have encountered in Yanagi's museum and elsewhere. In the years immediately following his Japanese sojourn, Price's presentation of his works became markedly more elaborate. Earlier pieces, such as *Chevrolet Brothers* and *Astronauts in the Ocean* (figs. 6, 7), were often enclosed in loosely painted boxlike forms, made under the spell of Joseph Cornell. (Price was apparently fond of quoting Cornell's aphorism "Tiny is the last refuge of the enormous.") After Japan, however, these boxes gave way to increasingly involved and playful arrangements, with still-tiny works presented on cushioned and shaped wood stands. For example, in *Specimen* (fig. 8), a pink egg sits atop a red velvet pillow, which, in turn, surmounts a green pedestal with a miniature railing. This type of pedestal was a fixture of the *Specimen* series for the next year or two. Price later described his approach: "Small objects are about intimate experience. And they tend to subvert detached analytical viewing by drawing you in closer to the physical reality of the piece."[13]

Little Rascals

Price's thinking about methods of display reached its complex apotheosis in the 1970s with *Happy's Curios*. This room-size installation consisted of pine cabinets holding hundreds of bowls, plates, vases, and cups depicting Pueblo vases, adobe buildings, pine trees and cacti, skeletons, sombrero-and-poncho-clad men, women carrying vases on their heads, and mountain backdrops, punctuated by posters and wall hangings with similar iconography (see figs. 10, 14, 15). As revealed in the associated sketches, the clusters of objects were carefully planned and laid out. Some units were relatively sparse; others, like *Death Shrine I* (The Harwood Museum of Art, Taos), were more involved and theatrical.

Price began working on *Happy's Curios* in 1972, soon after he and his wife, Happy Ward, relocated from Los Angeles to Taos, New Mexico. On surfing trips south of the border, Price and his friends had made a habit of stopping at curio stores in Tijuana, where Price felt he obtained an additional education in the art of earthenware pottery. The artist was drawn to these Mexican folk wares, which were produced at great speed for a tourist market by potters who did not consider themselves artists. He initially envisioned that *Happy's Curios* would take twelve months to complete, but it ultimately occupied him for five years and was finally presented in 1978 at LACMA, in his second solo museum show (see fig. 9). In the foreword to the accompanying catalogue, the curator, Maurice Tuchman, likened the undertaking's singular and uncompromising vision to all-consuming projects such as Kienholz's down-and-dirty tableaux and James Turrell's then-nascent *Roden Crater*.[14] That point was echoed more recently by the curator Douglas Dreishpoon, who suggested that *Happy's Curios* "may turn out to be one of the most quixotic enterprises in the history of American postwar art, on par with Jay DeFeo's *The Rose* and James Turrell's *Roden Crater*—obsessive projects without end."[15]

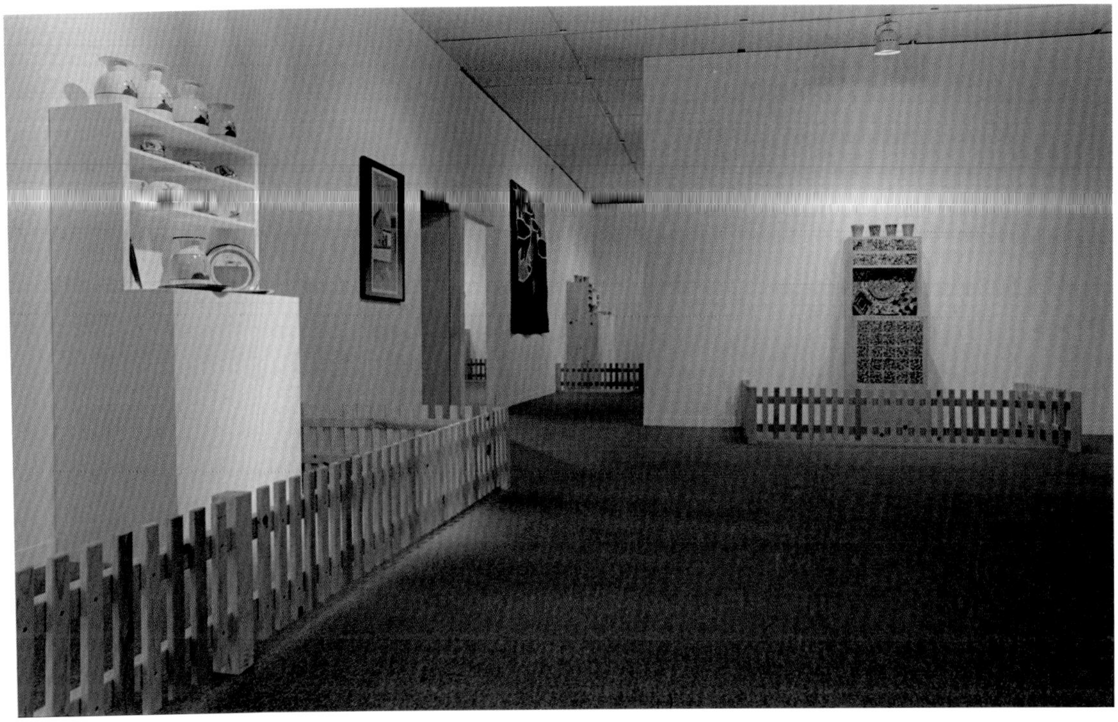

Happy's Curios has also been compared to Claes Oldenburg's *The Store* (1961), and its working title was, indeed, *Curio Shop*.[16] However, the sequence of displays inhabits a markedly different terrain from that explored by the New York–based Pop artists. Rather than honing in on mass commerce and consumption, factories and production lines, Price's installation thinks through the aesthetics, authorship, and economics of folk crafts. As the artist later explained, "I got turned on and thought I would make a tribute to Mexican pottery in the form of a curios store. It was kind of a fantasy. It was supposed to be a small store with some billboards outside, and a storefront window, and inside would be this bombardment of images and colors. . . . This stuff has humor in it, but it wasn't meant as a parody. It was actually meant as an homage to Mexican pottery."[17]

Price had become intrigued by what he called "wrong perspectives"—that is, the cultural position of artisans involved in the unsentimental activity of producing wares for American tourists. (An erotic component was also planned, although it was not included at LACMA.) This pretext offered him a release of sorts from the formal problem of "always trying to wed the color in the surface and the form and have the whole thing have the right feeling, so I would just decorate these little rascals, out-and-out decoration."[18] The rightness or wrongness of these perspectives has been variously interpreted. The design historian Glenn Adamson argued that the subject of *Happy's Curios* could be said to be "Price's inability, or unwillingness, to fully adopt the self-effacing mindset of a production potter."[19] In the way the installation's components seem to hover between cynicism and critique, Adamson identified them as being "among the earliest postmodern ceramics."[20]

FIG. 9. Installation view, *Ken Price: Happy's Curios*, Los Angeles County Museum of Art, 1978

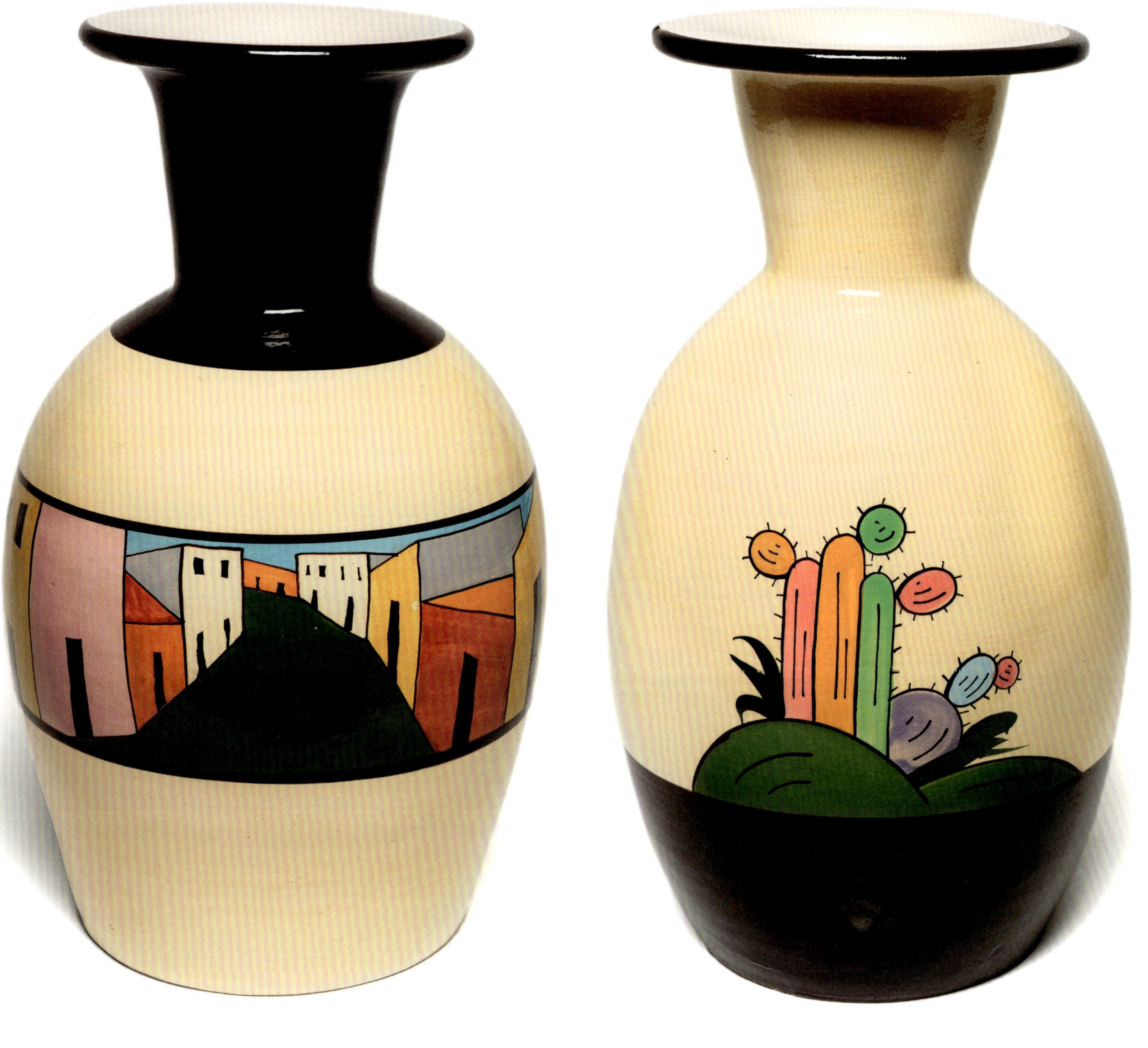

Learning How to See

Price made his clearest statement on how his works on paper intersect with his sculpture in 2003: "Drawing is a way of seeing what you're thinking about."[21] Even before surfing and music, drawing was one of his first loves; it played a generative and continuous role in his practice. At Otis, Price took Herbert Jepson's life-drawing class, which he later described as "essentially a course in learning how to see."[22] A couple of years after Otis, in the graduate lecture he delivered at Alfred University in 1959, Price quoted Rosanjin (who died that same year), arguing that potters must approach their craft through drawing.

While Price exhibited several works on paper in his first Ferus solo show in 1960, his drawings remained mostly private for much of the next two decades, until 1978, when he presented various studies as part of *Happy's Curios*. During those years, drawing, although somewhat backstage, was a vital activity in which he tested ideas, played, and planned. Early works on paper, such as a 1964 study for *Nose Table*, are technical sketches of sorts. You get the sense of dimensions and volumes being tinkered with, of things being worked out. Other drawings of that period, such as *Wart Nose* (fig. 11), have a cartoonish quality—they appear quickly done and are often comic. Drawing was, for Price, a place to experiment as well as a place to dream. In several works of the 1960s, cups are imagined taking on a life of their own, as in *Sea Turtle Cup* (fig. 12), in which the eponymous piece swims underwater surrounded by bubbles rising to the surface, as from a whale's blowhole.

Price believed that both very small and very large were powerful scales. He was concerned, he sometimes said, with the back-and-forth between the intimate and the monumental, a dialogue that was most strikingly enacted on paper. For example, most of Price's drawings of the 1960s adopt a slightly elevated angle, as in *Von Bayros Snail Cups* of 1968 (fig. 13)—although the claim that these are snails is little more than a ruse: they are clearly penises, albeit with shells. In other drawings, such as *Untitled*, 1967 (see p. 59), objects are viewed from below—a change of perspective that transforms an intimate vessel into something that looms. The domestic grows into the monolithic, becoming geological in scale.

FIG. 10. BOTH WORKS: *Untitled*, 1972–77. Glazed ceramic; 27.9 × 16.5 × 16.5 cm (11 × 6½ × 6½ in.), 29.2 × 15.2 × 15.2 cm (11½ × 6 × 6 in.)

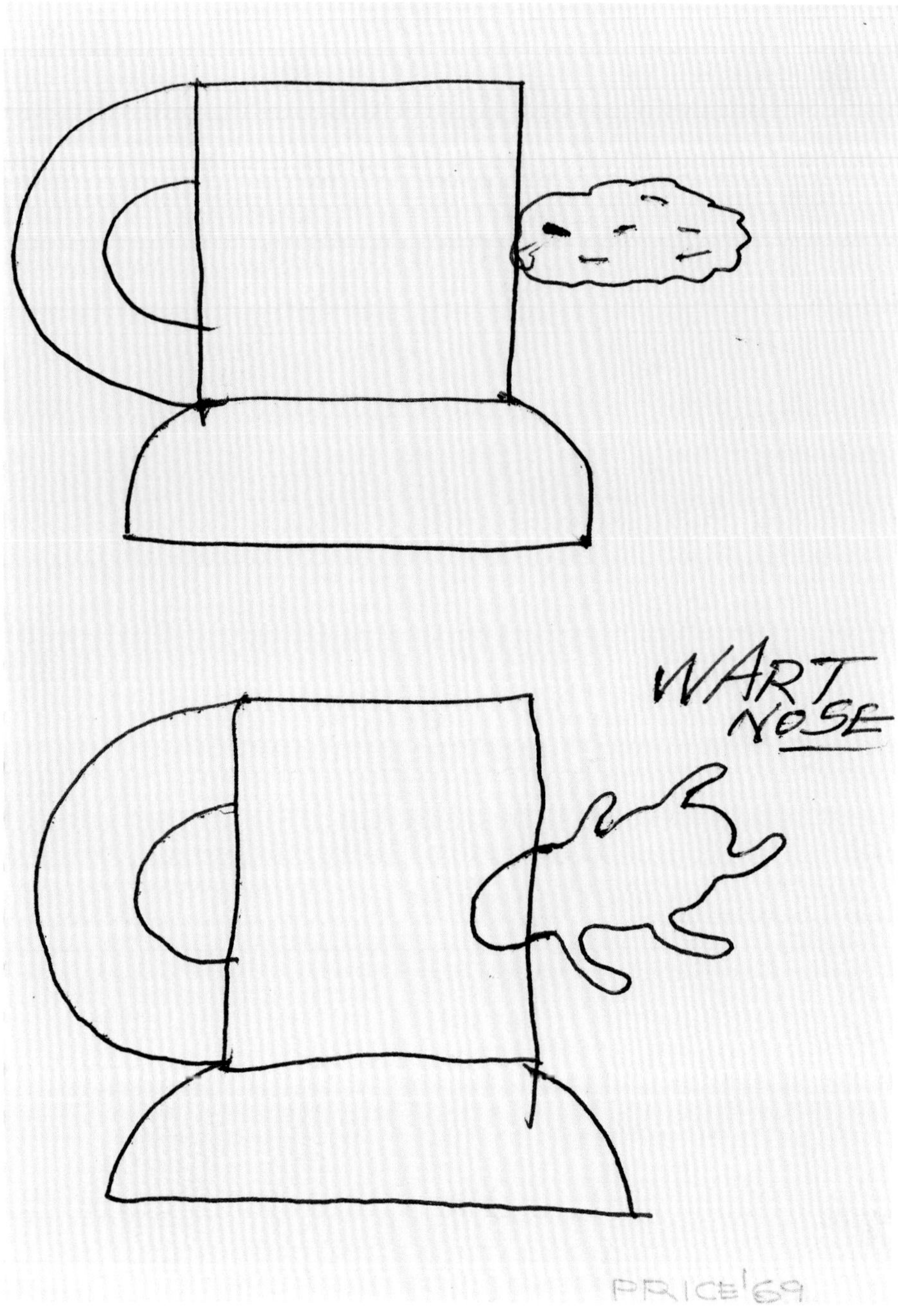

FIG. 11. *Wart Nose*, 1969.
Ink on paper, 15.2 × 11.4
cm (6 × 4½ in.)

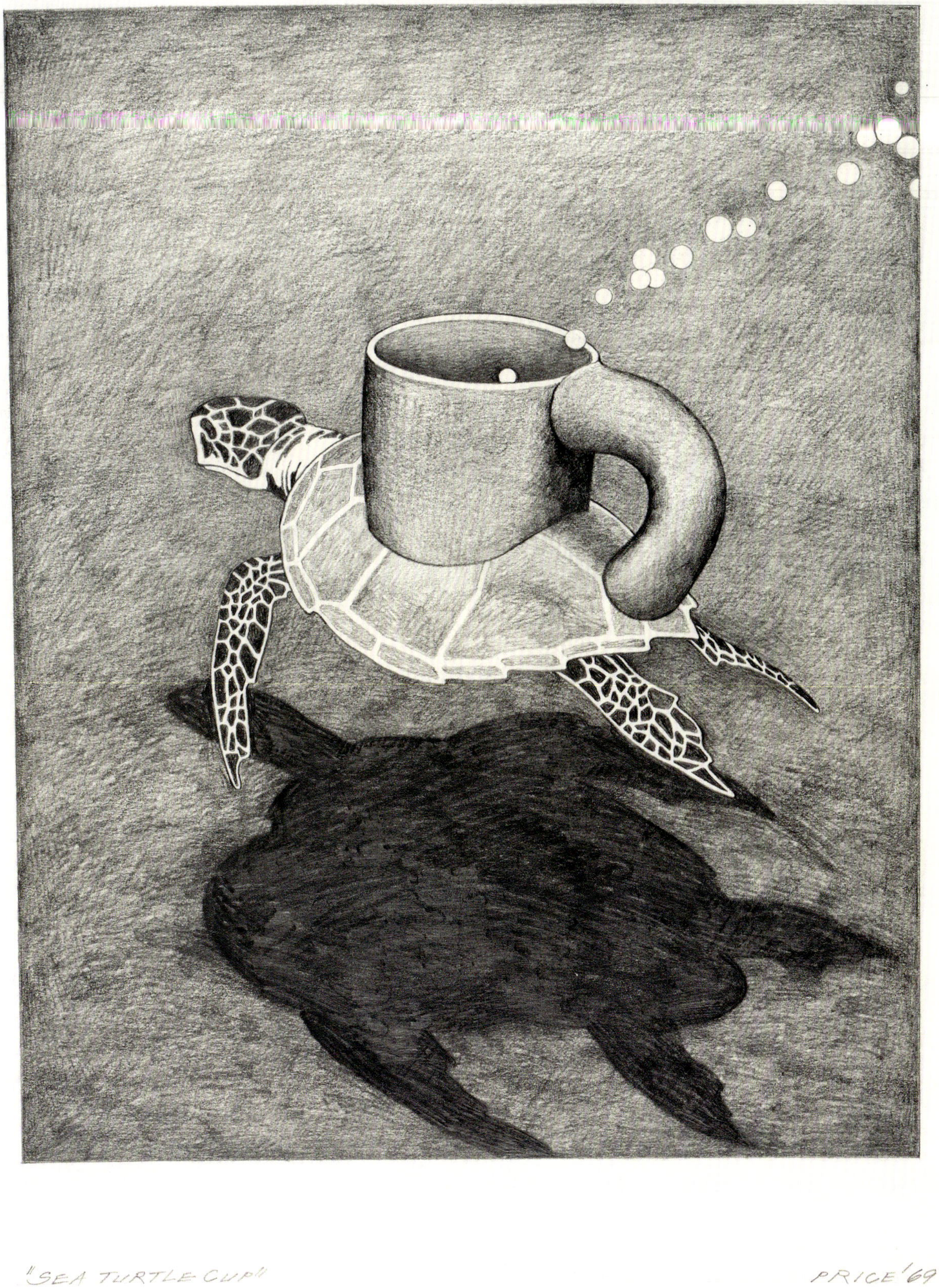

FIG. 12. *Sea Turtle Cup*, 1969. Graphite on paper, 34.9 × 27.3 cm (13¾ × 10¾ in.)

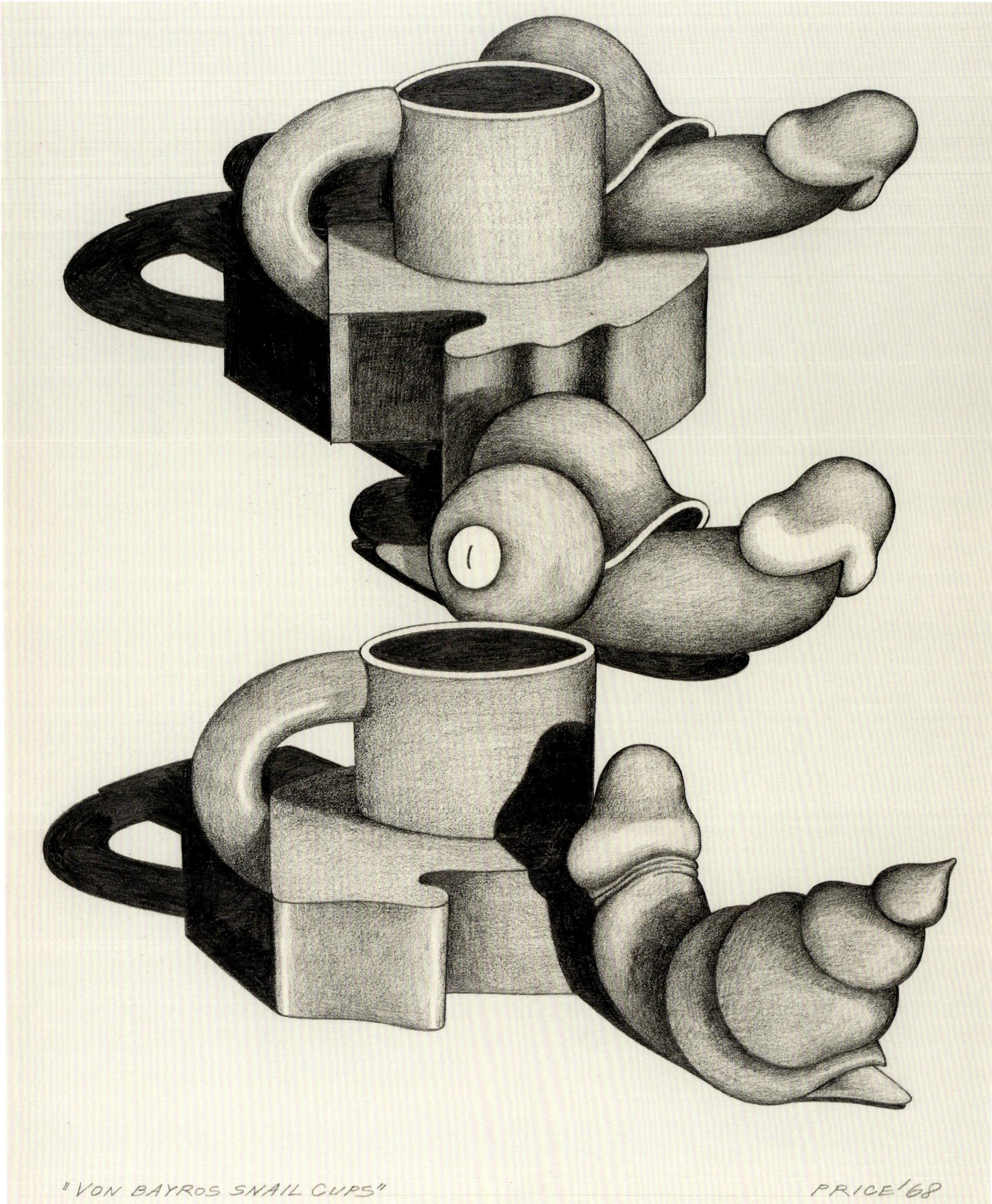
"VON BAYROS SNAIL CUPS"
PRICE '68

Many gouaches of the 1970s, such as *Untitled,* 1974 (see p. 73), relate directly to *Happy's Curios*, while others are independent, such as one that channels Fernand Léger in the desert, like a Purist painting uprooted from Paris to Mexico (fig. 16). It is in the works on paper of this period that we start to encounter not only animals and animal-like objects but people, too. One regular is Carmen (see p. 72); in the early 1980s, Carmen is replaced by Lorna, who engages mostly in B-movie-style adventures: diving, fighting sharks with a dagger, and so on (she returns in 1992 in a series of earthenware cups; see p. 116). Frequently, these works have erotic content, as in various nude studies of the late 1970s and *Mexican Girl with Doll Man* (1974), in which an Amazonian woman straddles a tiny, sombreroed man.

Peppered with annotations, the works on paper often feel diaristic. *Untitled,* 1980 (fig. 17), for example, was drawn on a sheet torn out of a notebook, dated May 23, with details about the placement of a white glaze and mention of a debt. Color is plotted out, plane by plane. In *Untitled*, 1987, there is a sense of eavesdropping on the artist as he works through formal and technical issues, methodically and unhurriedly (see p. 98, top). Elsewhere, we see the artist's notes to himself, such as "CAN'T PUT BOTTOM SLAB INSIDE—MAKE SOLID?" and "FLOATING SHAPE PIECES FOR NICHES?" In two drawings of 1988, he records the time for a gas hookup (see p. 104), reminds himself to do the cleaning, and ponders what to do on a Tuesday.

In the early 1990s, Price moved from the desert back to Los Angeles. This move is clearly registered in his drawings: the mesas, rock columns, and blue skies are replaced by infernal scenes of a polluted city, punctuated by plumes of smoke. In 1993, he made both a *Pollution* series and a whole series featuring oil refineries. In ink-and-acrylic works such as *Before the Earthquake* and *L.A. Sky* (both 1994; see p. 5), which were reproduced as limited-edition screenprints in an artist's book featuring poems by Charles Bukowski, we witness a forest fire in the hills, while *Downtown* (1994) shows traffic-choked streets (see p. 4). Even when Price turned his gaze back toward the desert, as in *Untitled*, 1993 (fig. 18), the polluted city remains visible on the horizon. At a moment when his abstract sculptures no longer required preliminary illustration, his drawings began to take their own path, diverging from—while remaining umbilically connected to—the three-dimensional work.

FIG. 13. *Von Bayros Snail Cups*, 1968. Graphite on paper, 40.6 × 31.8 cm (16 × 12½ in.)

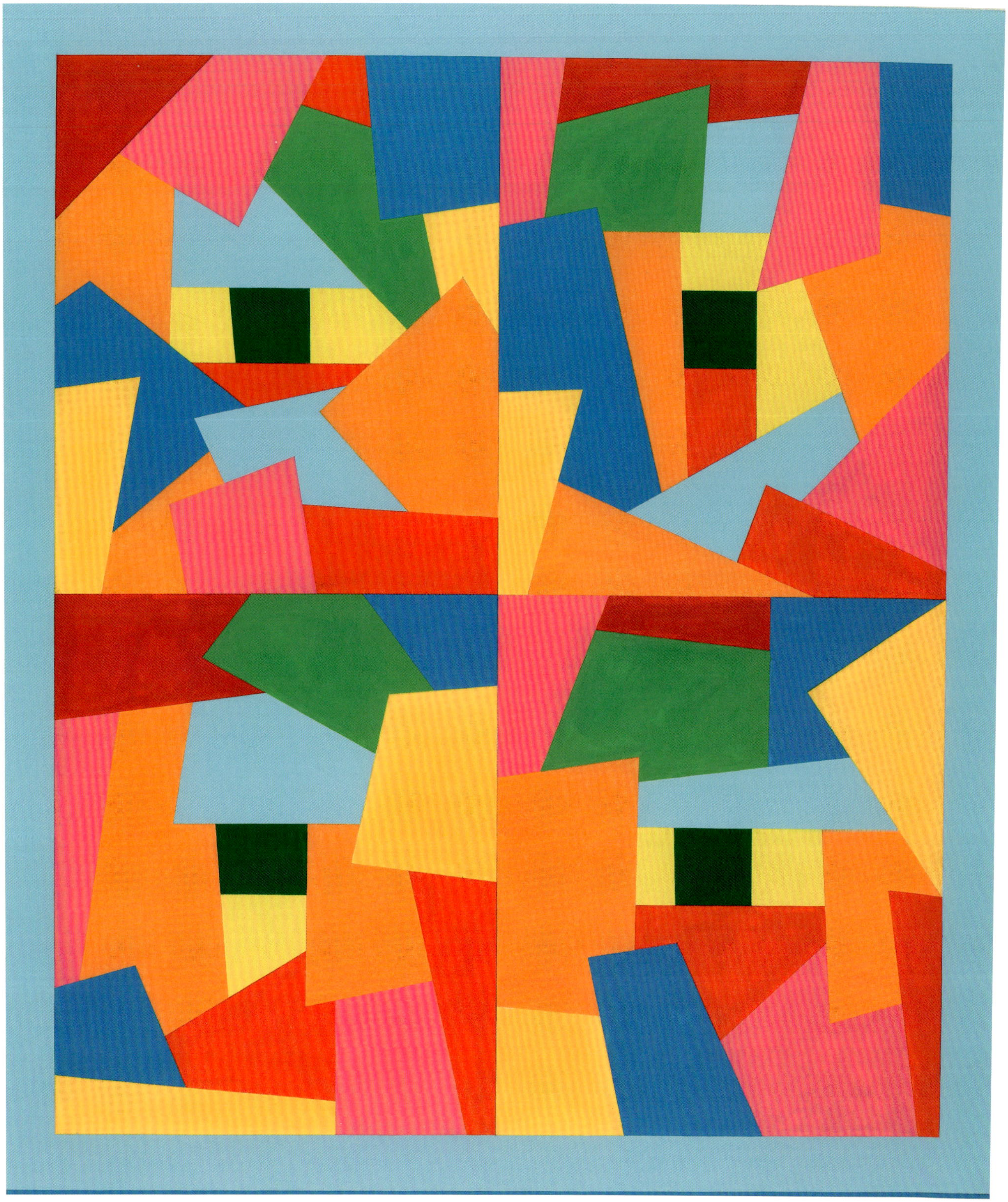

FIG. 14. *From Happy's Curios*, 1973. Poster paint on paper, 83.8 × 71.1 cm (33 × 28 in.)

FIG. 15. *Unit 6*, 1972–78. Ceramic with acrylic paint (6 vases); height of vases 19.1–24.1 cm (7½–9½ in.), cabinet 254 × 243.8 × 71.1 cm (100 × 96 × 28 in.).

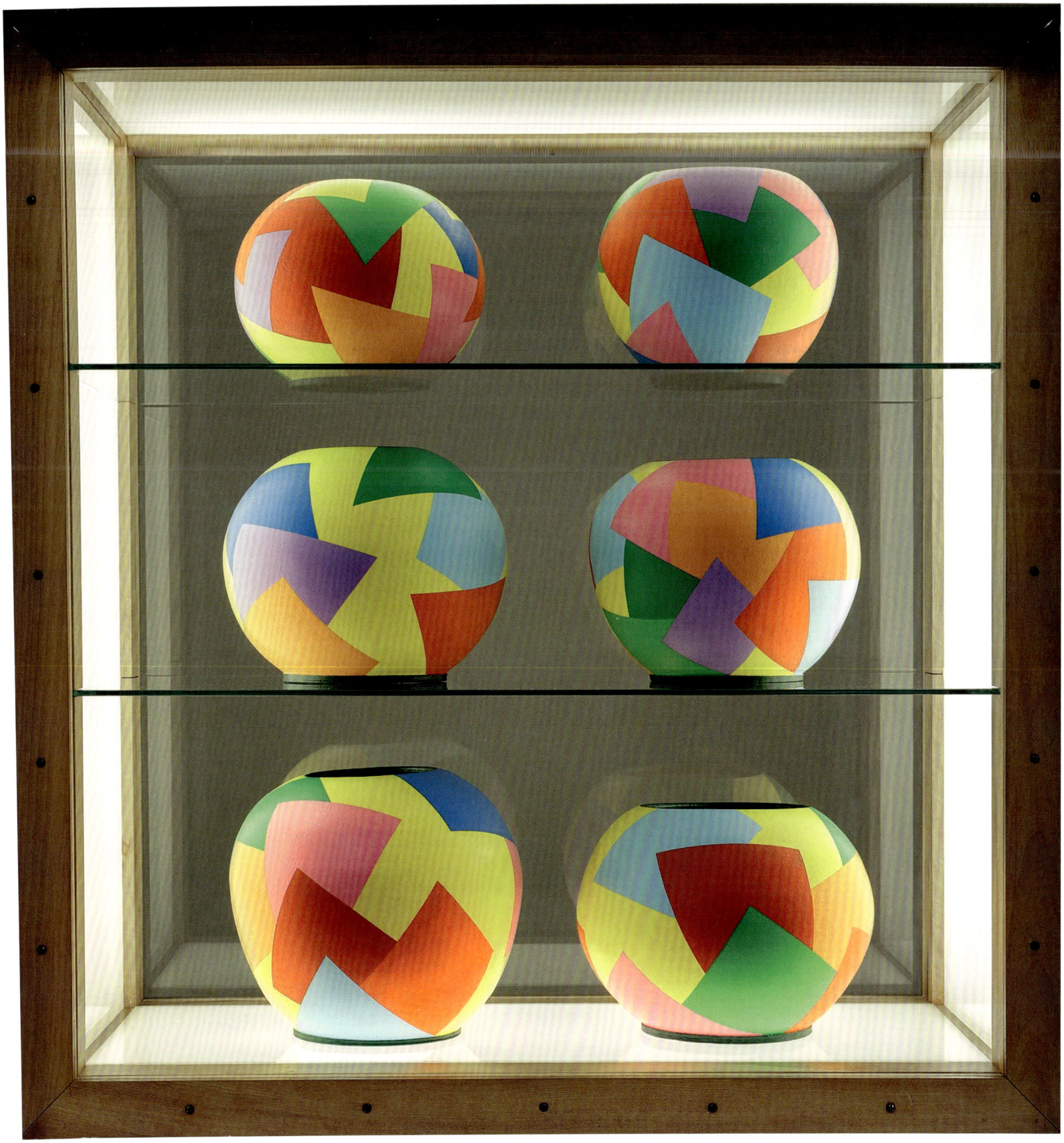

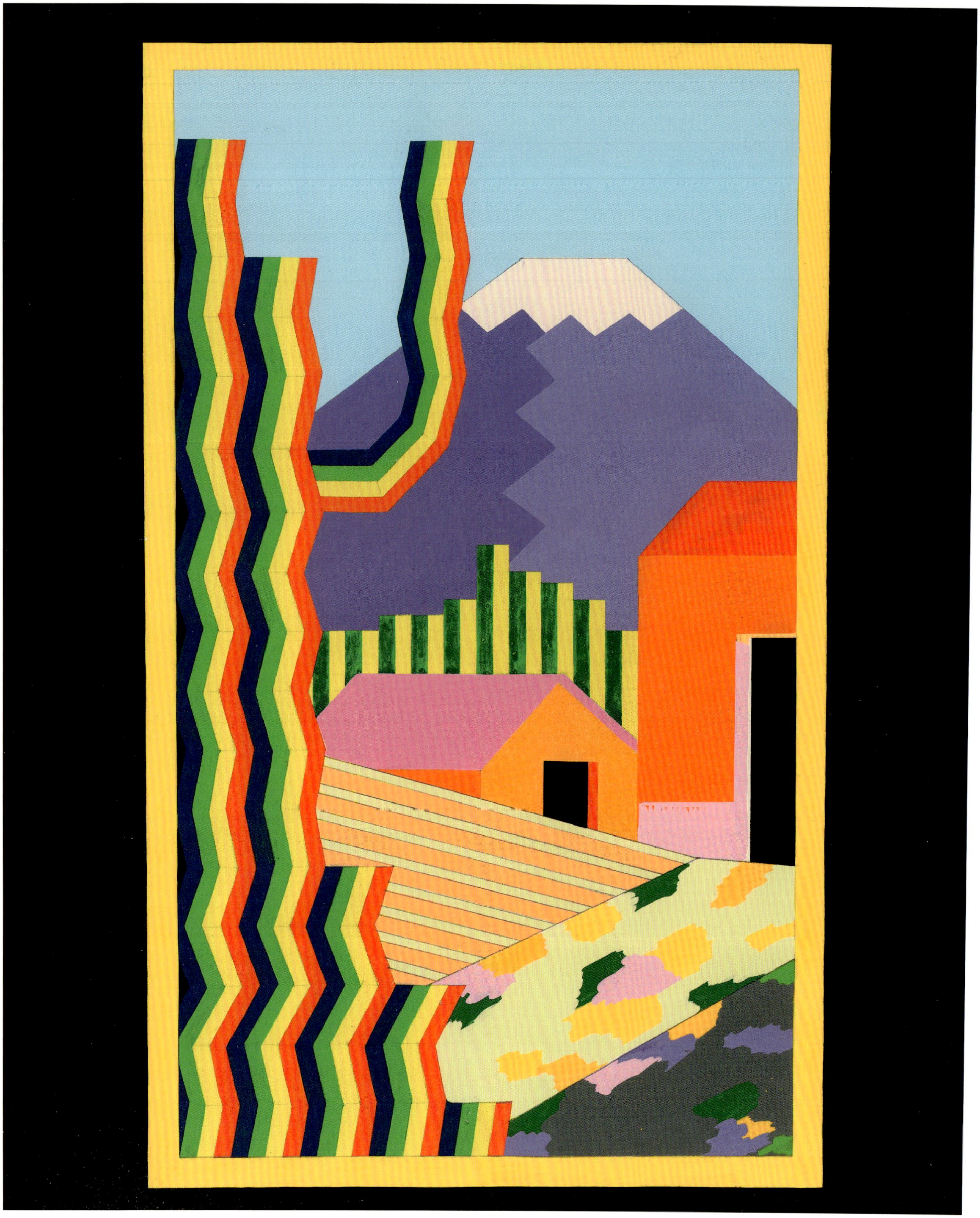

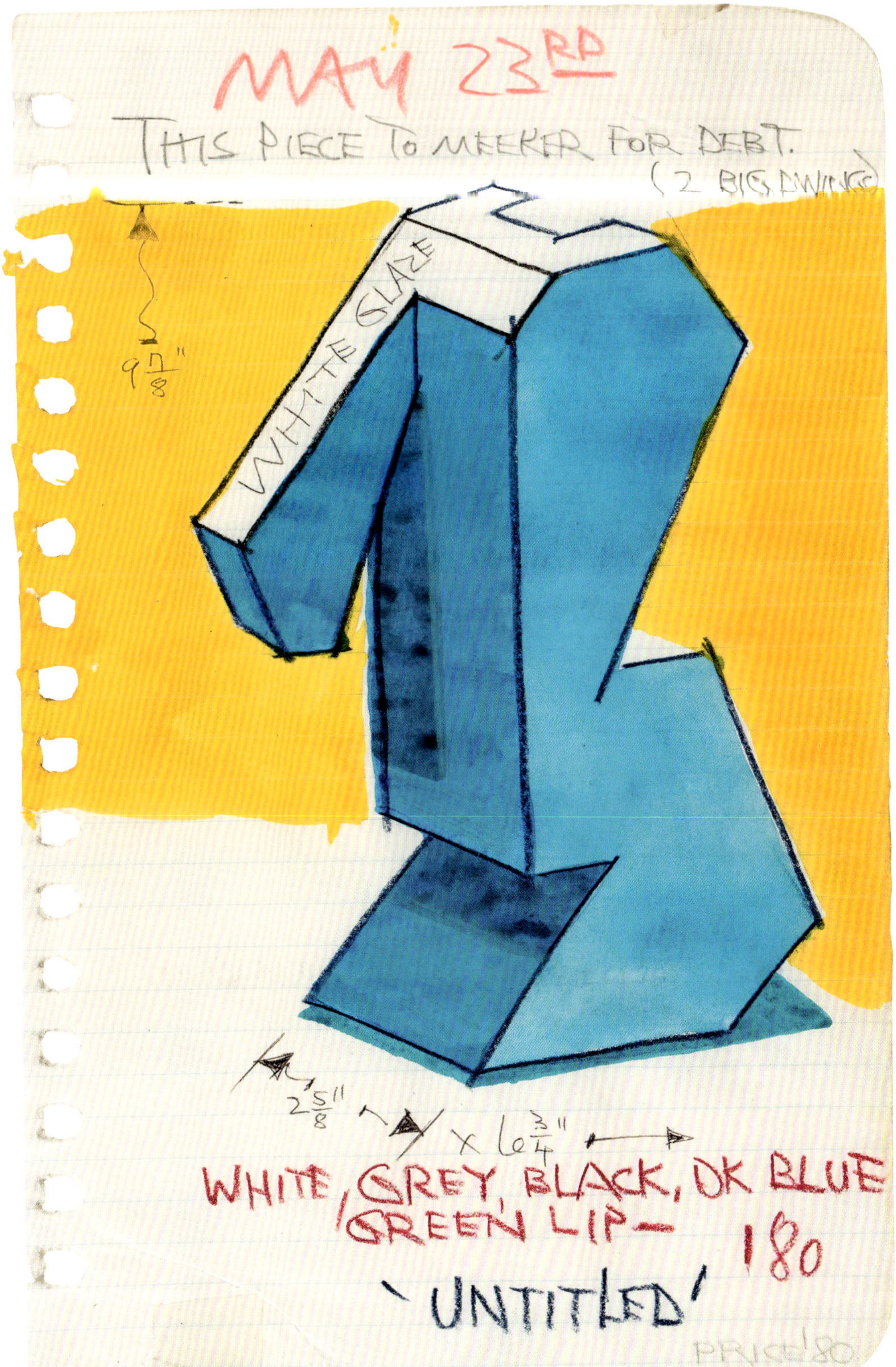

FIG. 16. *Untitled*, 1972–77. Tempera on paper, 31.8 × 24.1 cm (12½ × 9½ in.)

FIG. 17. *Untitled*, 1980. Watercolor and ink on paper, 24.1 × 15.2 cm (9½ × 6 in.)

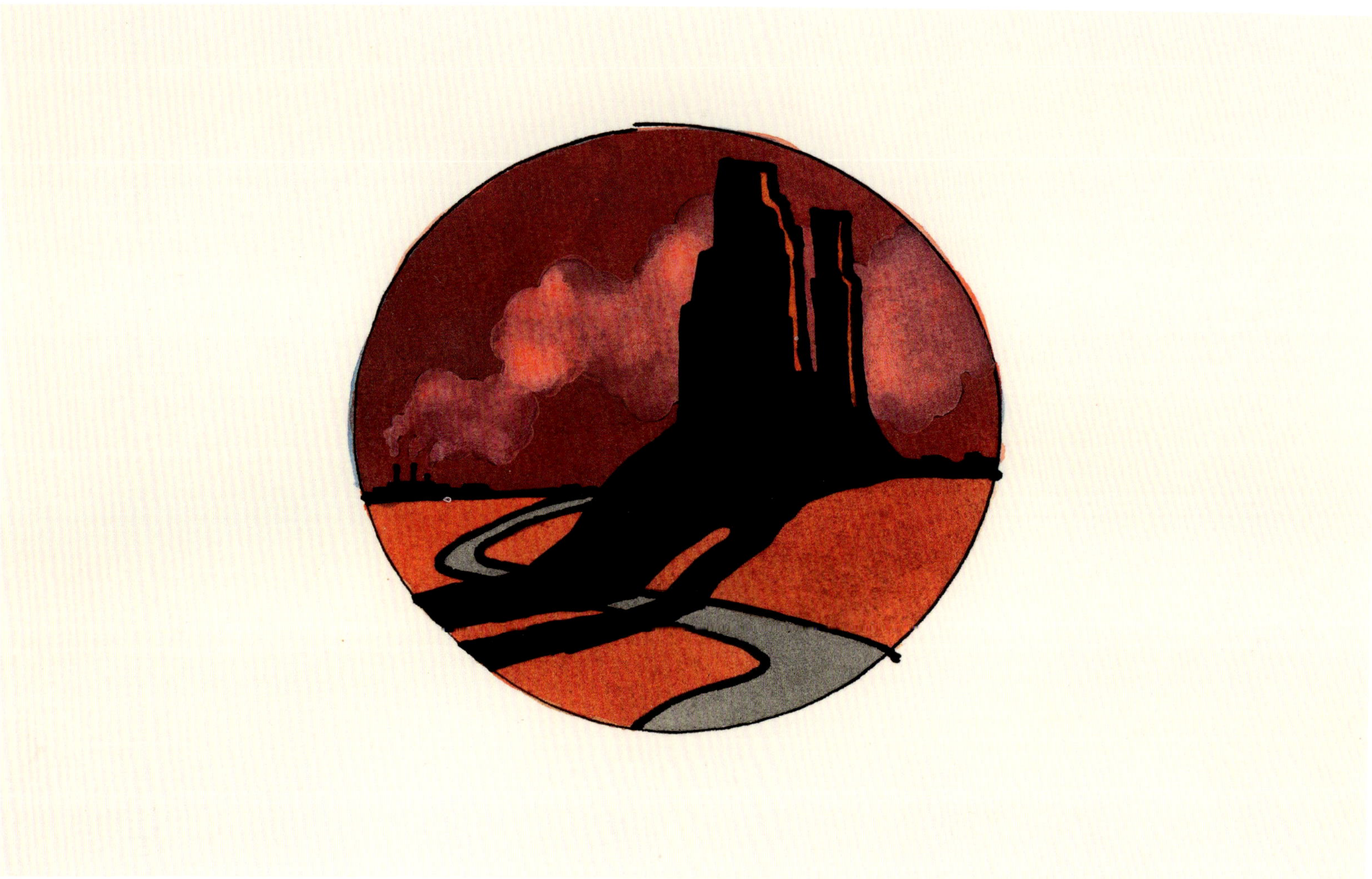

FIG. 18. *Untitled*, 1993. Watercolor and ink on paper, 20.3 × 20.3 cm (8 × 8 in.)

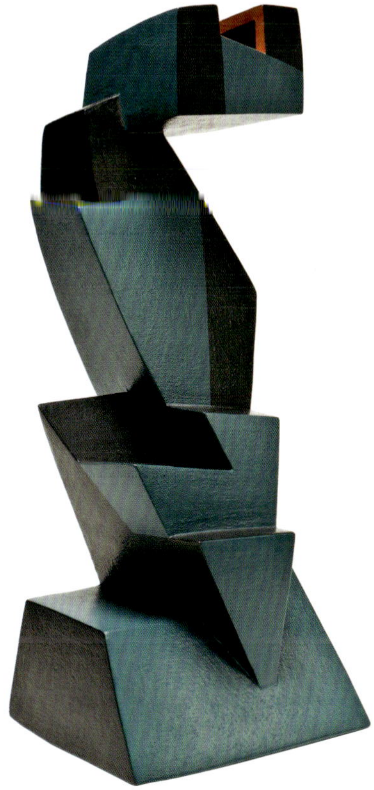

Color All the Way Through

In 1983, Price and his wife moved to coastal Massachusetts, where they stayed for the next eight years. The move coincided with the signal shift in Price's final three decades of work: from glazes to acrylic paints. In this sense, his career splits fairly evenly down the middle: the first half spent exploring the possibilities of glazes, moving far away from the conventional effects of ceramics but staying within that world, and the second half doing something quite different. Two sculptures of 1983 are titled *1914* (fig. 19) and *1917*; the dates, which are inextricably tied to the beginning of World War I and the Russian Revolution, respectively, are completely different from Price's usual titles and suggest that he understood these first unglazed works to be an important, even revolutionary, juncture in the progression of his work.

The technique that Price began to develop during this period involved priming the fired ceramic sculpture with more than a dozen layers of acrylic paint. Some of the earliest pieces made in this technique, such as *Egyptian* (1983) and *Chinese Block* (fig. 20), have the feel of nuggets of semiprecious metal ripped in pieces, with metallic interiors laid bare beneath obsidian surfaces. The colors soon grew brighter, and the cuts became ultraprecise: in *Mungor* (fig. 21), right-angled chunks have been seemingly removed from two volcanic-looking stones, revealing uniform planes of color. As Price noted in a 2005 lecture at the Chinati Foundation in Marfa, Texas, "I moved the geometry to the inside of the piece,

FIG. 19. *1914*, 1983. Fired and painted clay, 42 × 43.2 × 20.3 cm (16½ × 17½ × 8 in.). Collection of Emily Fisher Landau, New York

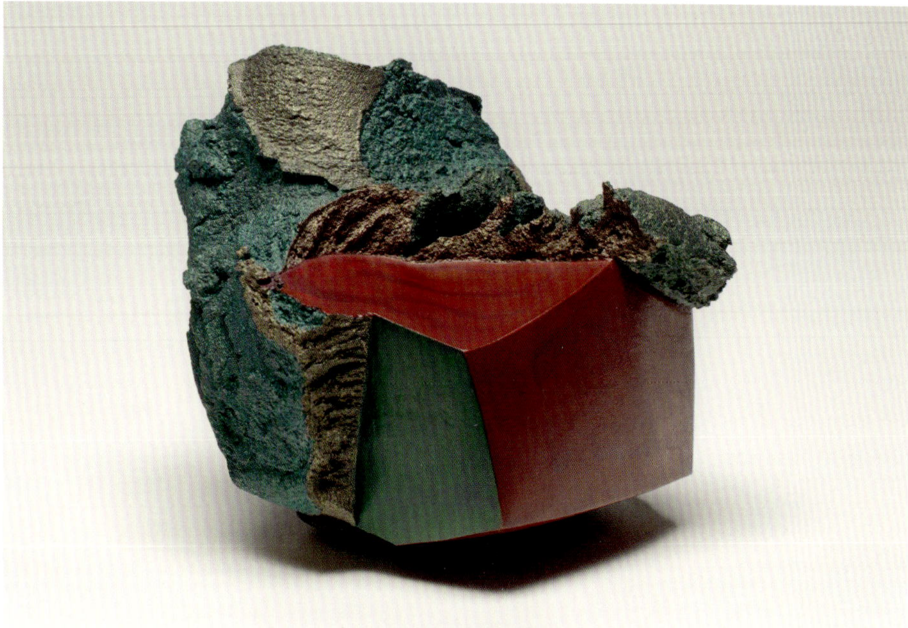

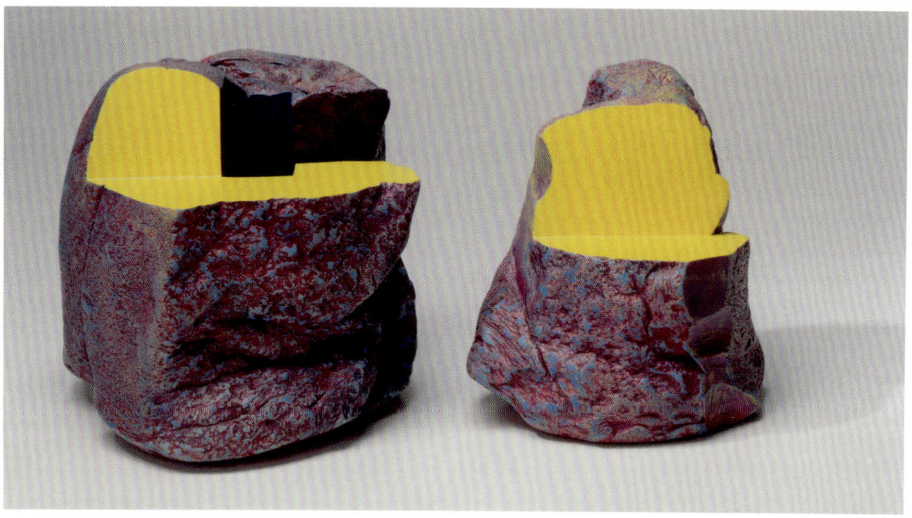

FIG. 20. *Chinese Block*, 1984. Fired and painted clay, 11.4 × 11.4 × 12.7 cm (4½ × 4½ × 5 in.). Happy Price

FIG. 21. *Mungor*, 1985. Fired and painted clay; two parts: 19.8 × 19 × 18 cm (7¾ × 7½ × 7 in.); 18.2 × 16 × 13.5 cm (7¼ × 6¼ × 5¼ in.). Stedelijk Museum 's-Hertogenbosch

and made the outer forms more amorphous."[23] In *Ultra-Purple* (1987), a textured exterior surface is broken by a flat turquoise slit that leads to a jet-black interior (see p. 43). Of these pieces, the artist Robert Irwin observed, "You had the feeling that if you cut that thing in half, it would be that color all the way through."[24]

The Golden Period

In 1991, Price was appointed head of the ceramics department at the University of Southern California, a position he held for a decade. During that time, back in Los Angeles, his son, Jackson, began to work with him in the studio, and Price experimented with using a cloth or cotton swab soaked in alcohol to work through layers of paint. This technique allowed him to meticulously blur colors together, creating

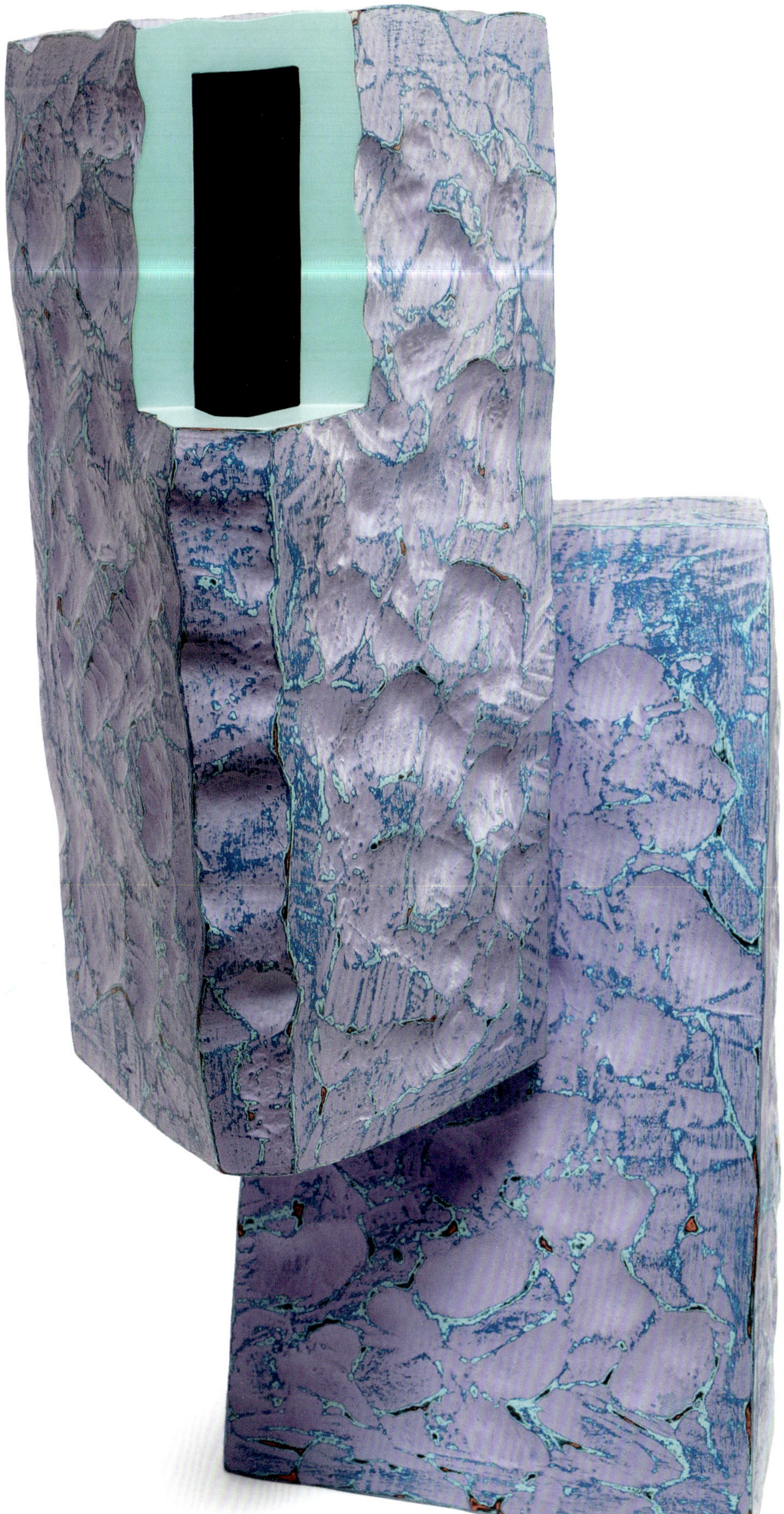

FIG. 22. *Ultra-Purple*, 1987.
Fired and painted clay,
58.4 × 27.9 × 38.1 cm
(23 × 11 × 15 in.)

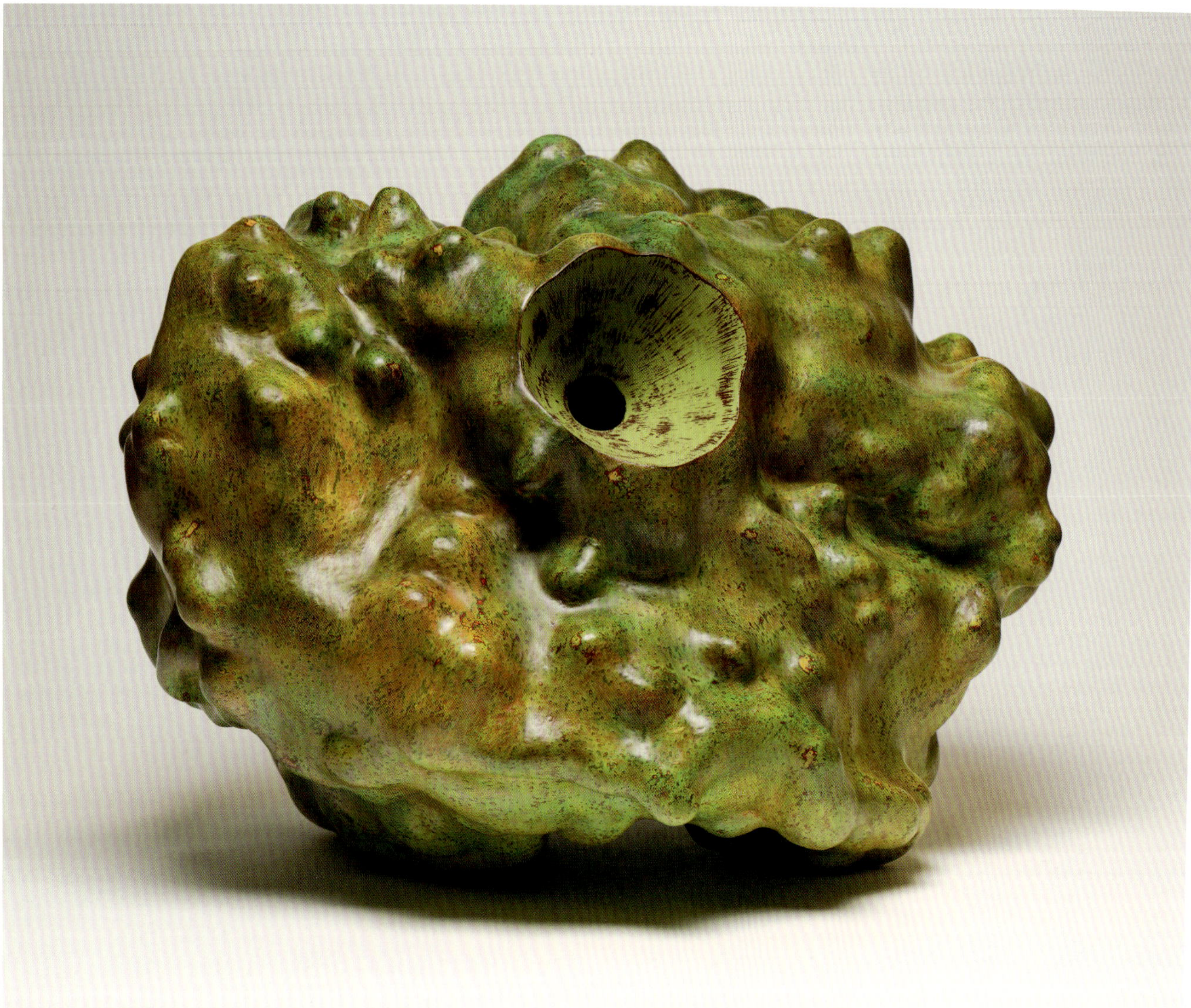

an almost digital smoothness. By the middle of the 1990s, Price was making works that were among the largest of his career: a series of volcanic forms, each about two feet wide or high, with titles like *Pagan*, *Phobia* (fig. 23), and *Underhung*. But these masterful pieces were still not widely appreciated by critics or the public. Writing in the *Village Voice* in 1994, Peter Schjeldahl called Price "maybe the most underrated living American artist."[25]

In the late 1990s, Price refined his technique still further, beginning to dry-sand the painted surfaces. Dave Hickey noted that the artist borrowed this technique from the surfboard workshop: "Back in the day, monochrome layers of paint, in different colors, were applied one after another to the super-slick surface of an aerodynamic surfboard, then sanded down to reveal rainbow streaks along the sleek length of the board, like flames on a lowrider."[26] Price applied as many as a hundred layers of paint to a piece, in up to seven different colors.

FIG. 23. *Phobia*, 1995. Fired and painted clay, 43.2 × 58.4 × 47 cm (17 × 23 × 18½ in.). The Museum of Modern Art, New York, Gift of Edward R. Broida

Although the artist's sculptures slowly grew in size over the course of the 1990s, they remained compact by most measures. Before 2000, Price had made very few series that topped twenty inches in height. This limit would rise in what was to be his final decade, which Price referred to as his "golden period." In 2003, he moved back to Taos and began to revisit certain mound-like pieces with which he had tinkered as early as the 1960s but had had to abandon after the particles from the fiberglass with which he had been experimenting, in lieu of clay, made him ill. In the flawless surfaces and liquid curves of works such as *Marti*, *Lazo*, *Go-No-Go,* and *Not from Yesterday* (fig. 24), several viscous forms seem to be piled casually atop one another, both drooping down and rising erotically up. It is difficult to describe these architectonic slumps more clearly than by citing the titles with which Price christened another three works of 2006: *Geodesic Pile*, *Slippery*, and *Slack*. Rather than assuming a single rounded or boulderish form, these pieces now grew protuberances, moving in multiple directions at once, completely fluid. Seeing them in reproduction rather than in person, it is possible to have the distinct impression that they are computer-generated. Their stippled and psychedelic surfaces keep them in motion; they are as concerned with weight as with weightlessness. Possessed of a shimmering and mercurial energy, these are sculptures with a life of their own, intent on survival.

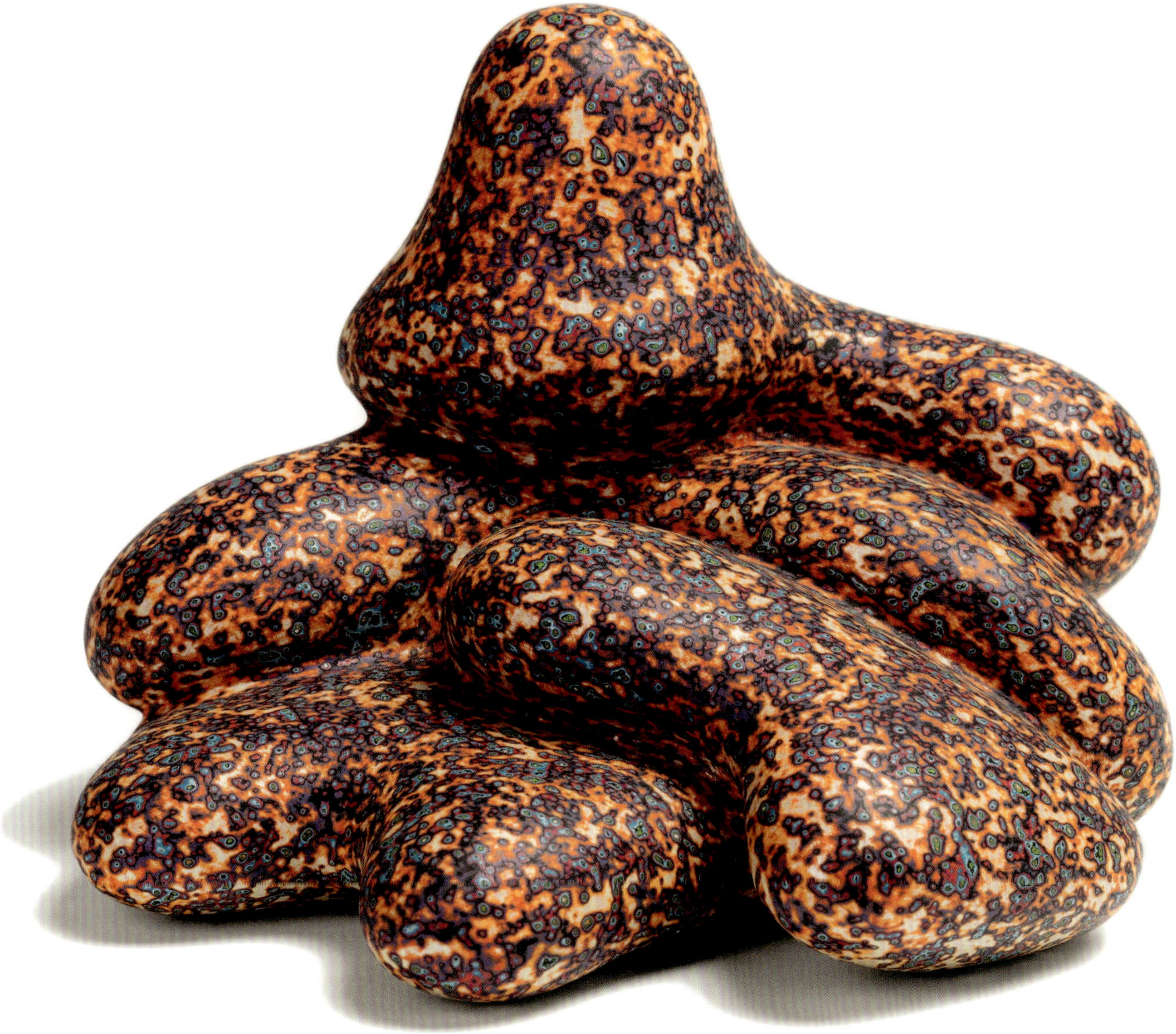

FIG. 24. *Not from Yesterday*, 2006. Fired and painted clay, 14 × 21.6 × 17.8 cm (5½ × 8½ × 7 in.)

NOTES TO PAGES 17–19, EROTIC BIOMORPHISM: THE WORKS OF KEN PRICE

1 Quoted in *Ken Price: Slow and Steady Wins the Race; Works on Paper, 1962–2010*, exh. cat. (New York: The Drawing Center, 2013), p. 18.

2 Douglas Dreishpoon, "Drawing Is a Way of Seeing What You're Thinking About," in ibid., p. 29.

3 Ken Price, "Japanese Pottery," in *Ken Price Sculpture: A Retrospective*, exh. cat. (Los Angeles: Los Angeles County Museum of Art, 2012), p. 193.

4 Quoted in Joan Simon, "An Interview with Ken Price," *Art in America*, January 1980, pp. 98–104.

NOTES TO PAGES 21–46, LIVES OF THEIR OWN: KEN PRICE'S SCULPTURES AND WORKS ON PAPER

1 Hunter Drohojowska-Philp, "A Life in Clay" (interview with Ken Price), *artnet Magazine*, October 22, 2008, http://www.artnet.com/magazineus/features/drohojowska-philp/drohojowska-philp10-22-08.asp.

2 John Coplans, "Circle of Styles on the West Coast," *Art in America*, August 1964, p. 9.

3 Peter Plagens, *Sunshine Muse: Contemporary Art on the West Coast* (New York: Praeger, 1974), p. 95.

4 Henry T. Hopkins, "Kenneth Price, Untitled Ceramic," *Artforum*, August 1963, p. 41.

5 Ken Price, "Ken Price: Personal Influences," *Ceramics Monthly*, September 1994, pp. 31–35.

6 "Ken Price in Conversation with Vija Celmins," *Ken Price: Sculpture and Drawings*, exh. cat. (Göttingen: Steidl Publishers; New York: Matthew Marks Gallery, 2007), p. 7.

7 William Wilson, "In the Galleries: Couple of Bogey Men Add Luster to an Art Tradition," *Los Angeles Times*, July 11, 1966, p. C10.

8 Edward Lebow, "The Ceramics of Ken Price," in *Ken Price*, exh. cat. (Houston: Menil Collection and Houston Fine Art Press, 1992), p. 20.

9 Karen Tsujimoto, "Confluence: People, Ideas, and Art; Southern California, 1945–1970," in *Clay's Tectonic Shift: John Mason, Ken Price, Peter Voulkos, 1956–1968* (Los Angeles: Getty Publications, 2012), p. 41.

10 Stephanie Barron, "Lumps, Bumps, Grooves, and Curves: Fifty Years of Ken Price Sculpture," in *Ken Price Sculpture: A Retrospective*, exh. cat. (Los Angeles: Los Angeles County Museum of Art; Munich: Prestel, 2012), p. 17.

11 John Coplans, "California Sculpture Today," *Artforum*, August 1963, p. 4.

12 Soetsu Yanagi, "Introduction: Leach in Japan," in Bernard Leach, *A Potter's Book* (London: Faber and Faber, 1940), p. xvii.

13 "Ken Price: A Talk with Slides"/"Ken Price: Una charla con diapositivas," *Chinati Foundation Newsletter* (in English and Spanish), no. 10 (2005), p. 31.

14 Maurice Tuchman, "Foreword and Acknowledgments," in *Ken Price: Happy's Curios*, exh. cat. (Los Angeles: Los Angeles County Museum of Art, 1978), p. 5.

15 Douglas Dreishpoon, "Drawing Is a Way of Seeing What You're Thinking About," in *Ken Price: Slow and Steady Wins the Race; Works on Paper, 1962–2010*, exh. cat. (New York: The Drawing Center, 2013), p. 39.

16 Barron, "Lumps, Bumps, Grooves, and Curves," p. 24.

17 Price, "A Talk with Slides," pp. 27–28.

18 Joan Simon, "An Interview with Ken Price," *Art in America*, January 1980.

19 Glenn Adamson, *Thinking through Craft* (London and New York: Bloomsbury, 2007), p. 53.

20 Ibid, p. 54.

21 Dreishpoon, "Drawing Is a Way of Seeing," p. 18.

22 Drohojowska-Philp, "A Life in Clay."

23 Price, "A Talk with Slides," p. 32.

24 Quoted in Suzanne Muchnic, "A Burgeoning Art Scene with Room for Ceramics," in *Clay's Tectonic Shift*, p. 180.

25 Peter Schjeldahl, "The Most Beautiful Show in Town; Ken Price: Career Survey," *Village Voice*, May 17, 1994.

26 Dave Hickey, "The Price of Everything," in *Ken Price Sculpture*, p. 164.

PLATES

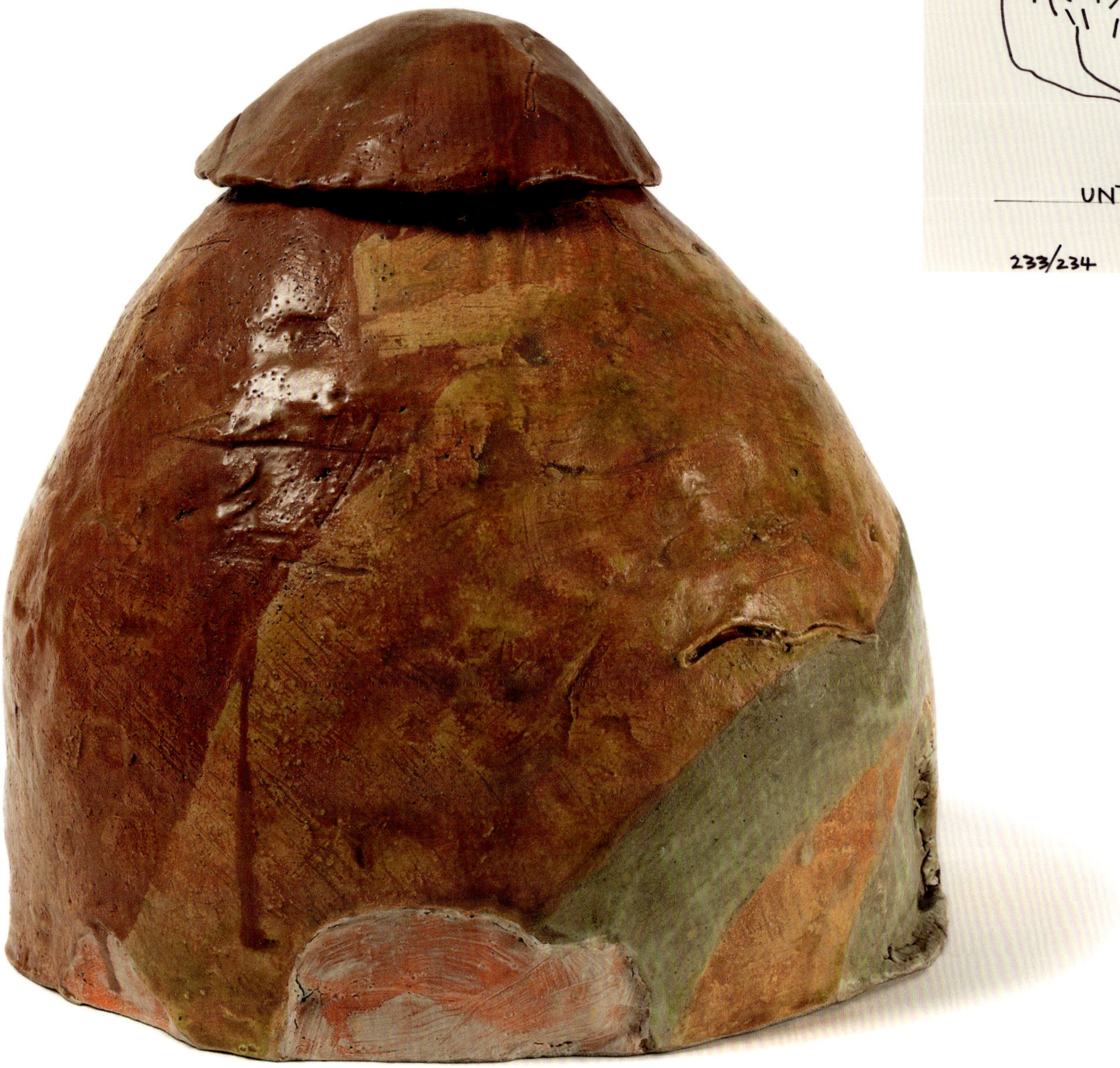

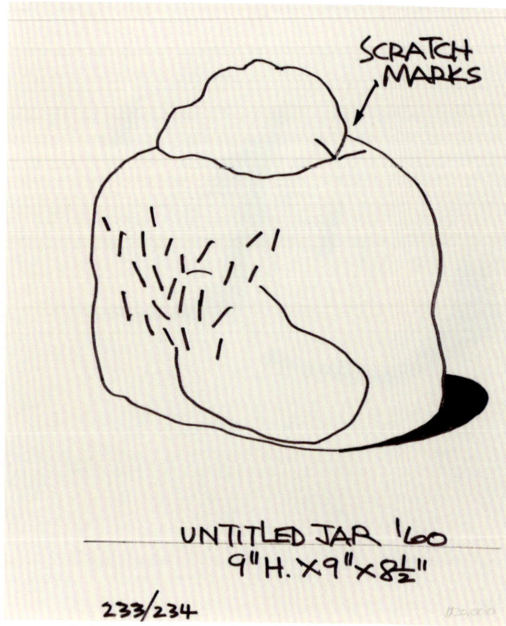

LEFT:

Untitled, 1960

RIGHT:

Untitled Jar, no date

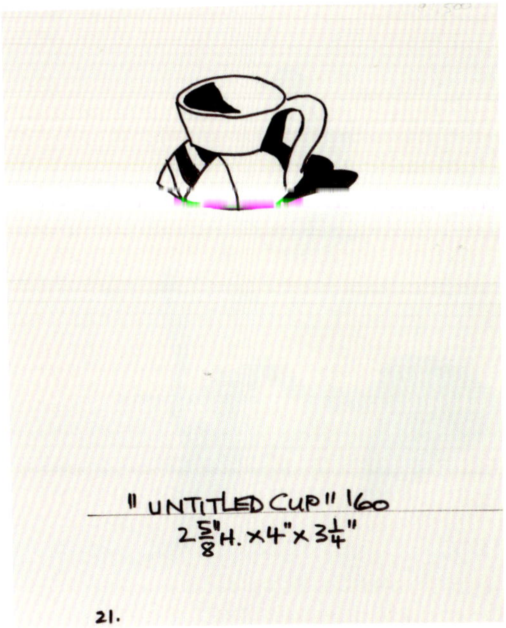

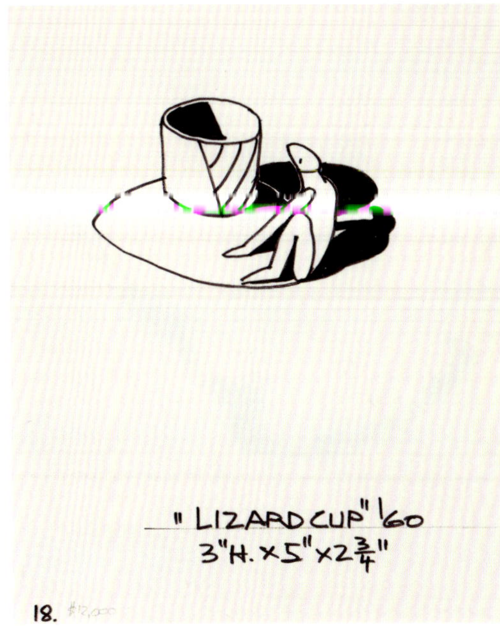

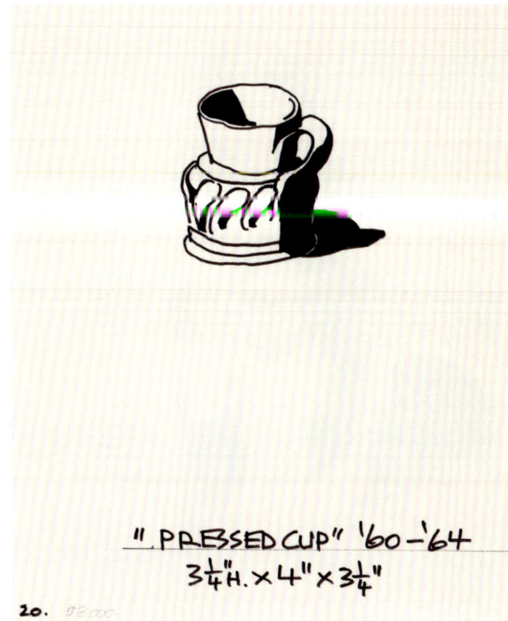

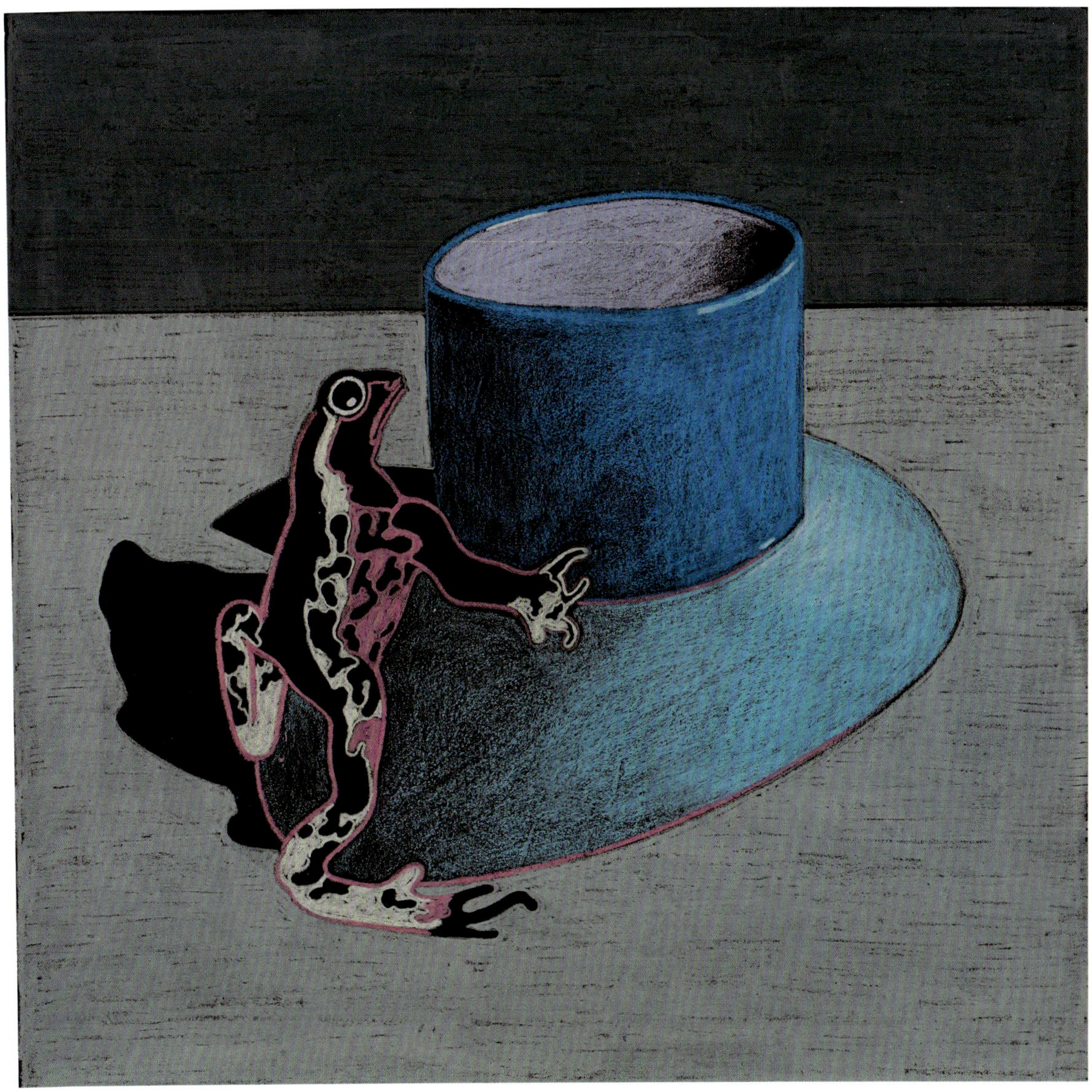

TOP ROW, LEFT TO RIGHT:
Untitled Cup, no date
Lizard Cup, no date
Pressed Cup, no date
LEFT:
Frog Cup, 1967

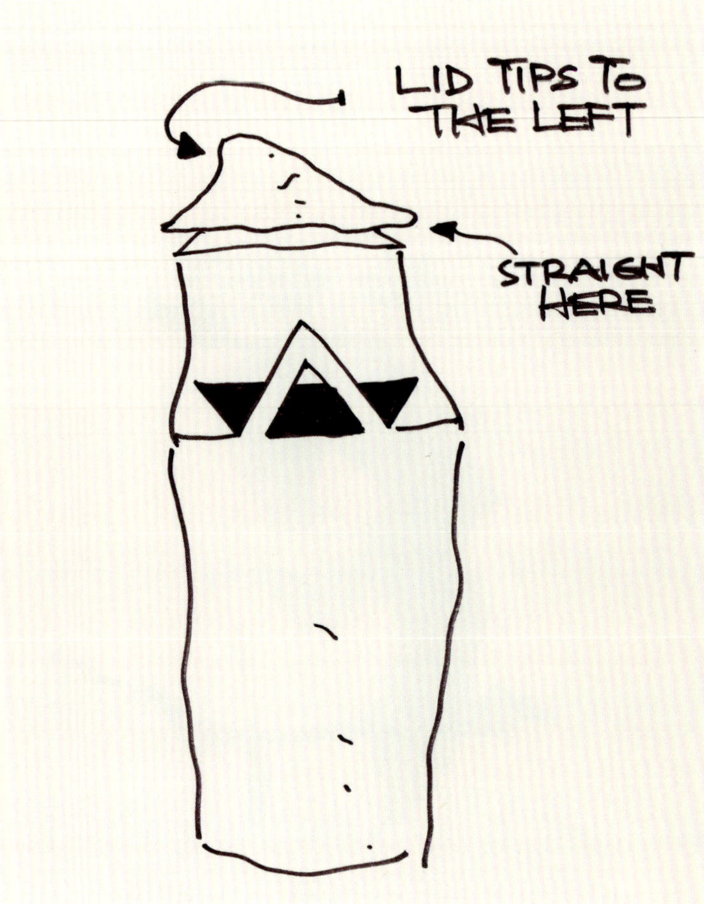

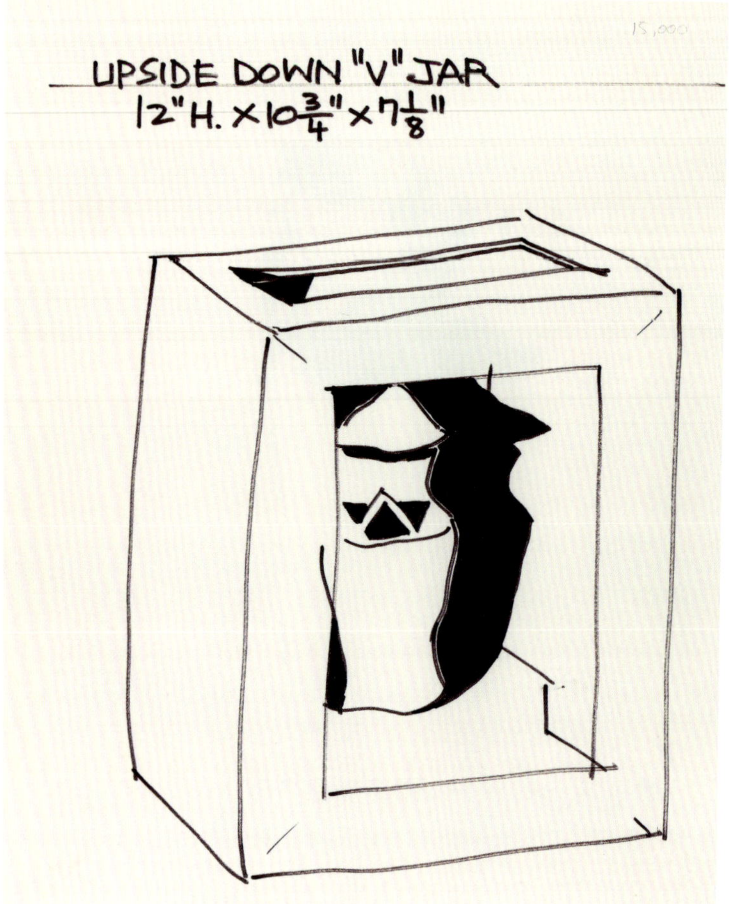

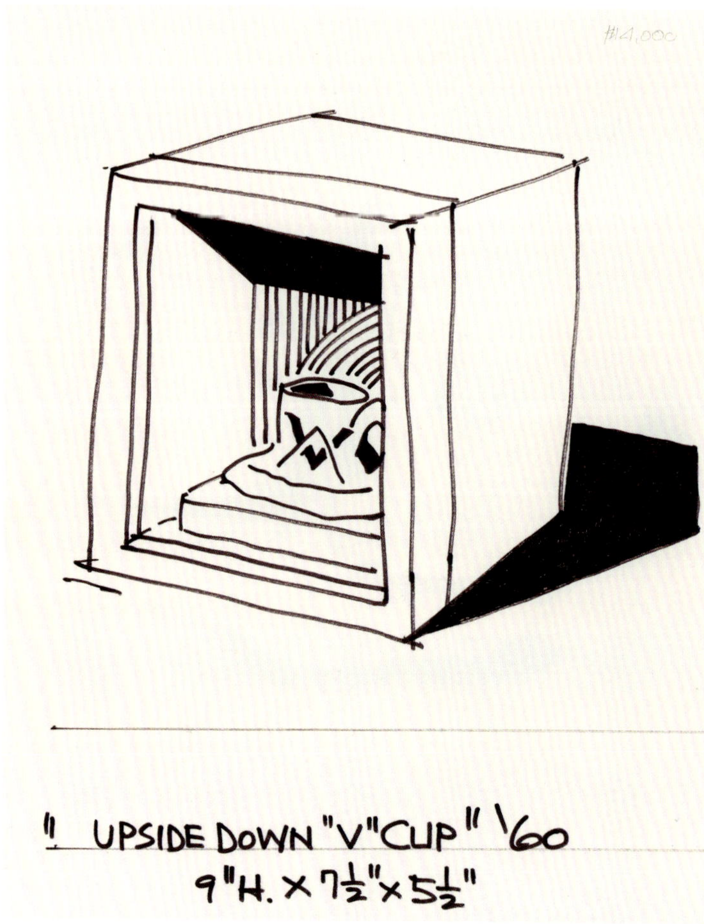

CLOCKWISE FROM TOP LEFT:
Lid Tips to the Left, no date
Upside Down "V" Jar, no date
Upside Down "V" Cup, no date

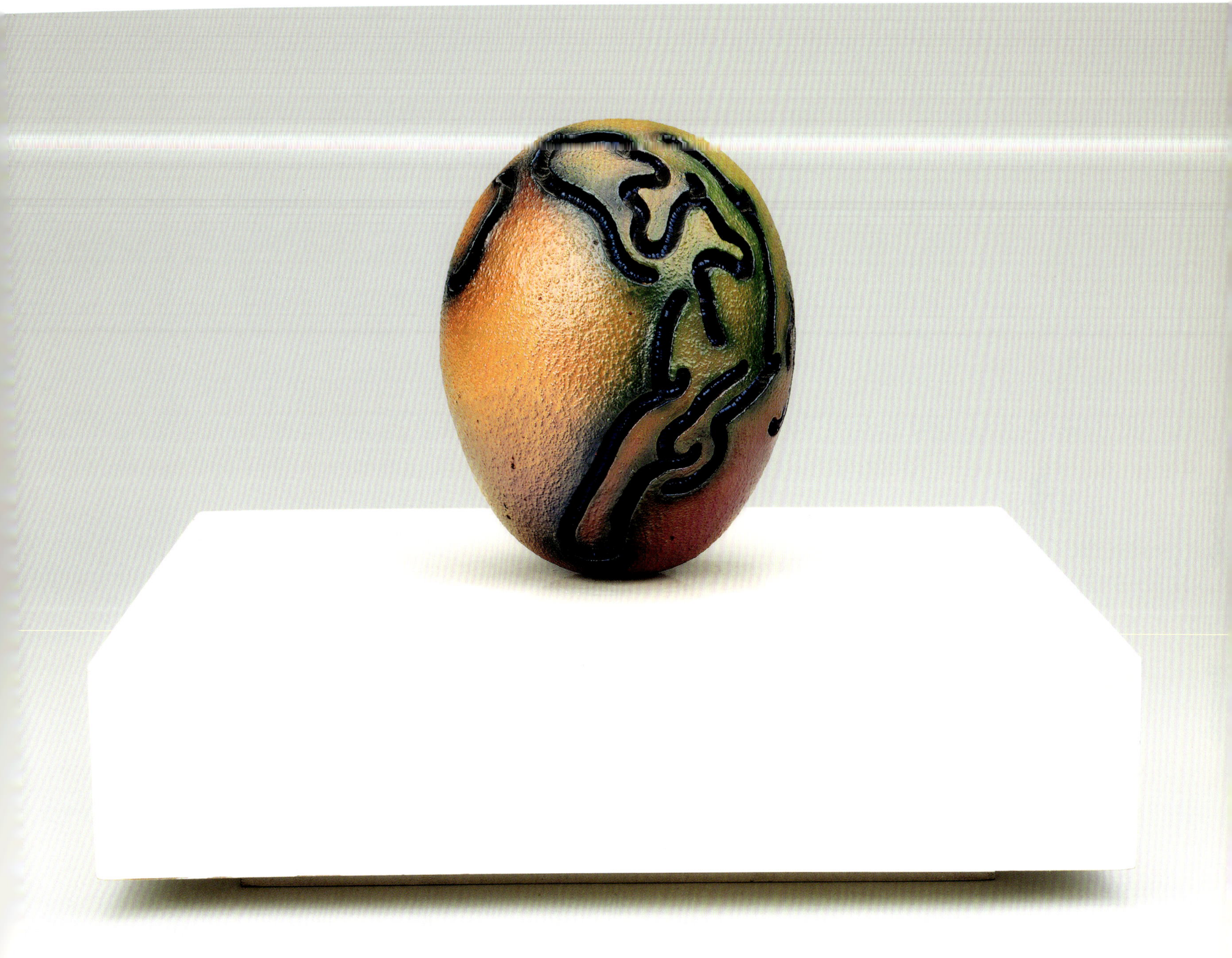

Untitled, c. 1962

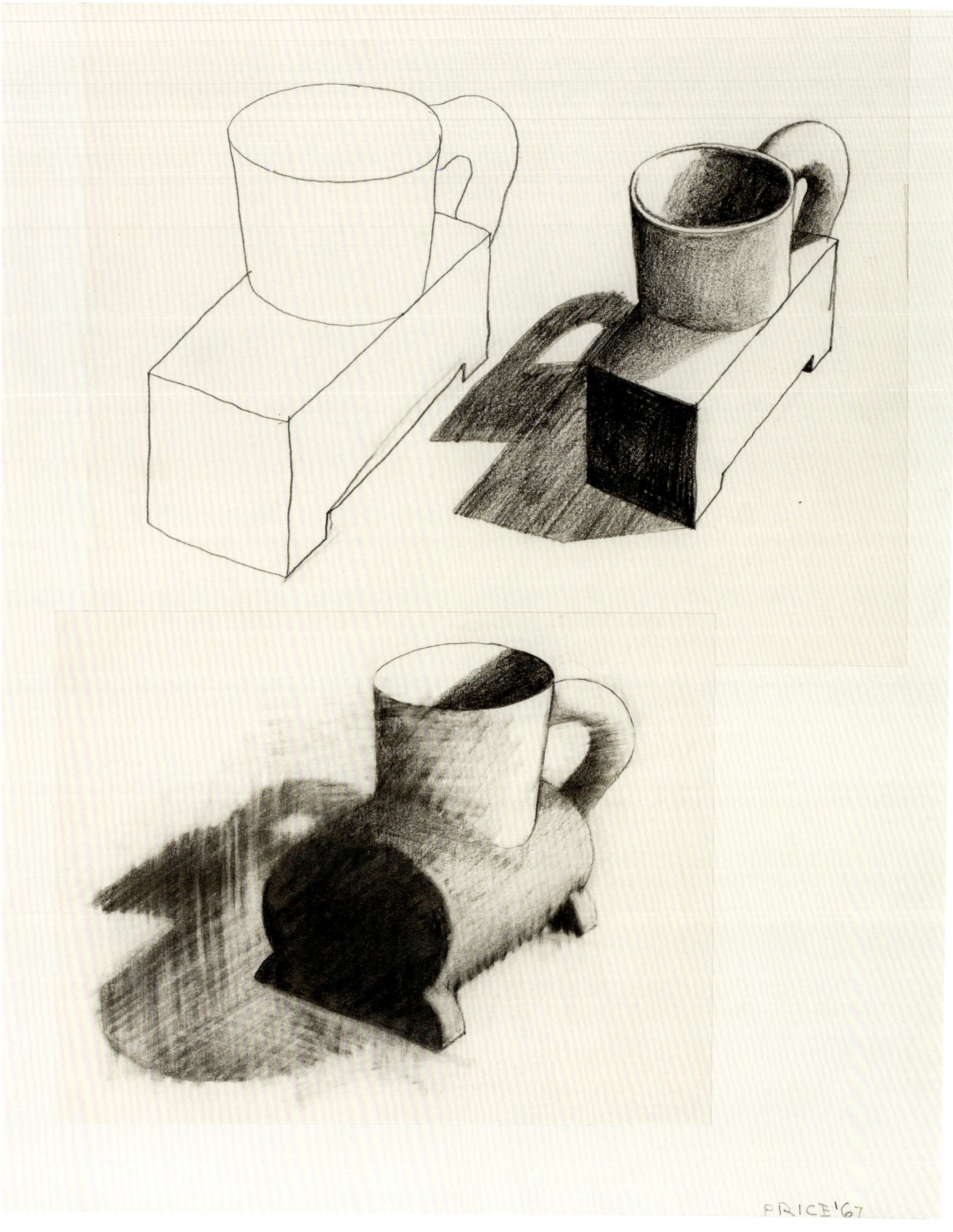

Untitled, 1967

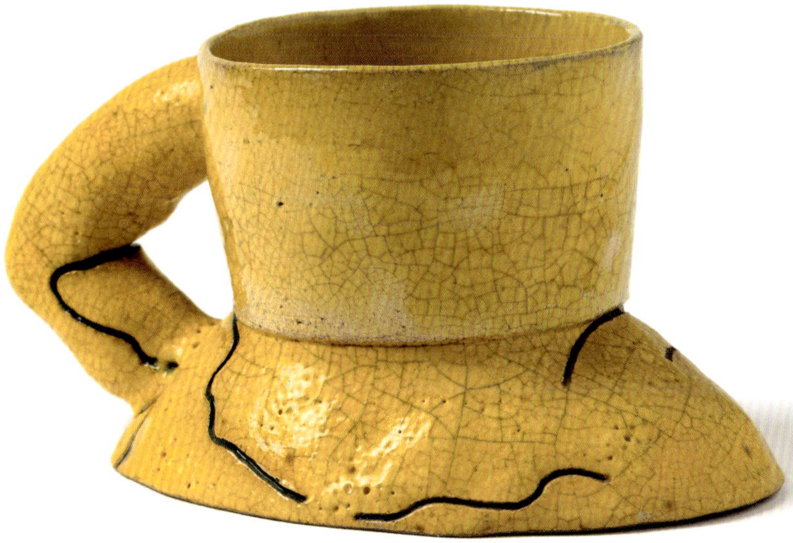

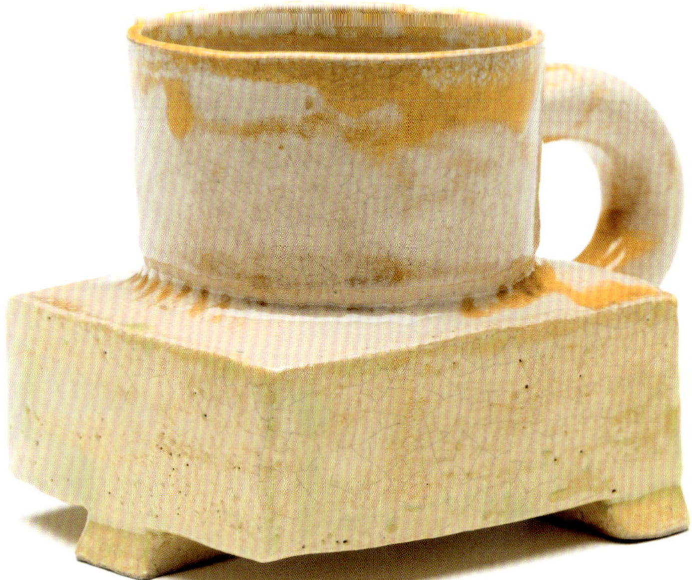

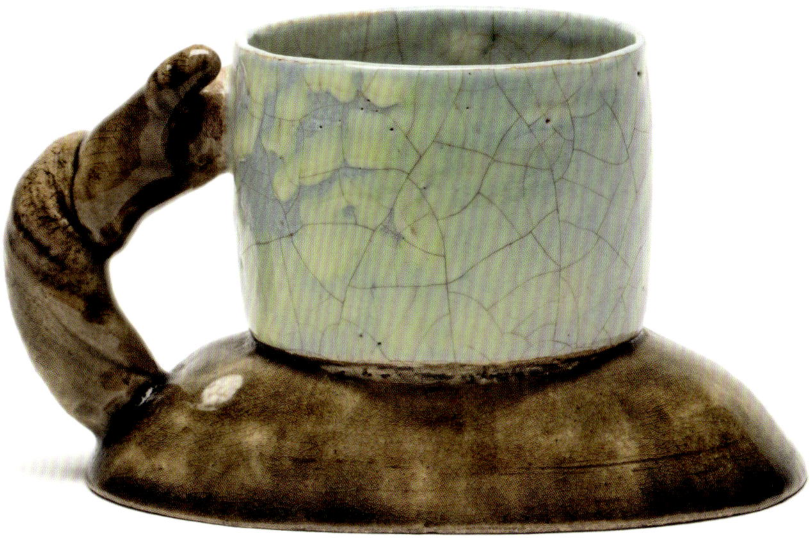

CLOCKWISE FROM TOP LEFT:
Electric Cup, c. 1966
Untitled, 1968
Twisted Twig Cup, 1966

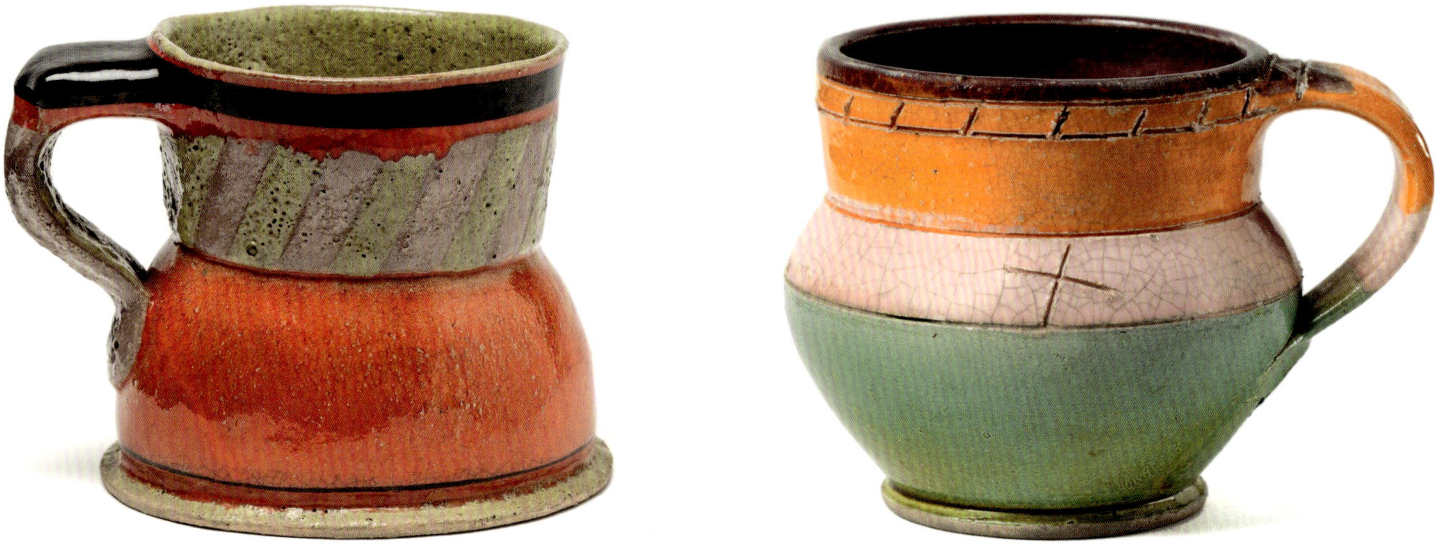

Untitled, 1965
Untitled, 1976

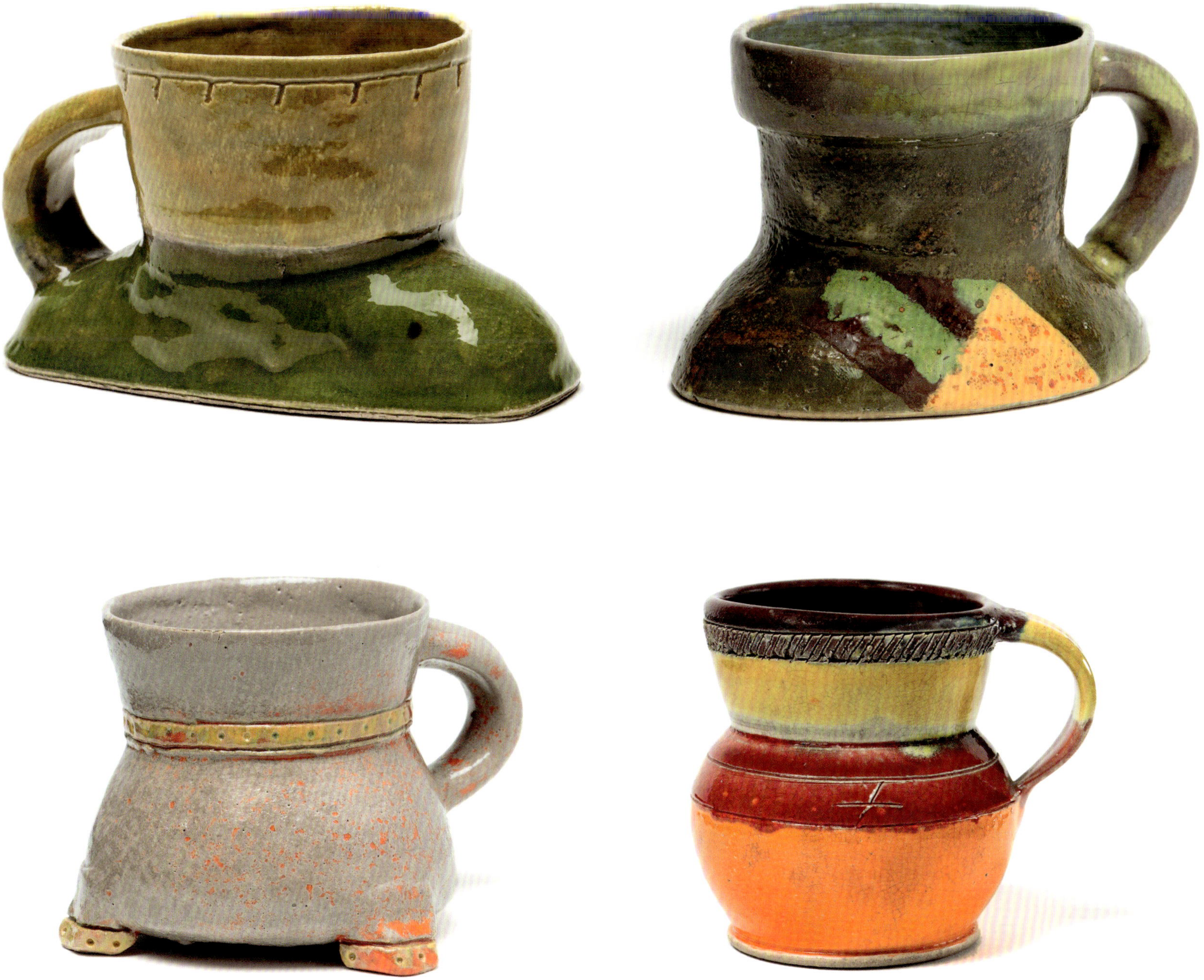

CLOCKWISE FROM TOP LEFT:
Untitled, c. 1966
Untitled, 1960
Untitled, 1976
Untitled, 1964

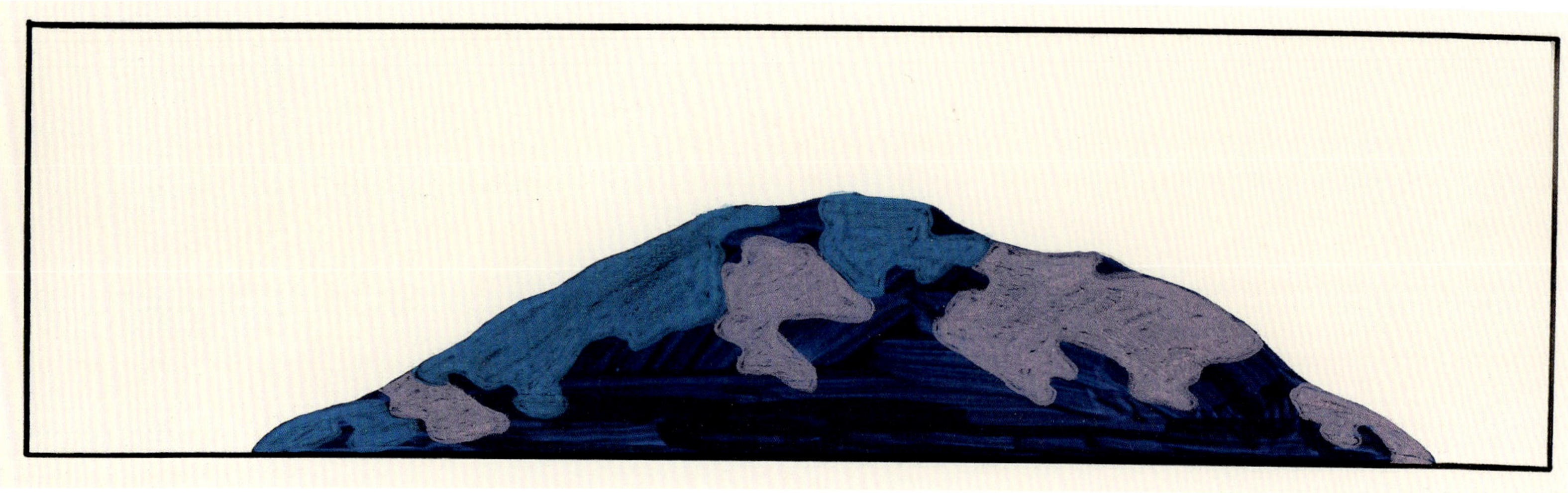

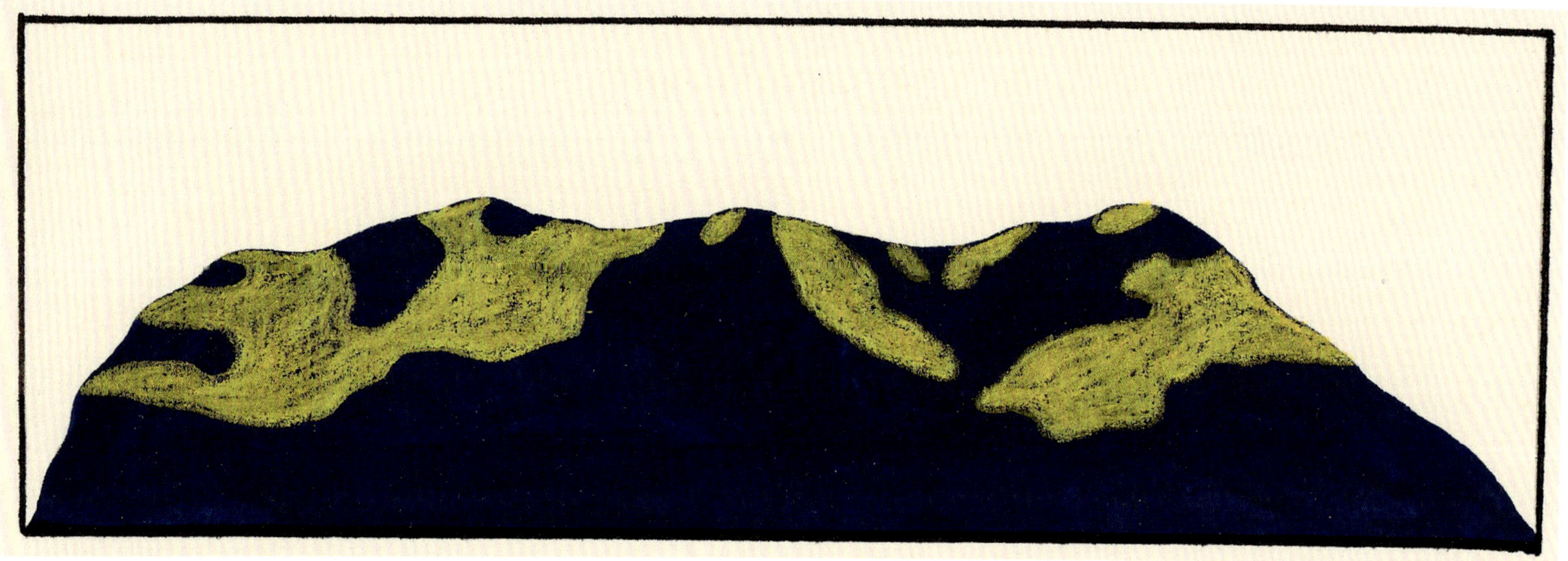

BOTH WORKS:
Reflecting Bump, 1967

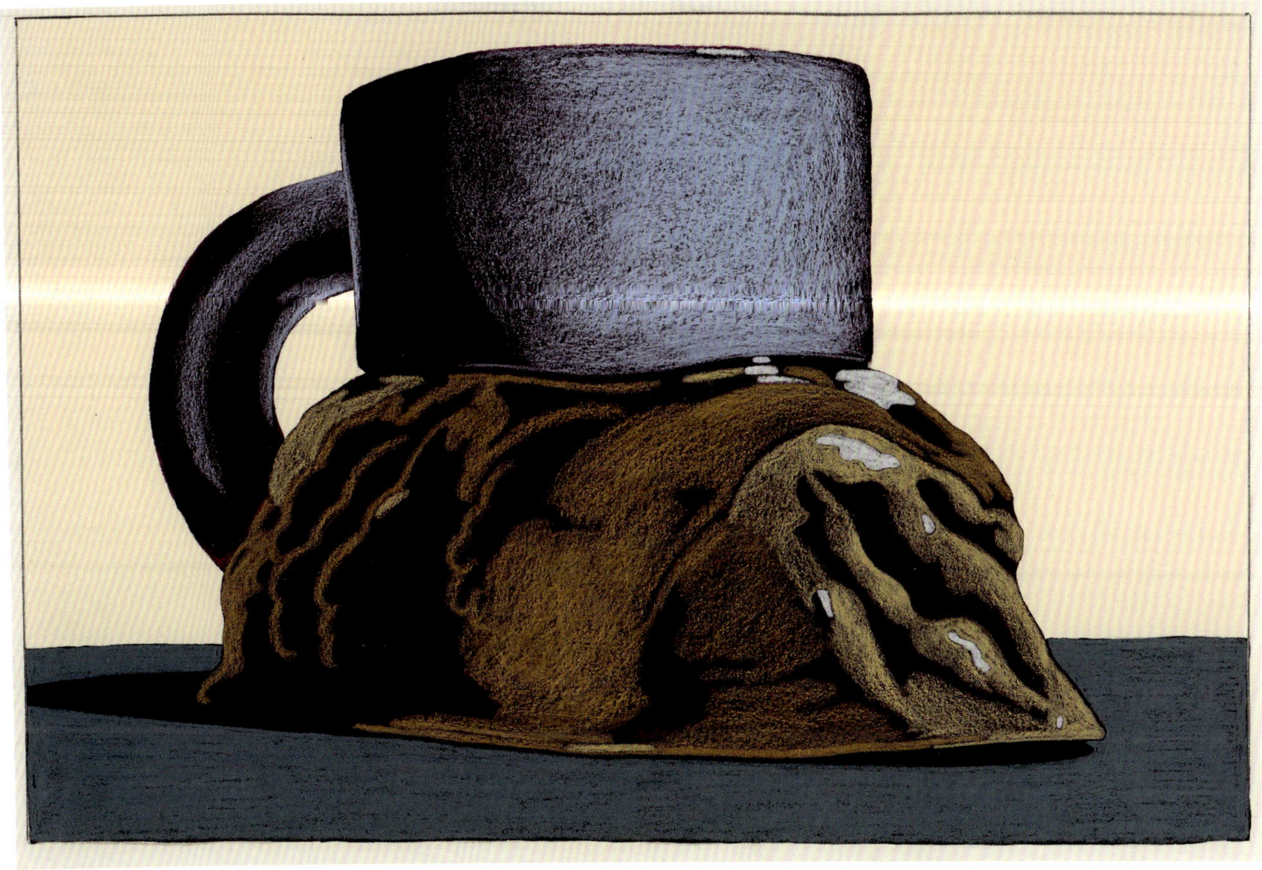

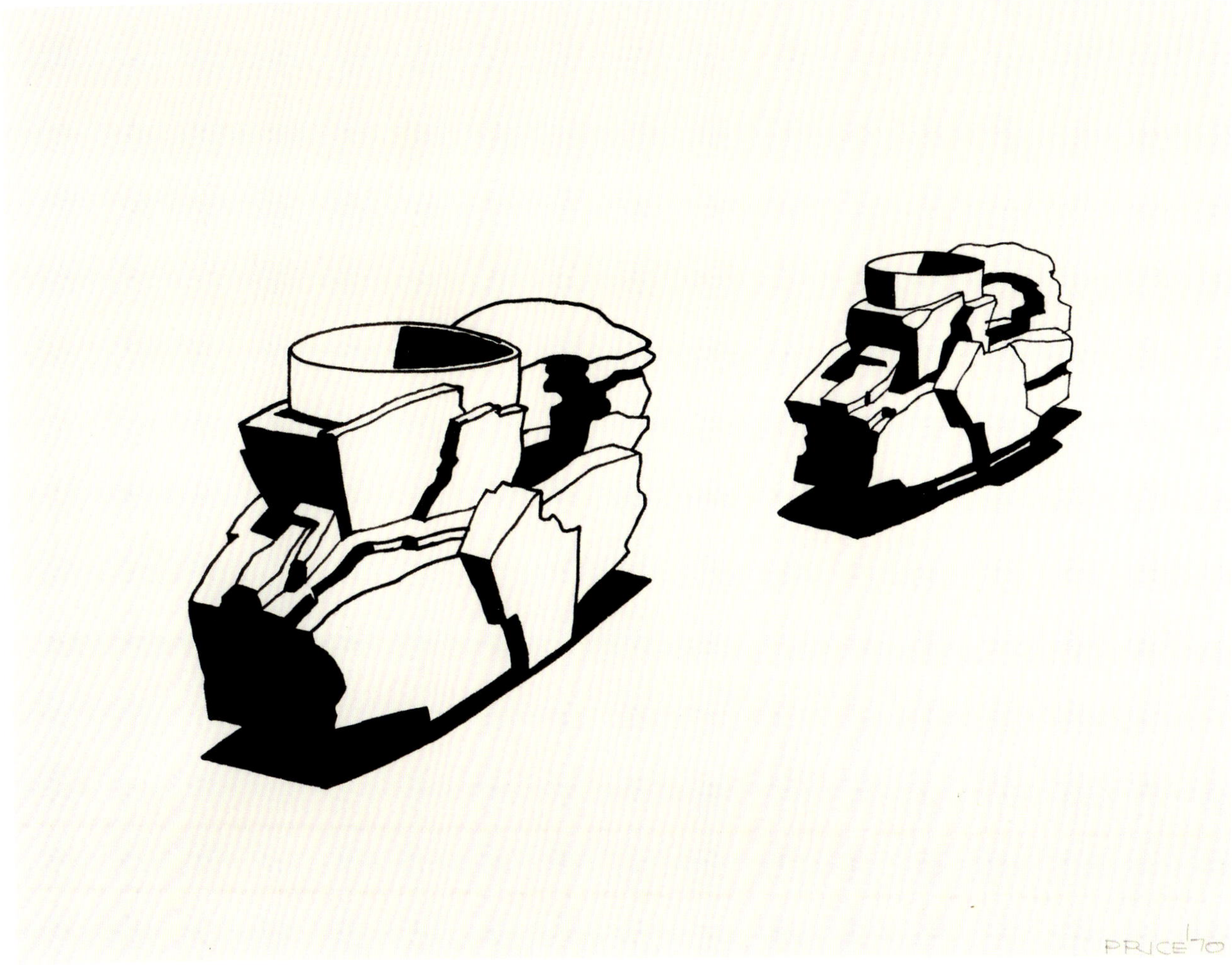

Untitled, 1967
Untitled, 1970

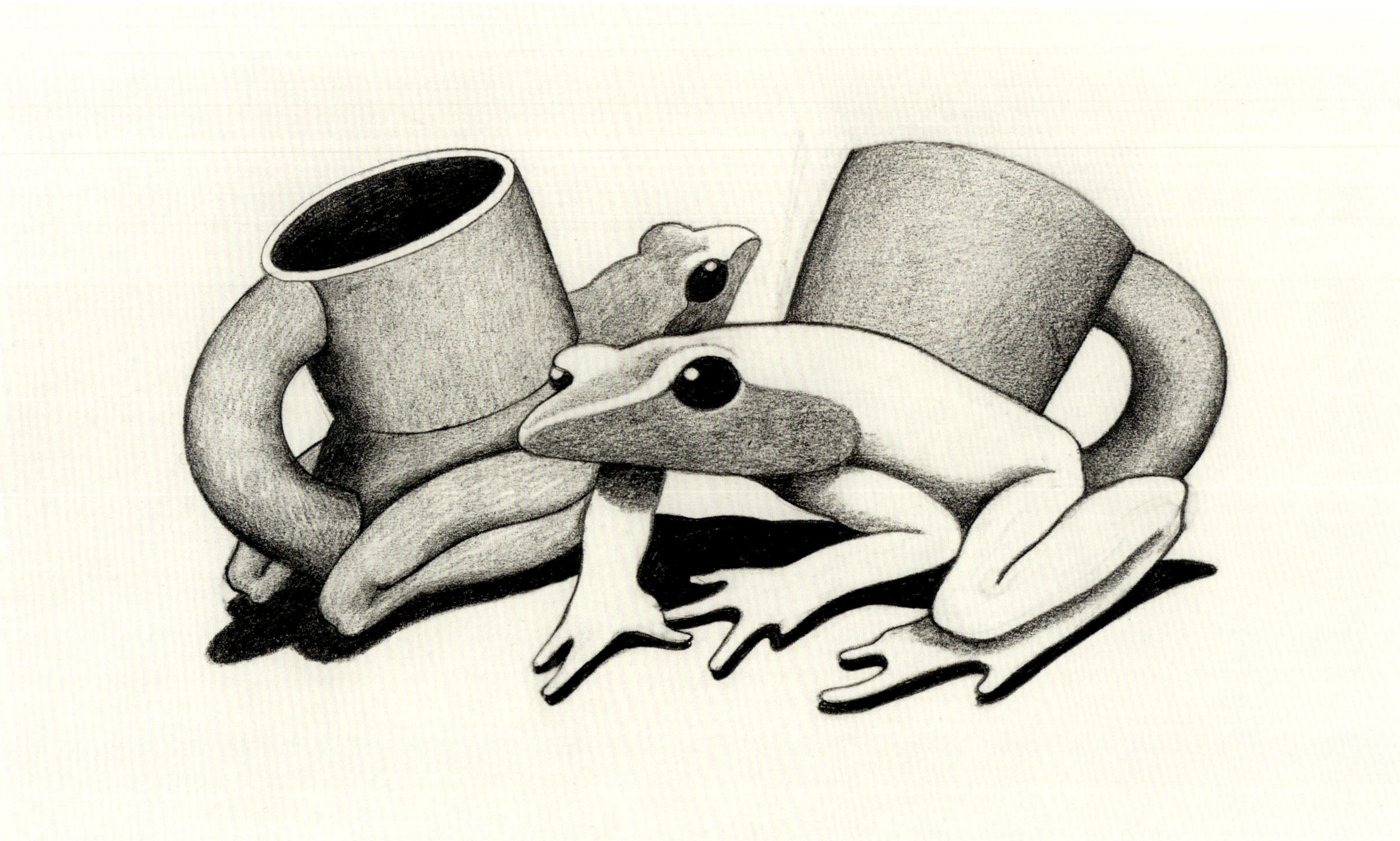

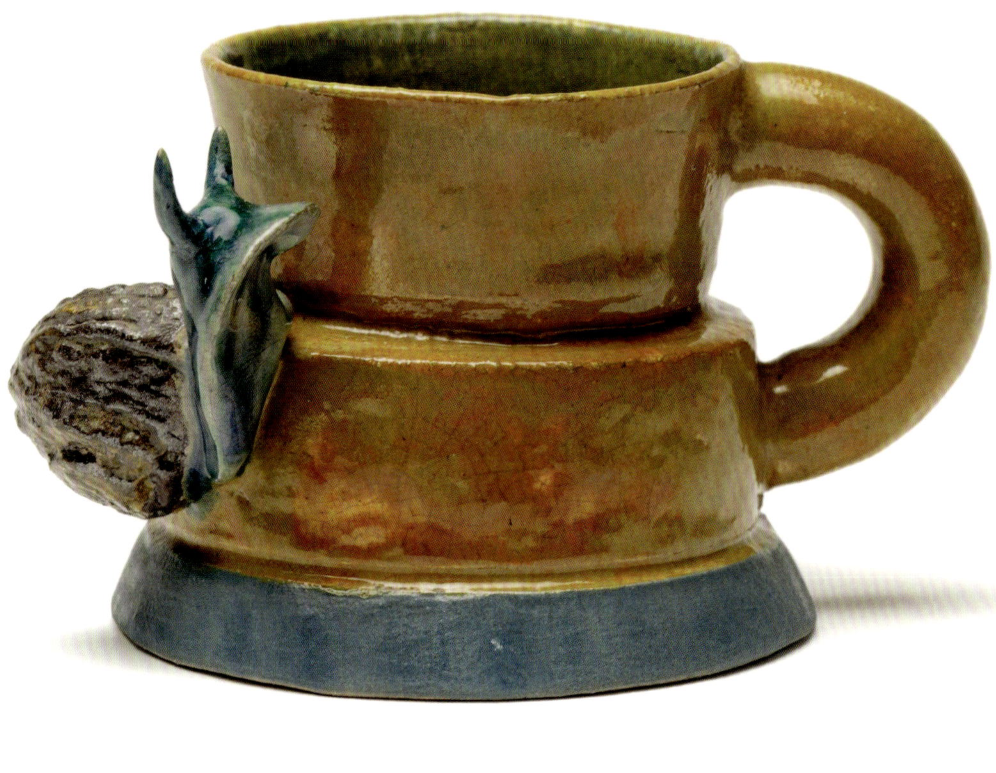

Two-Frog Cup, 1968
Round Snail Cup, 1968

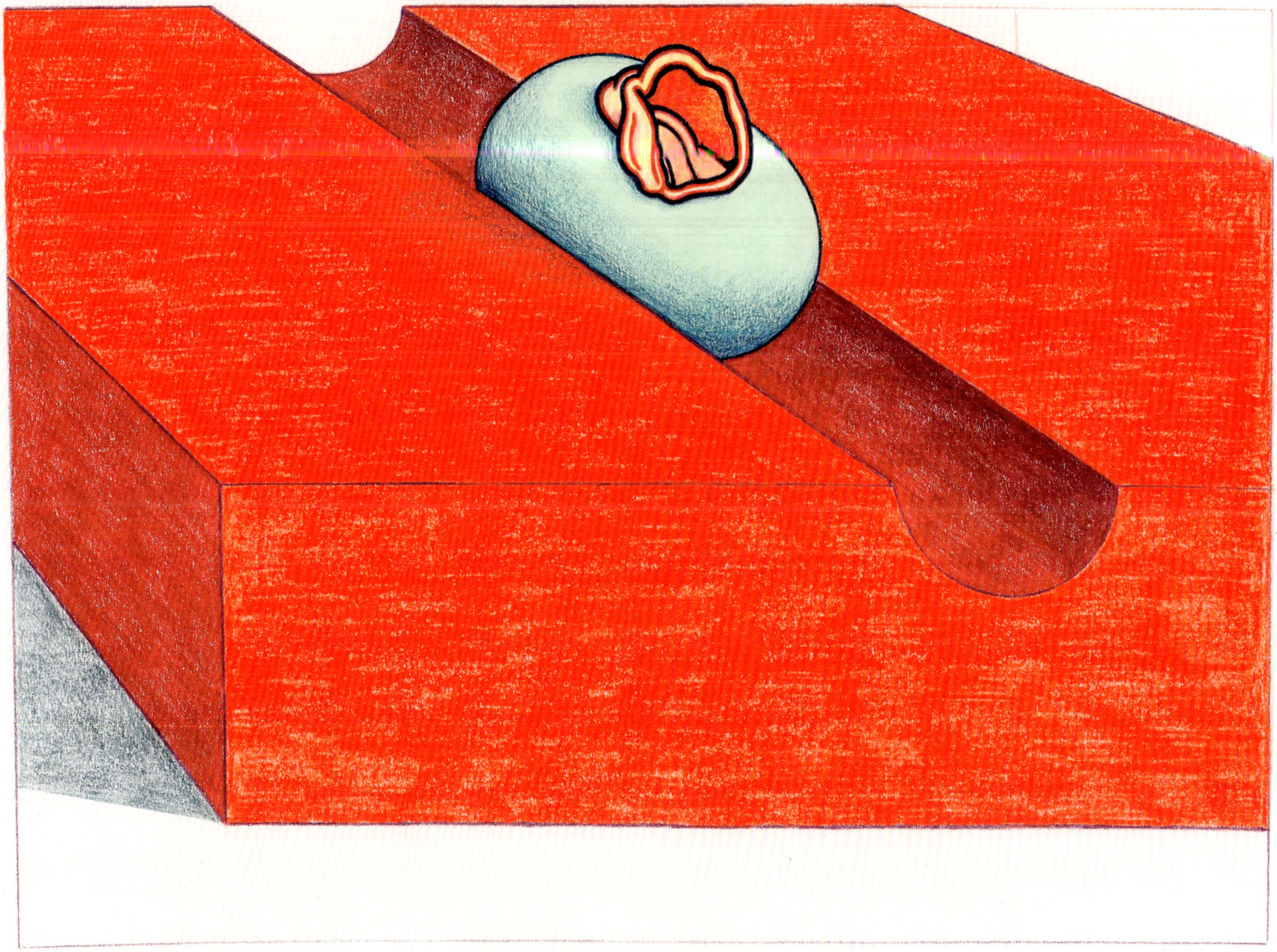

Specimen, 1968

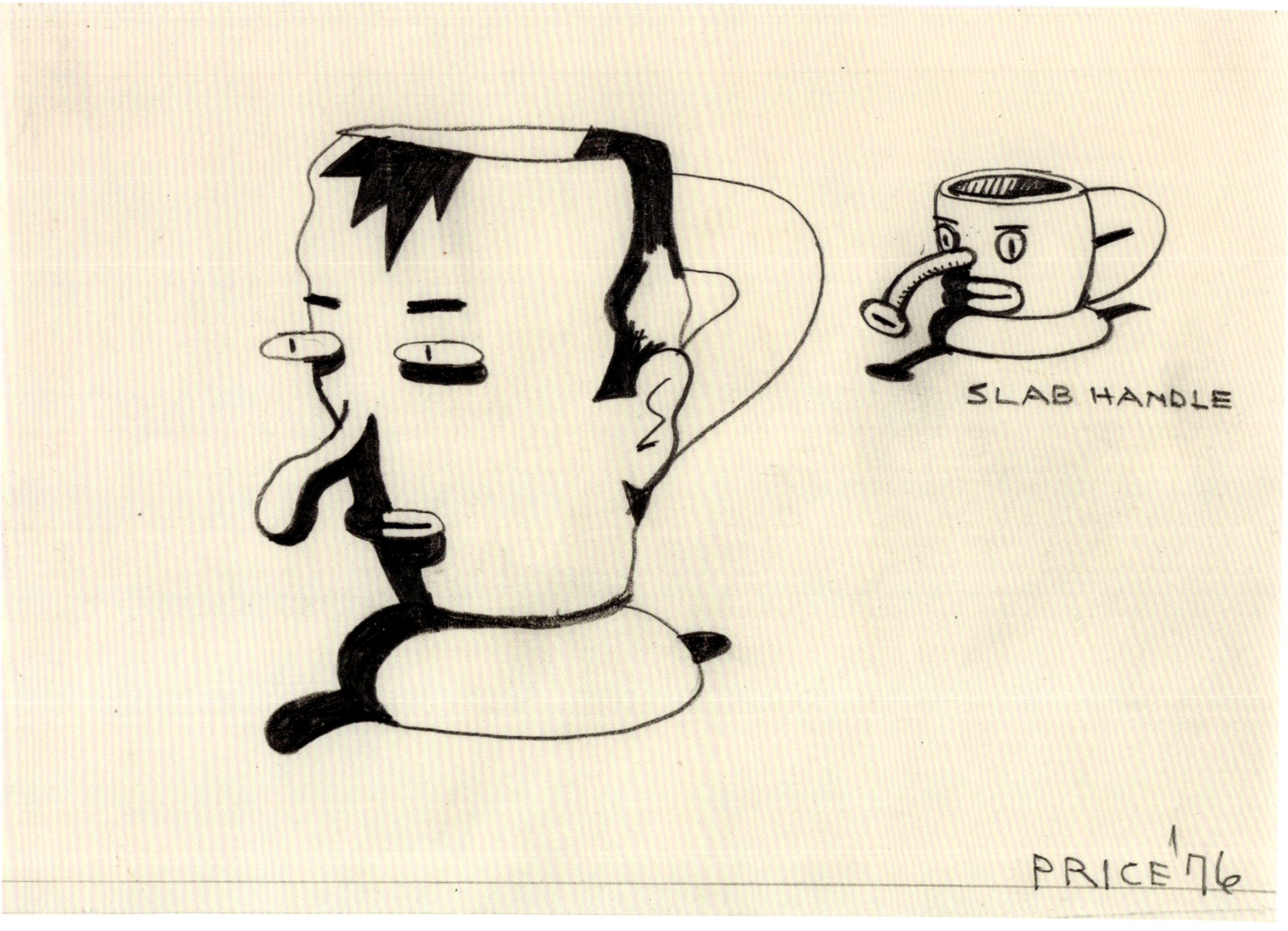

Slab Handle, 1976

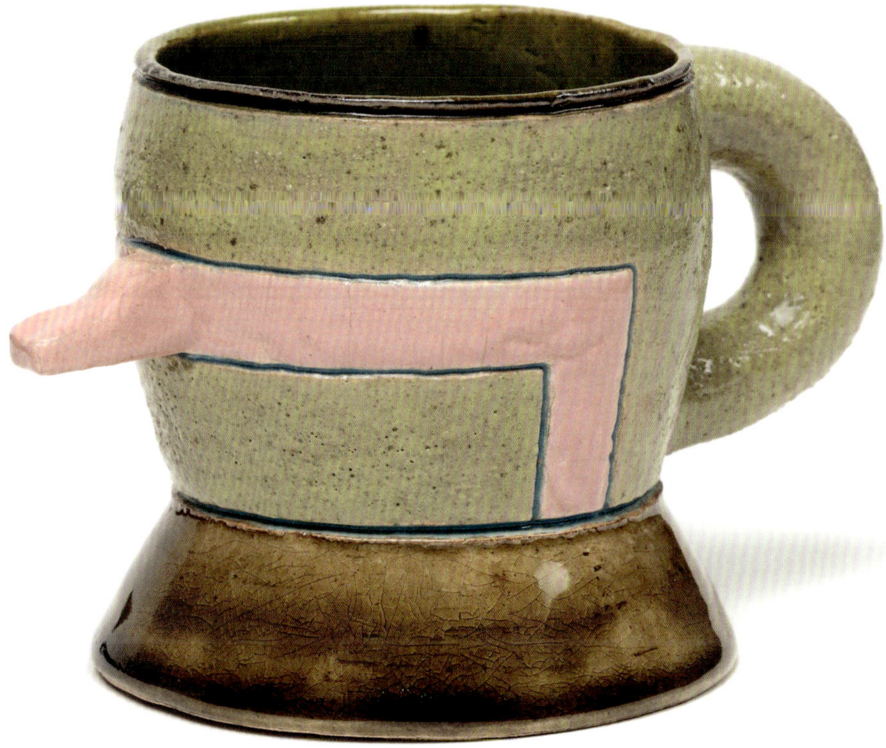

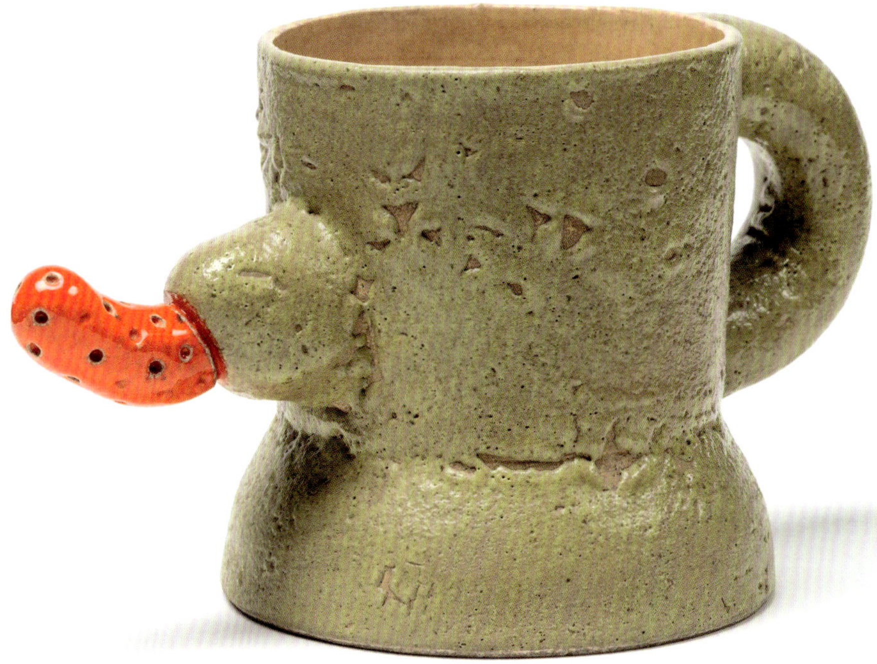

Nose Cup—Late '30s, 1969
Untitled, 1968–69

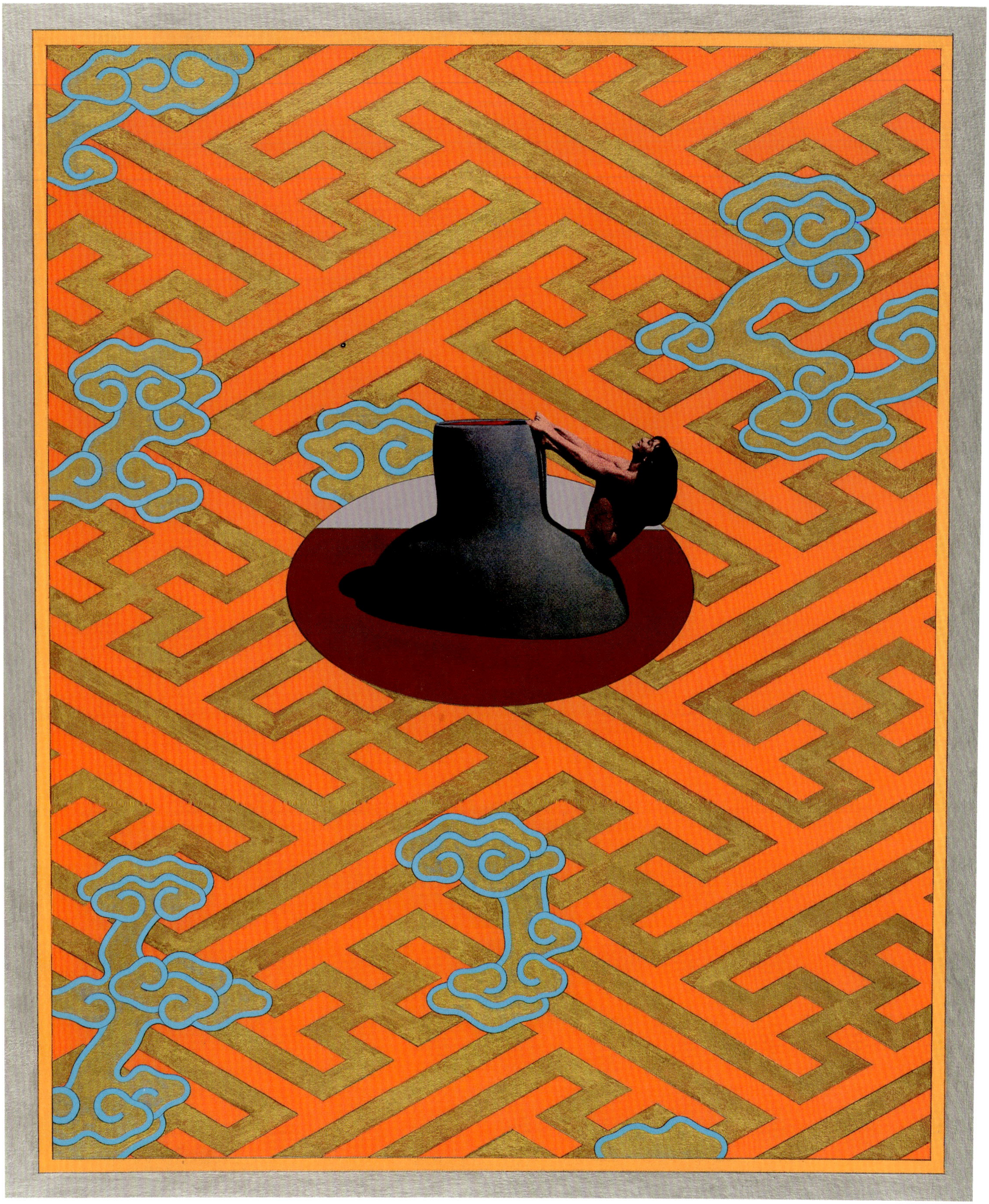

Study for Chinese Figurine Cup, 1969

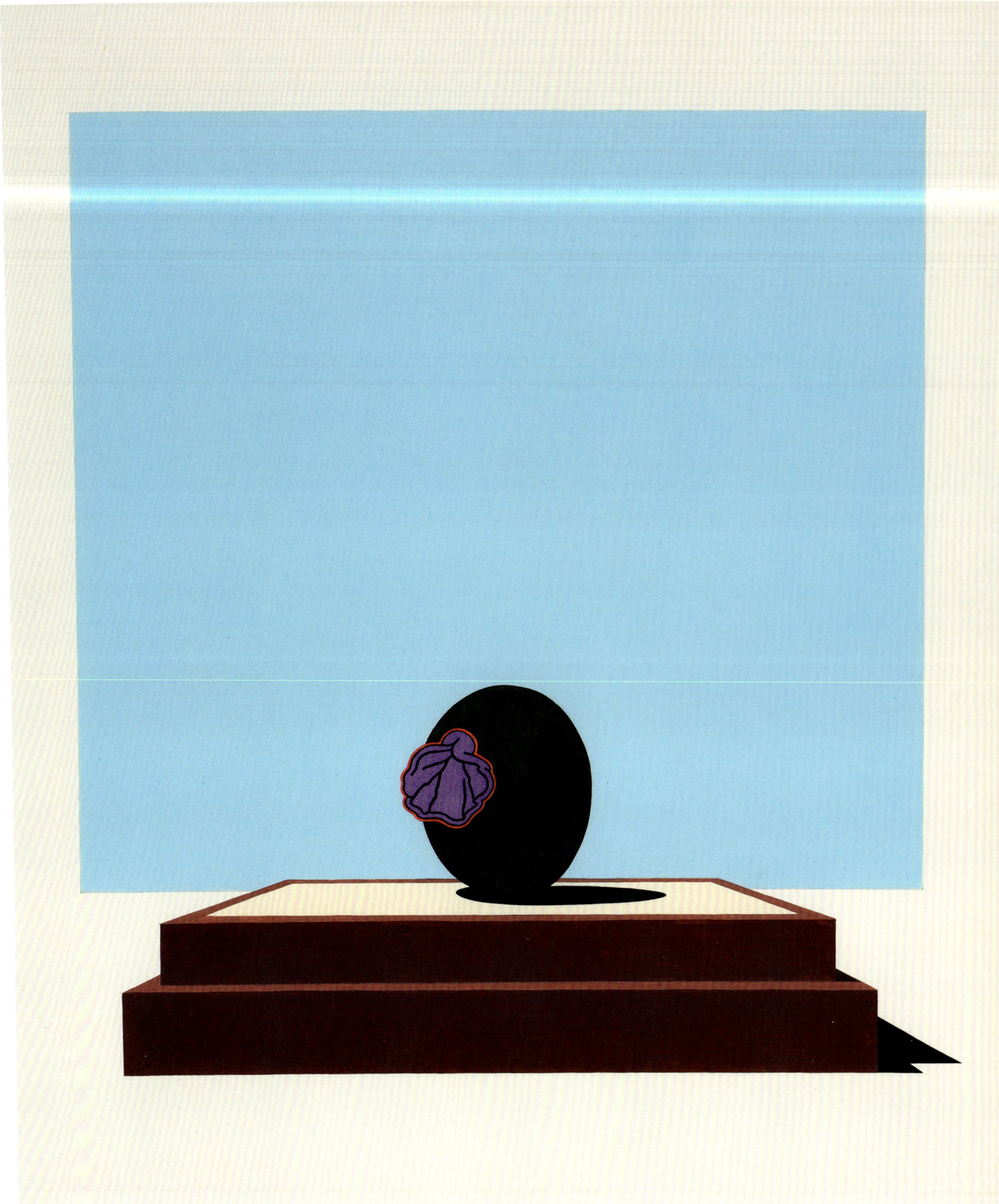

Specimen G5228, 1971

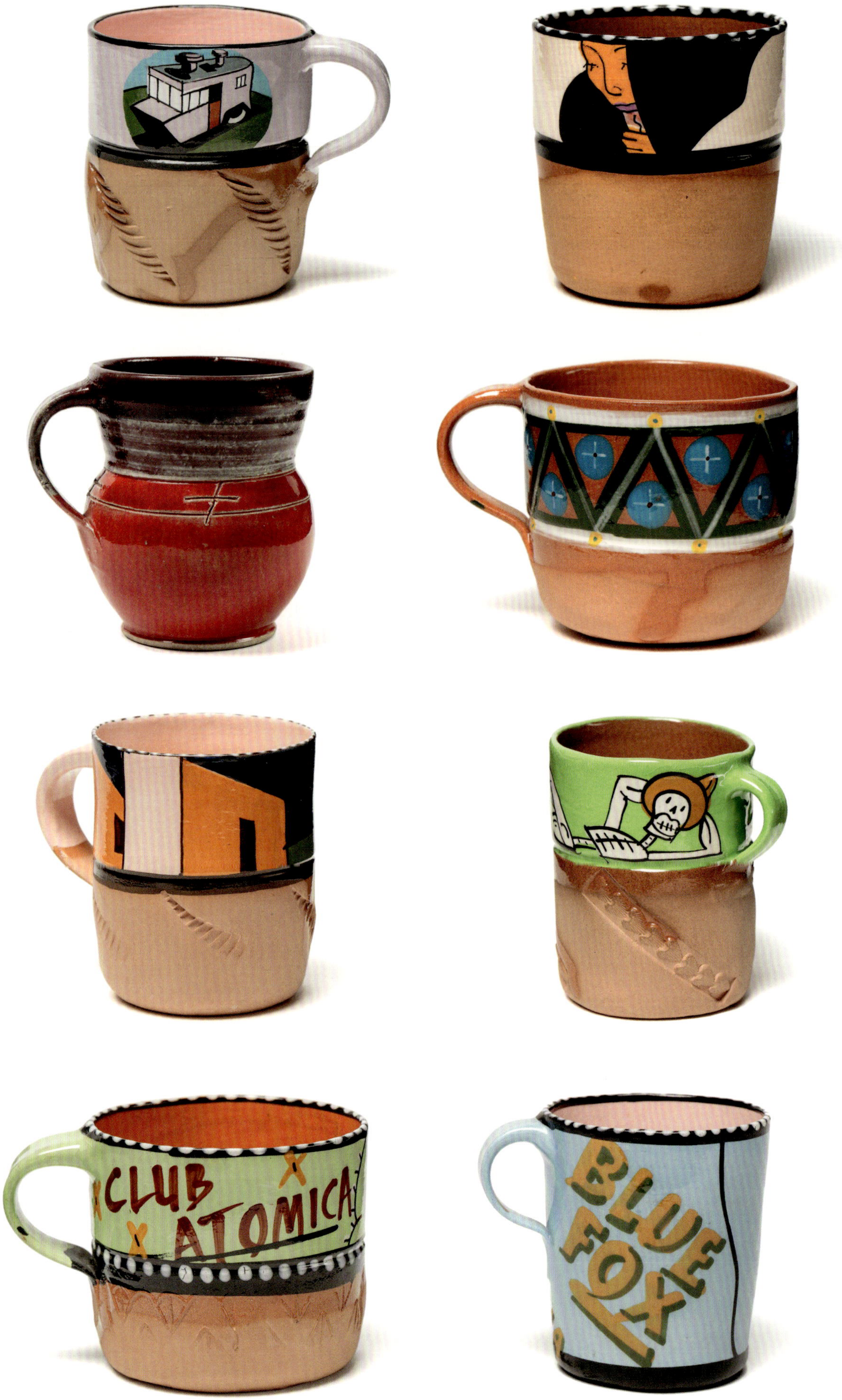

CLOCKWISE FROM TOP LEFT:
Untitled, 1972–77
Untitled, 1972–77
Untitled, 1972–77
Untitled, 1972–77
Untitled, 1982
Untitled, 1976
Untitled, 1972–77
Untitled, 1976

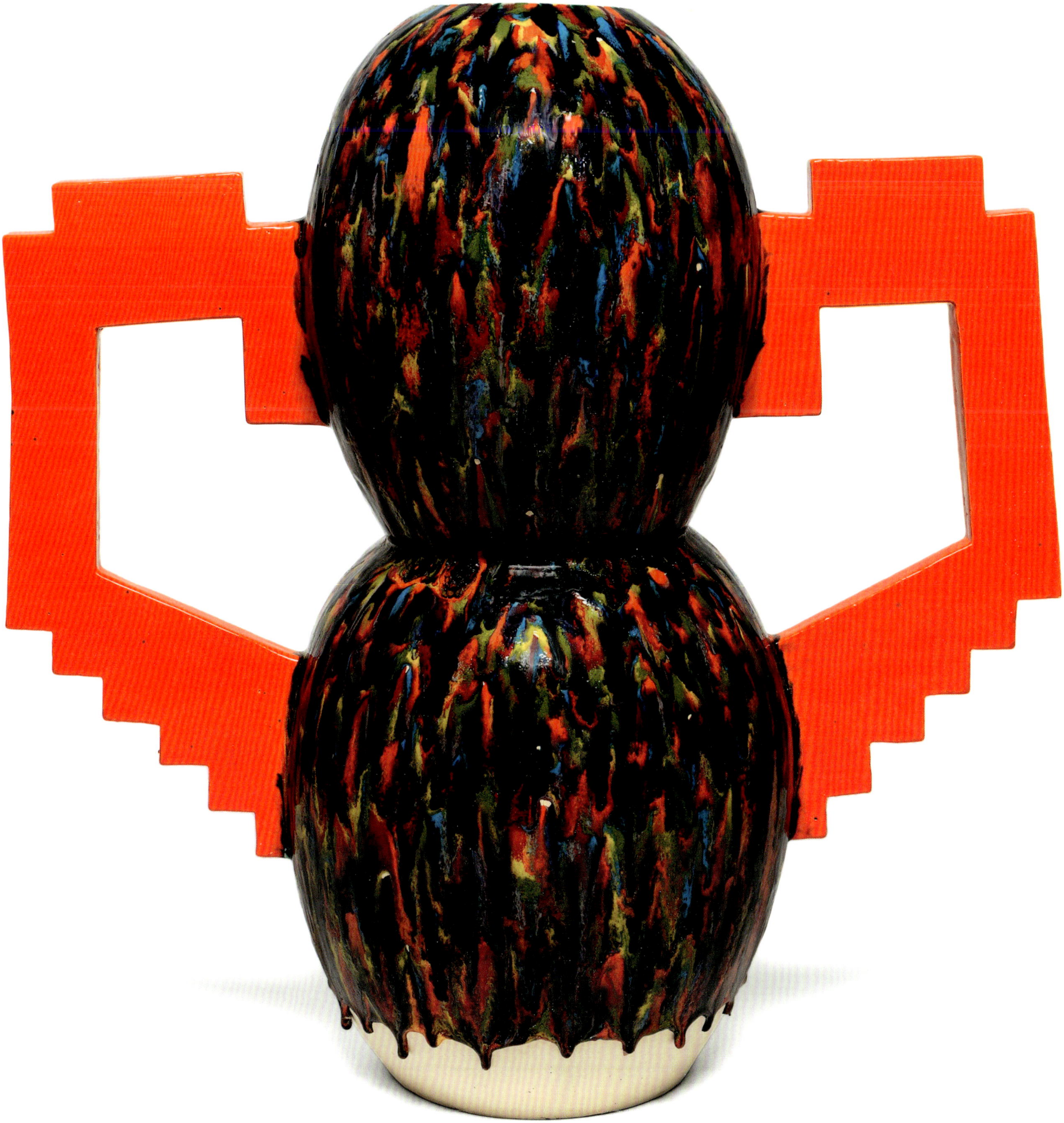

Untitled No. 312, 1972–77

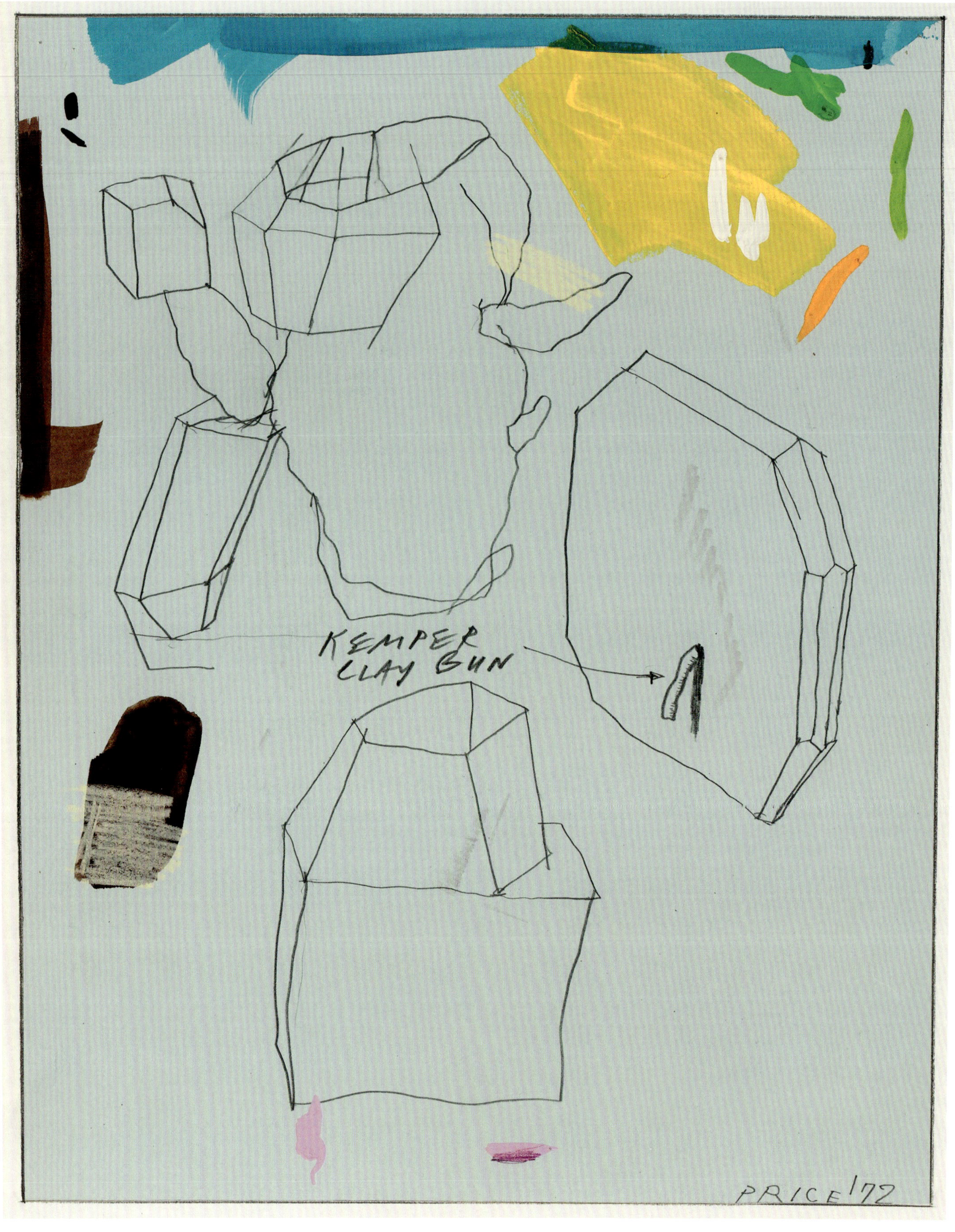

Kemper Clay Bun, 1972

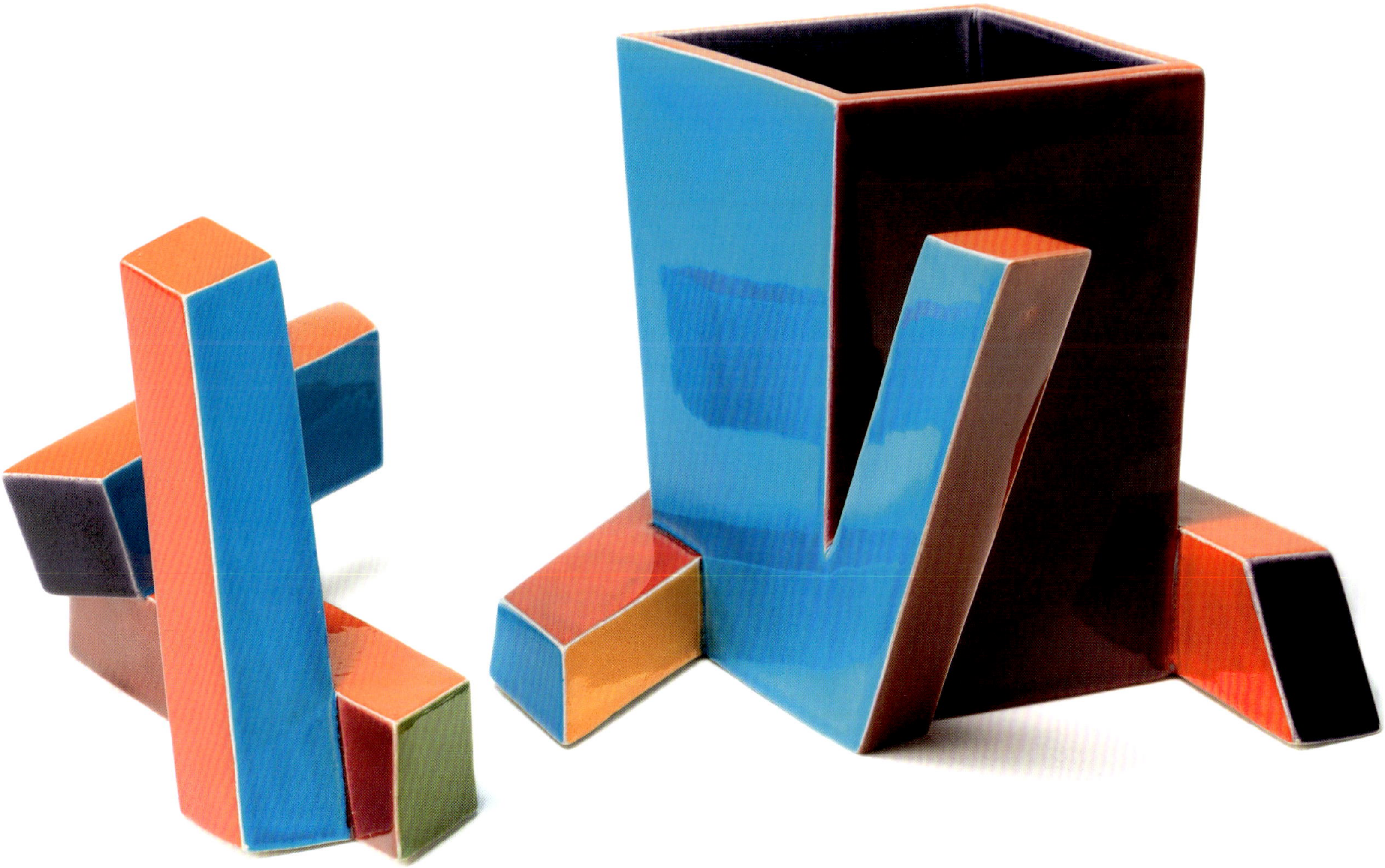

Untitled #7, 1974

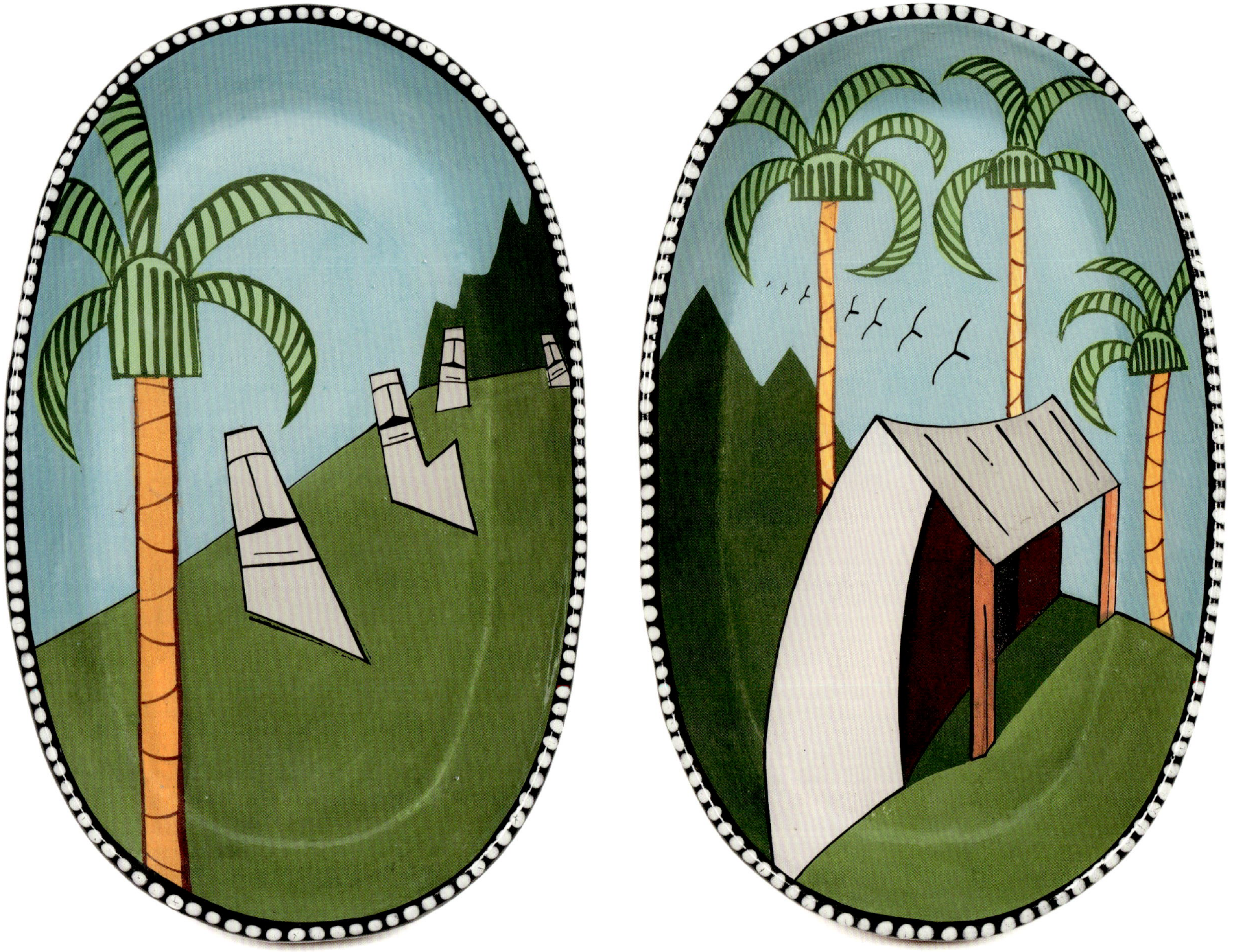

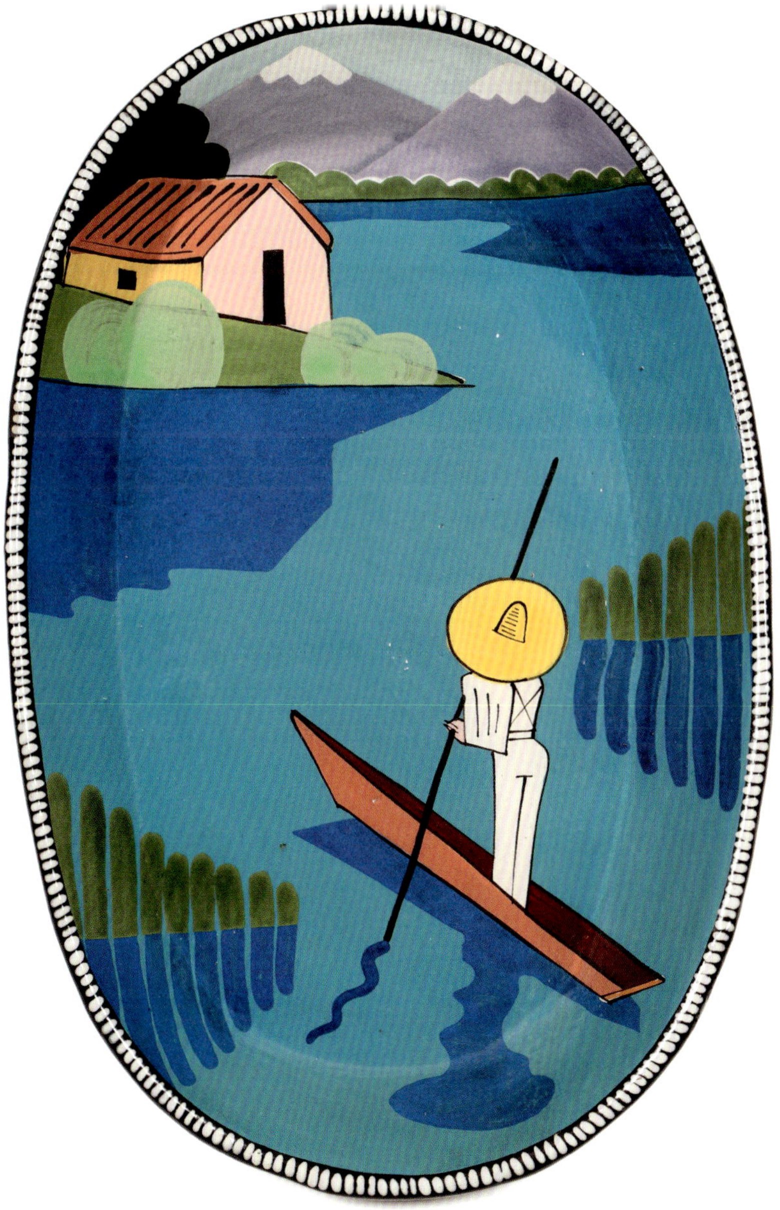

LEFT TO RIGHT:
Untitled, c. 1980
Untitled, c. 1980
Untitled, 1972–77

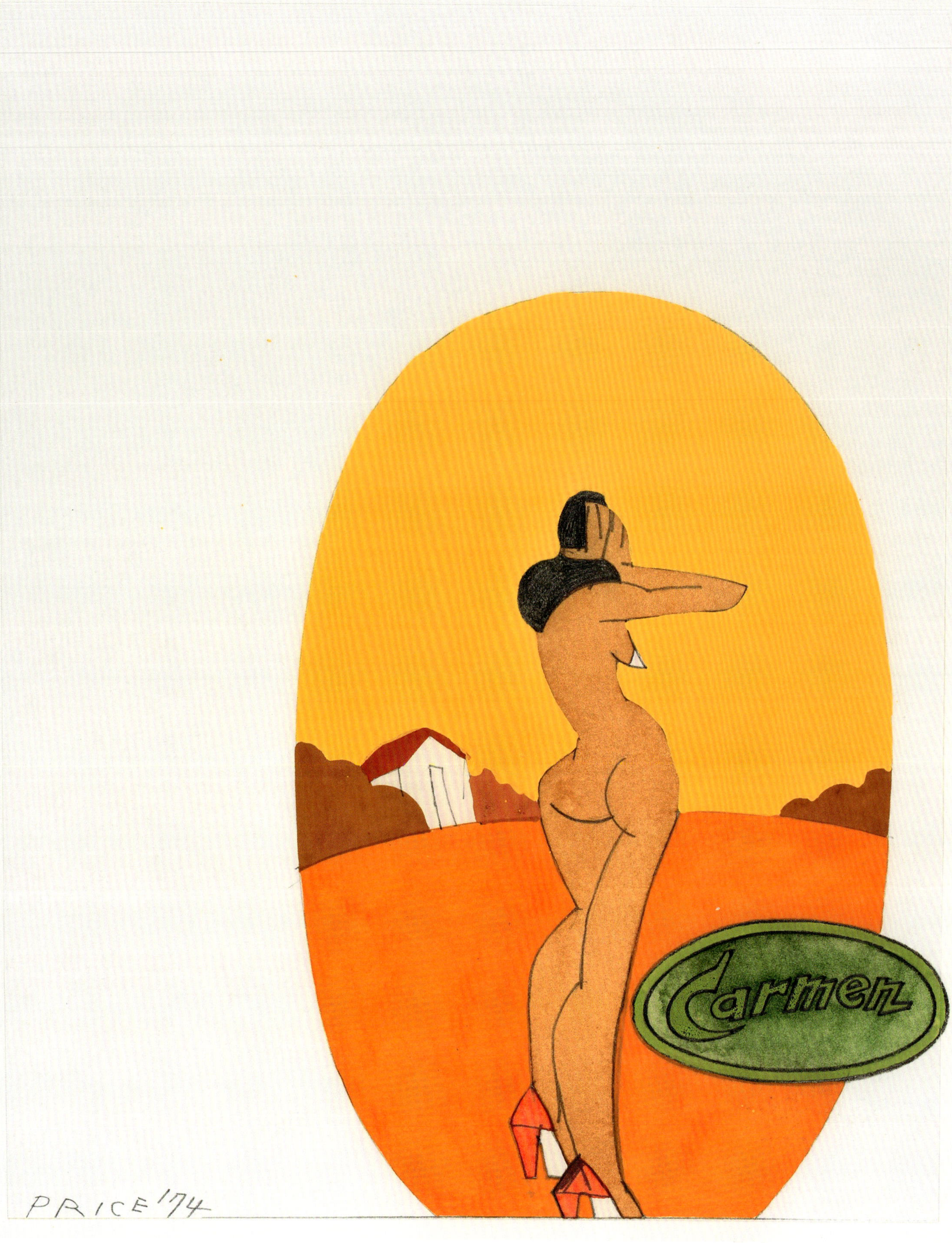
Carmen
PRICE '74

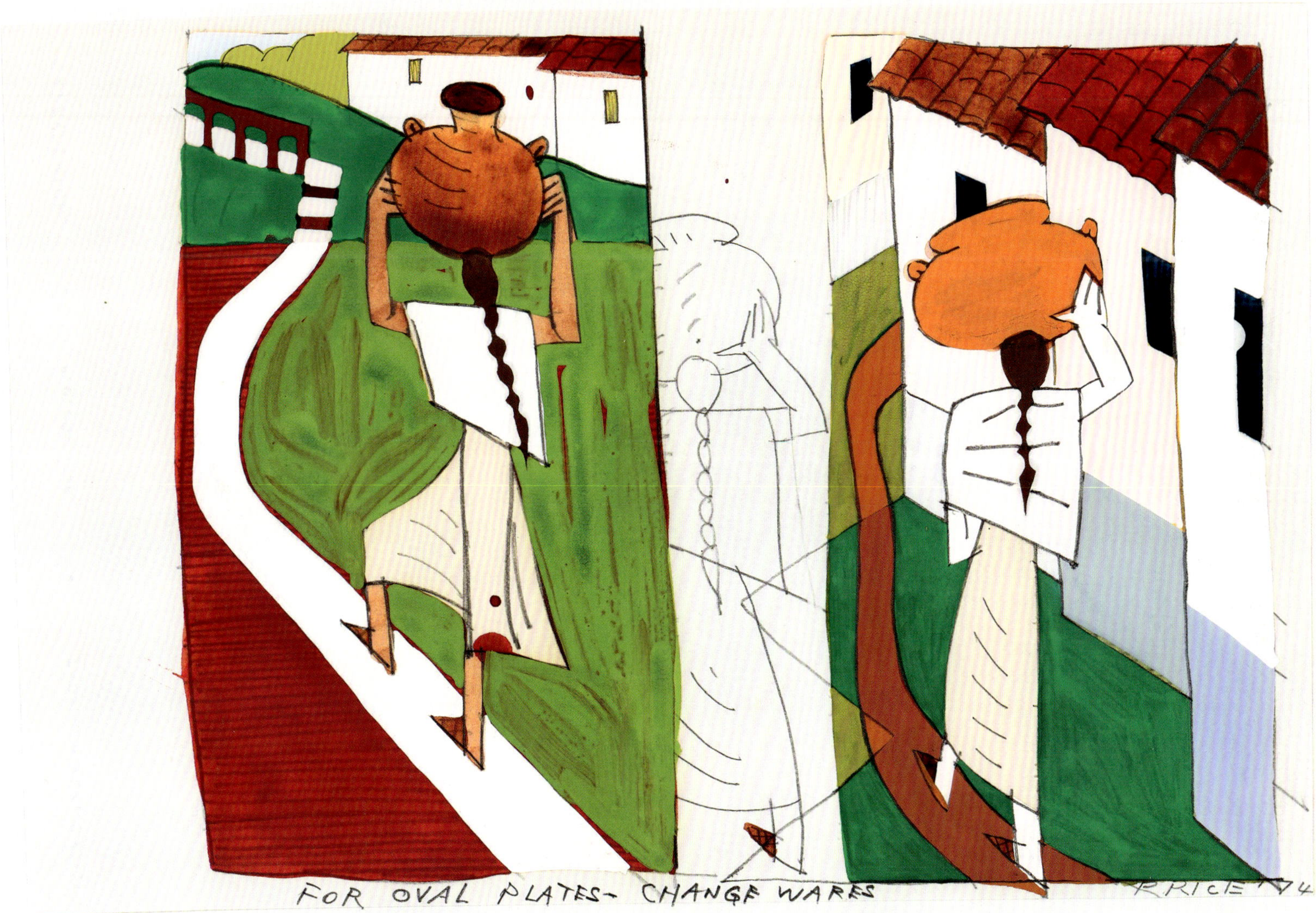

Untitled, 1974
OPPOSITE:
Carmen, 1974

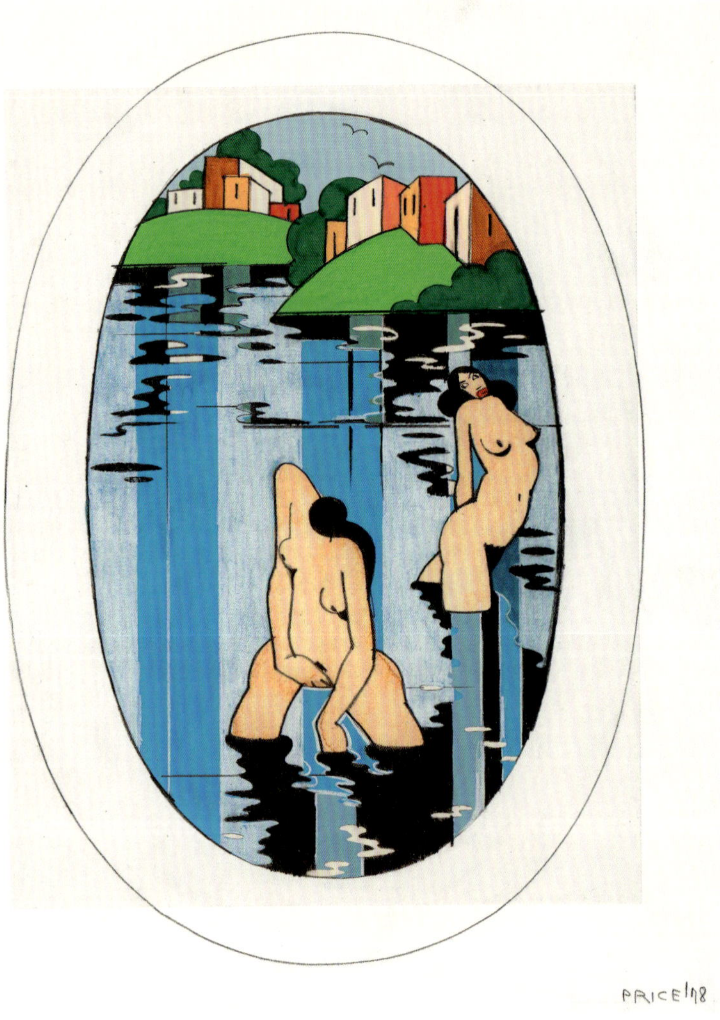

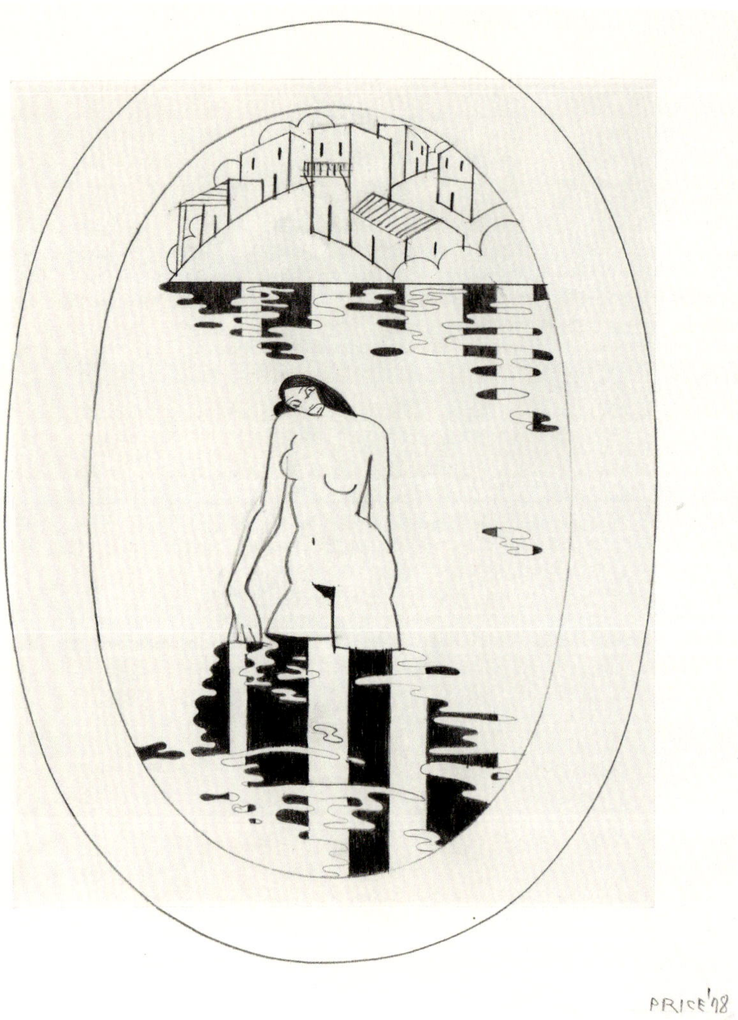

ALL WORKS:
Untitled, 1978

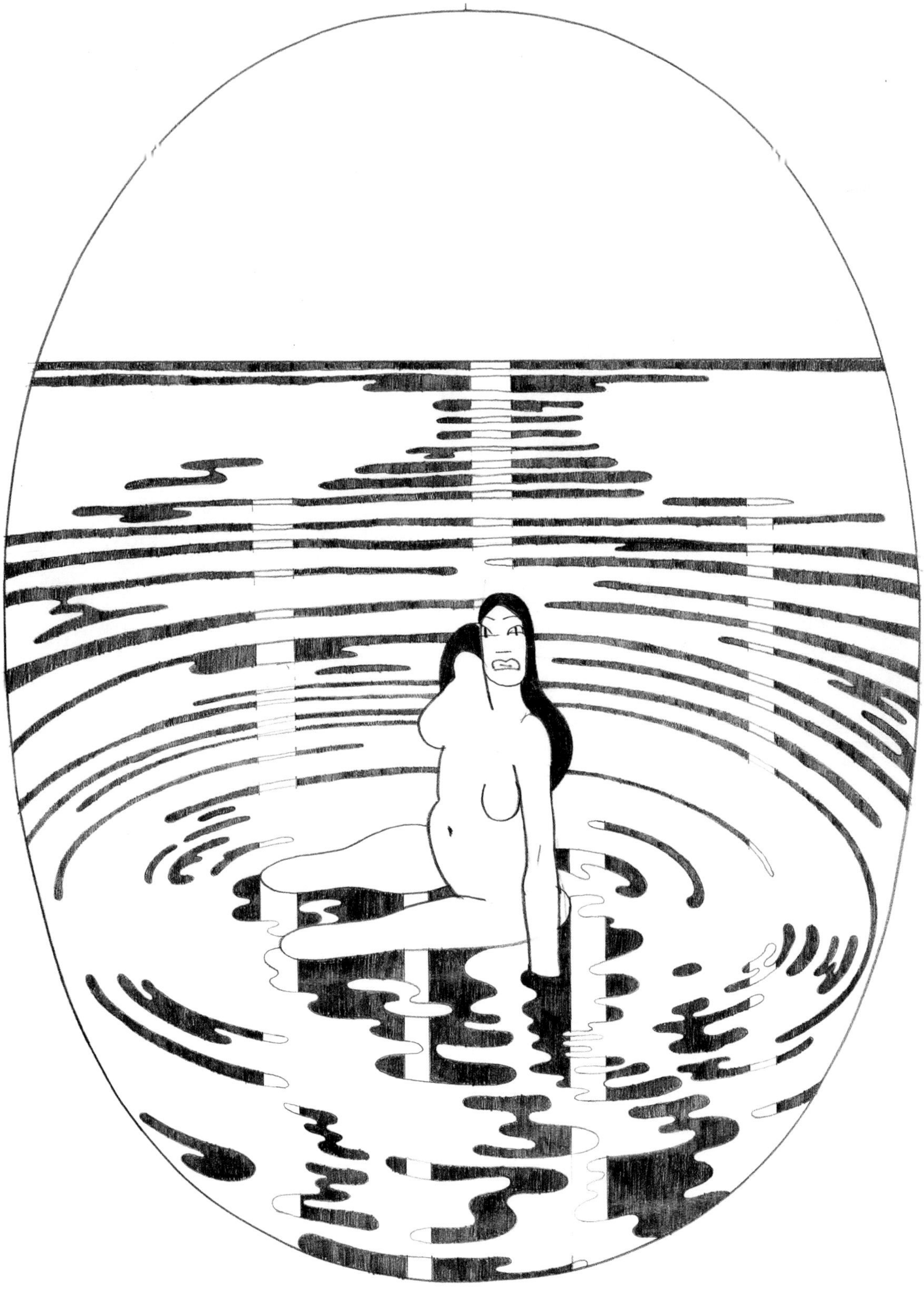

PRICE '08

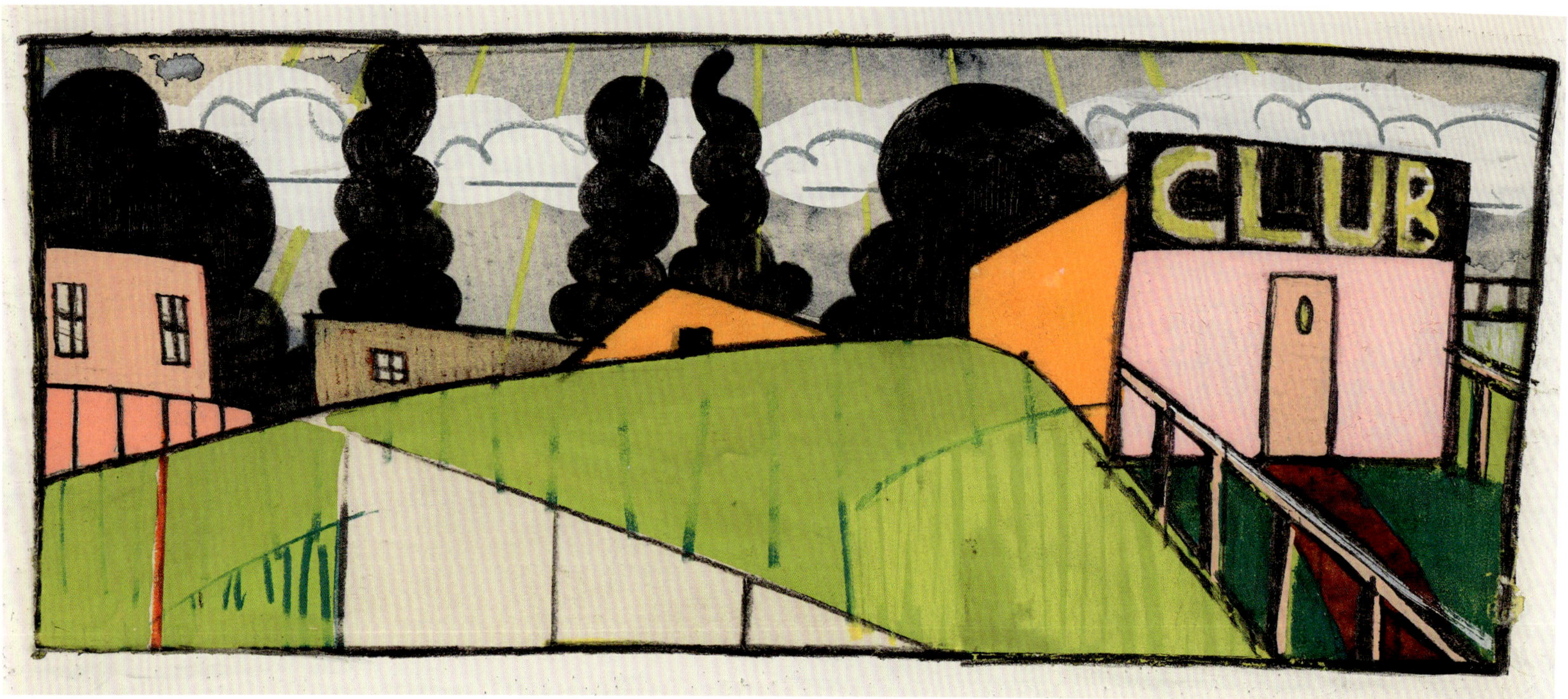

Untitled, 1978

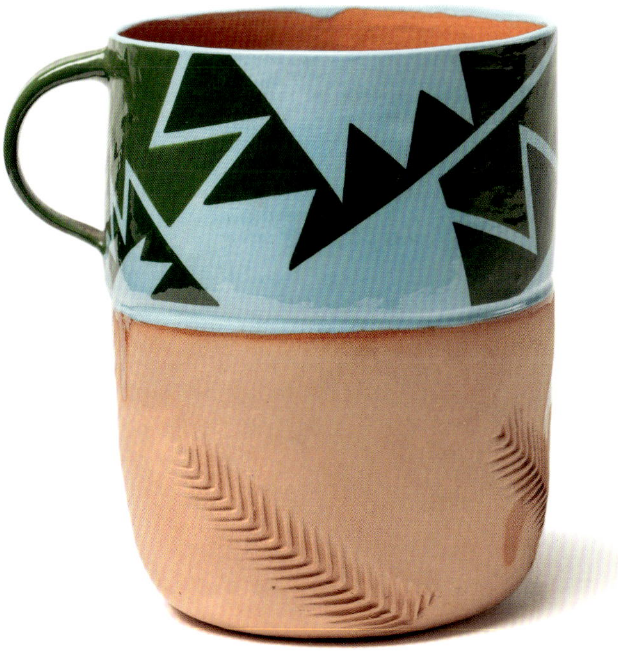

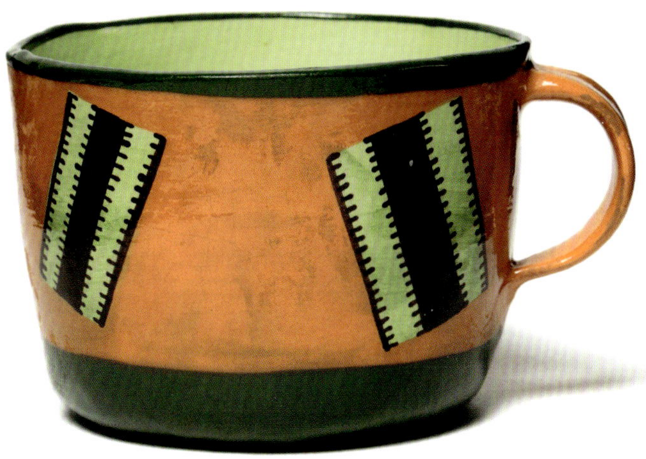

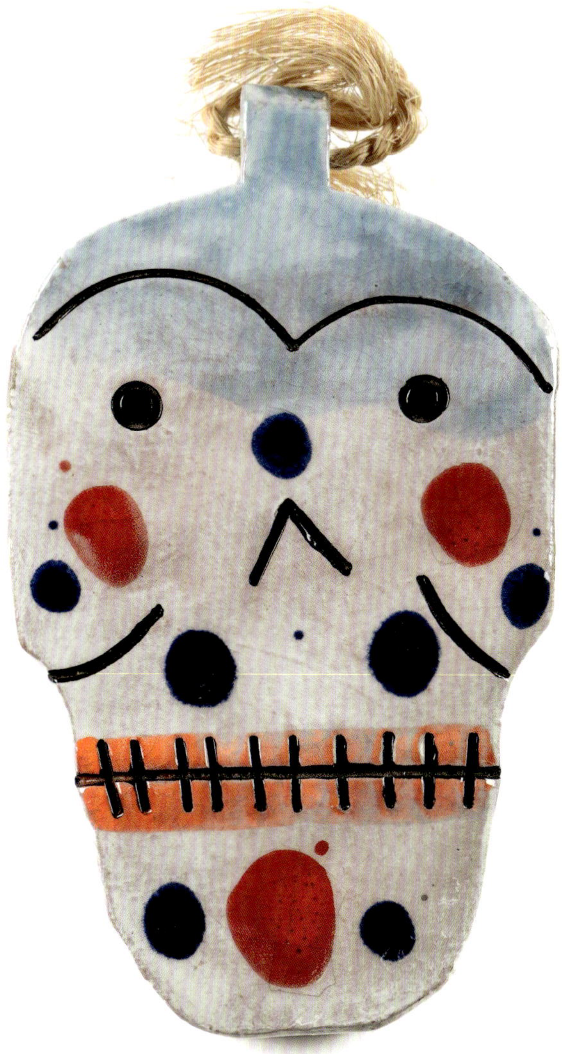

CLOCKWISE FROM TOP LEFT:
Untitled, 1972–77
Untitled, 1972–77
Untitled, 1978

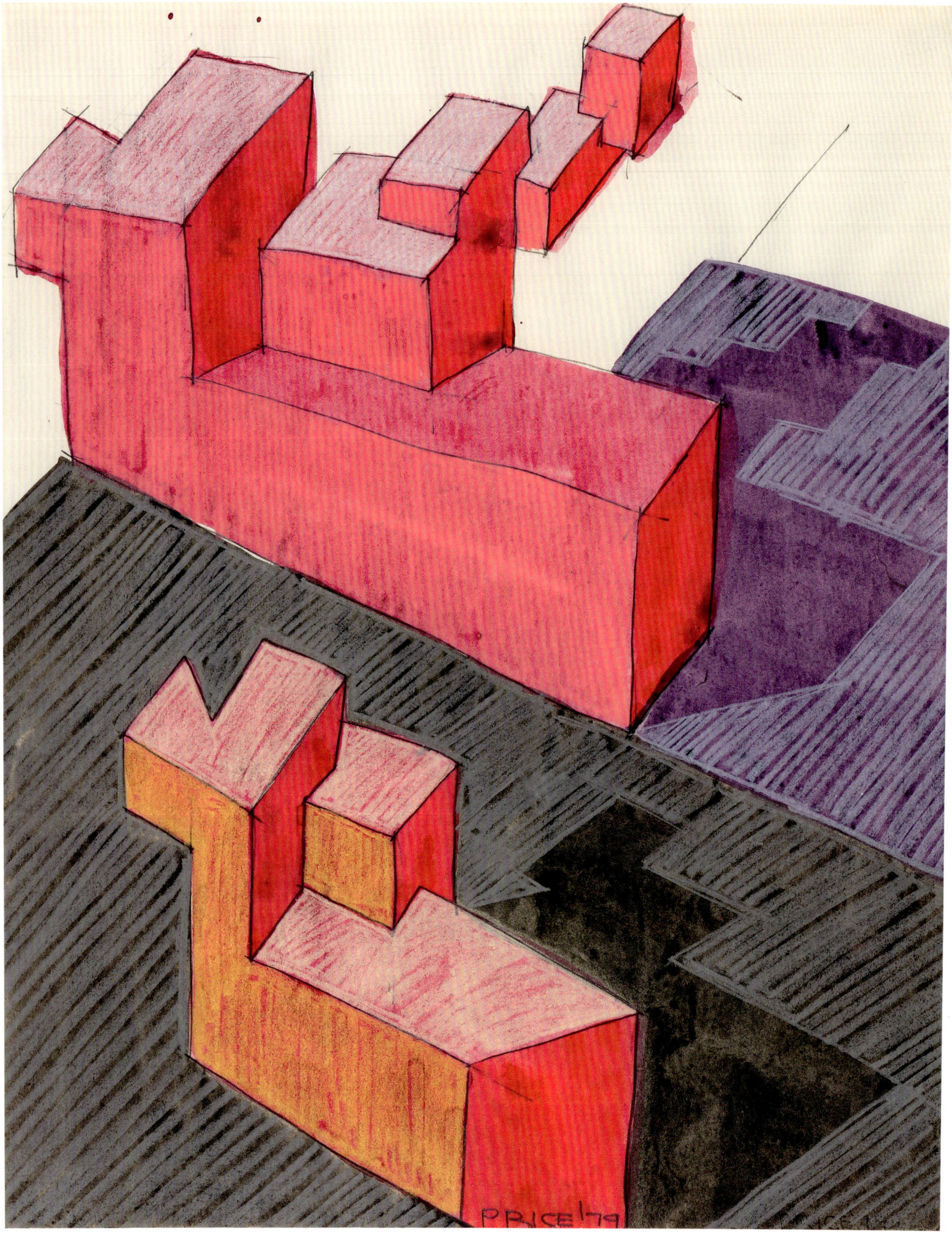

Untitled, 1979

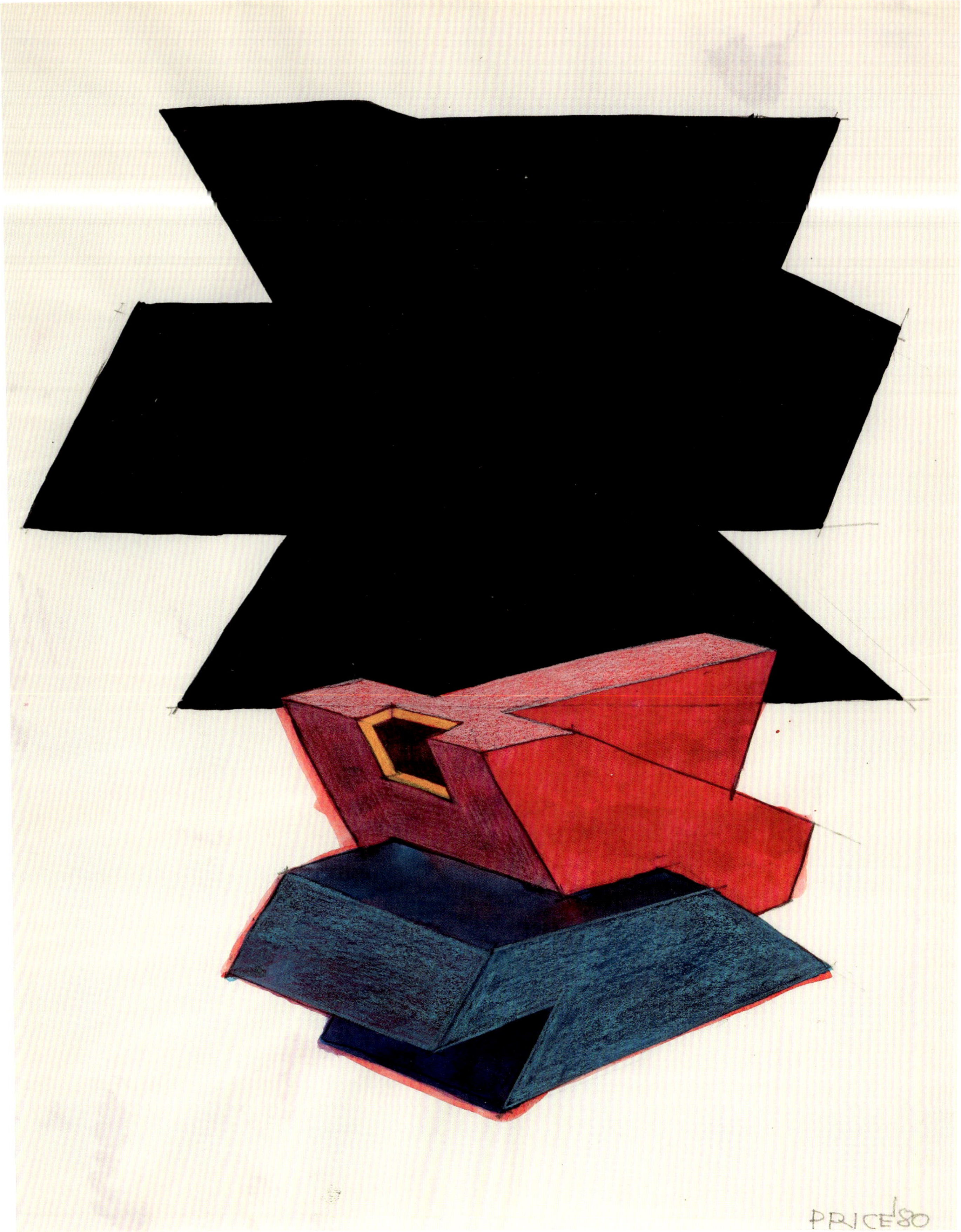

Untitled, 1980

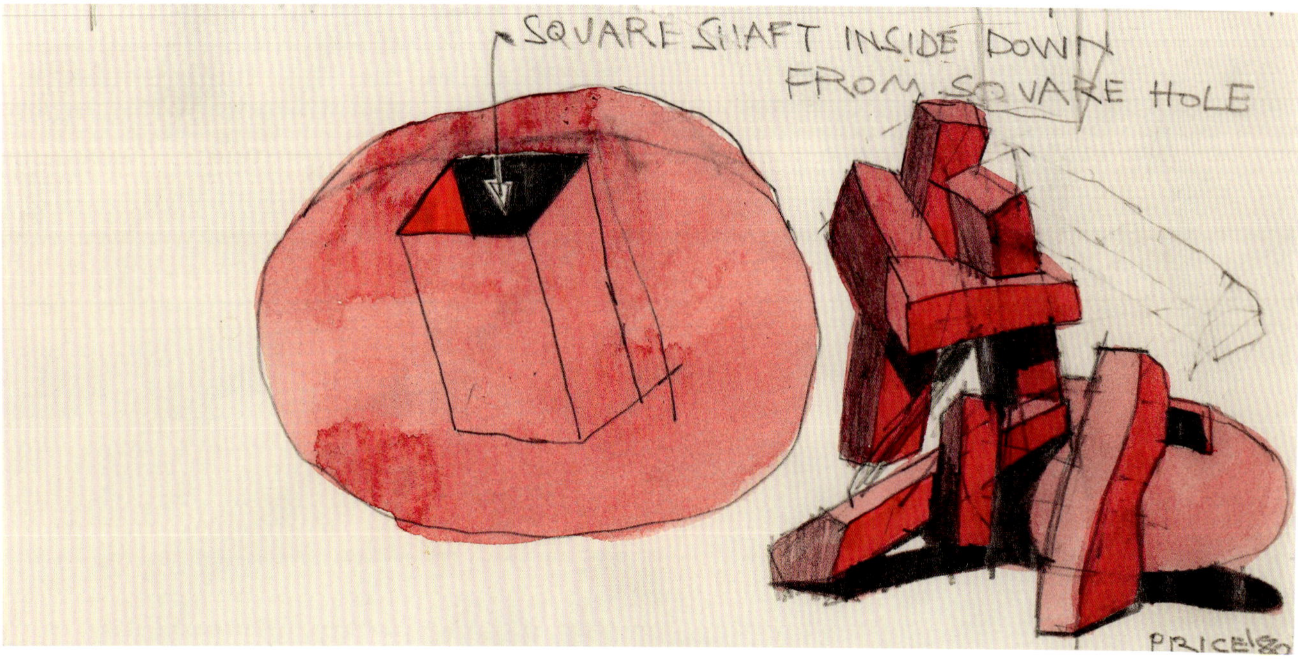

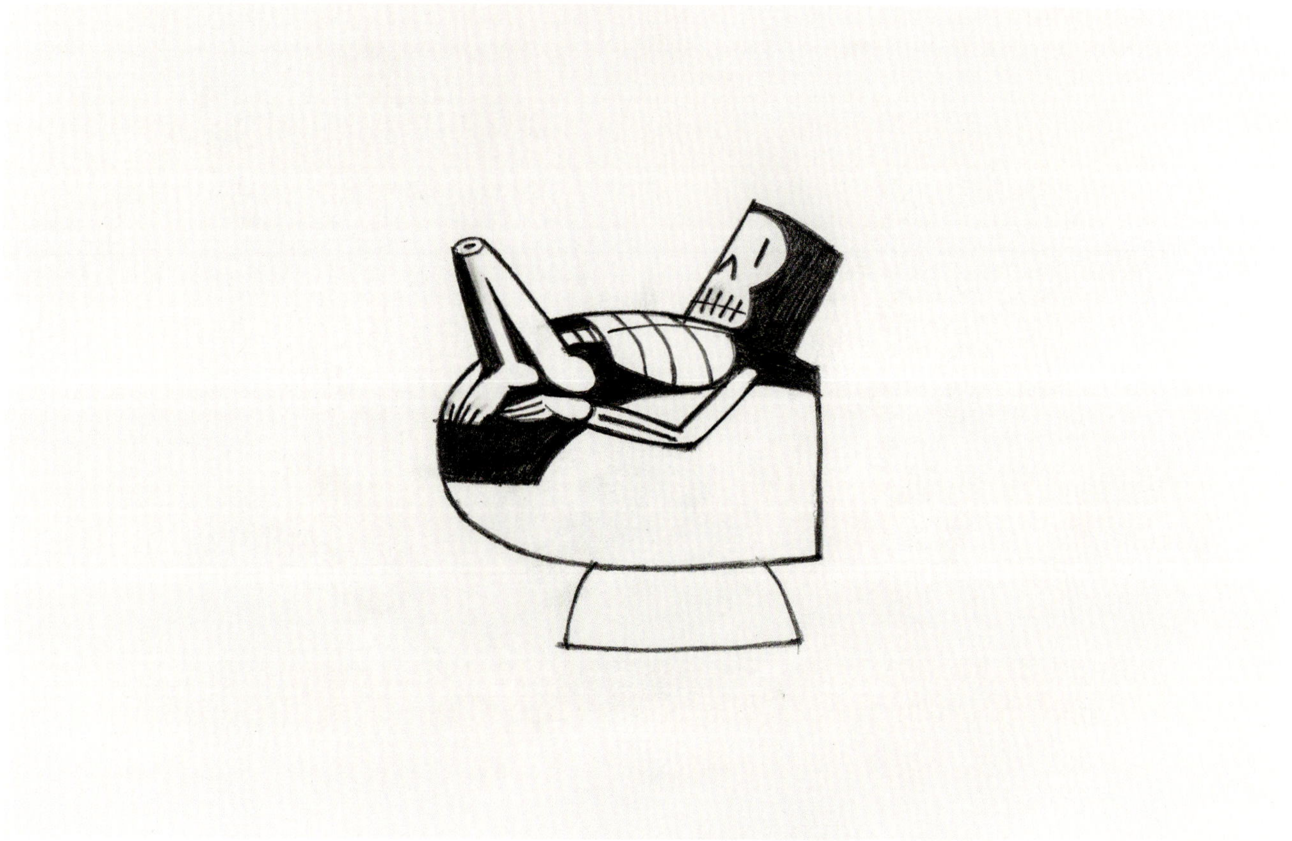

Untitled, 1980
Untitled, 1979

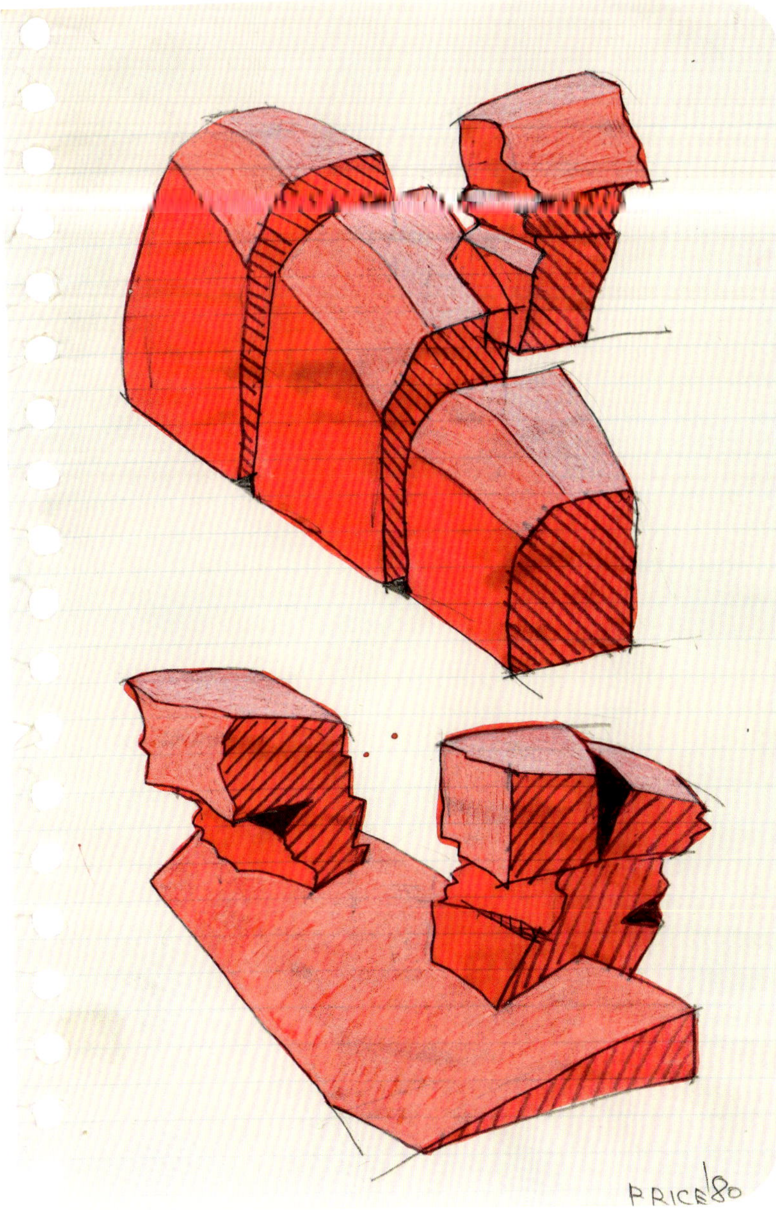

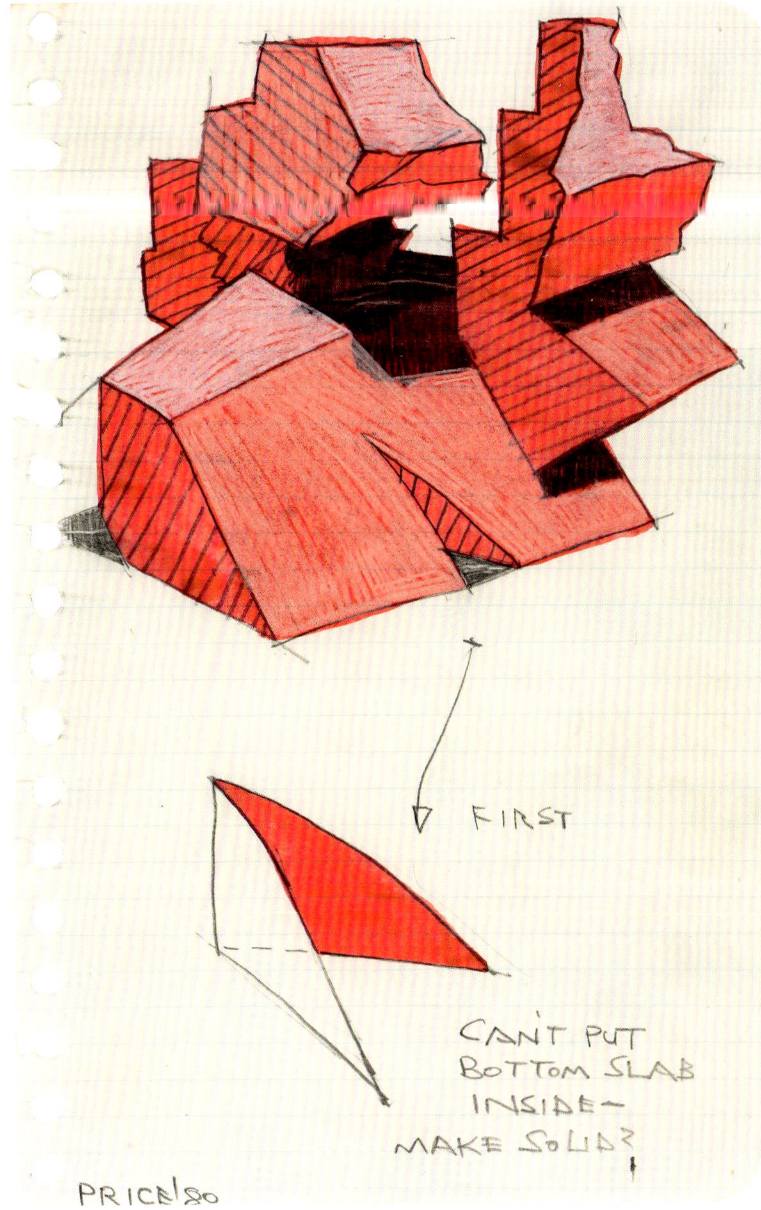

BOTH WORKS:
Untitled, 1980

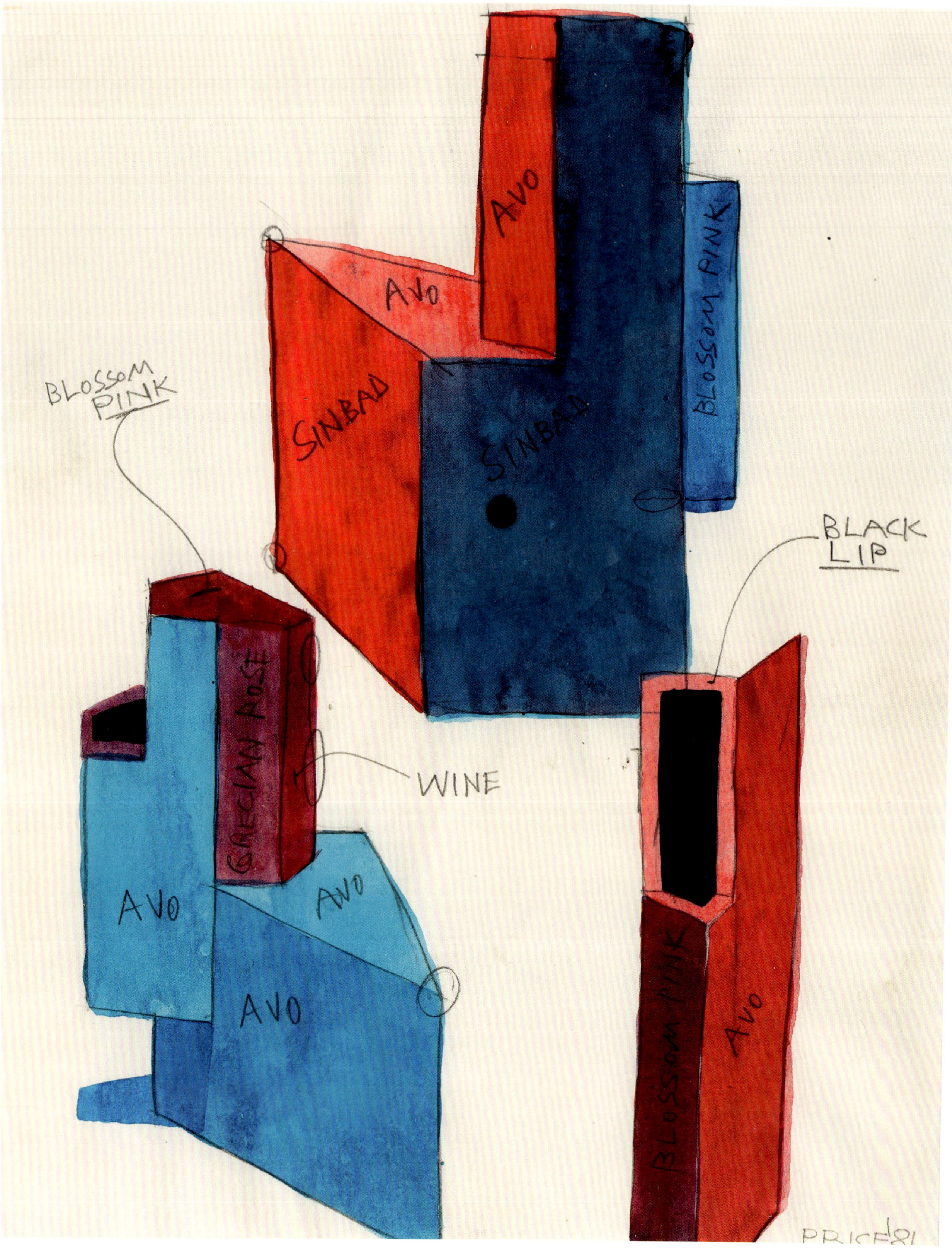

Untitled, 1981

OPPOSITE, CLOCKWISE FROM TOP:

Nonquitt Cove/Nonquitt Rocks, 1981

Untitled, 1980

Rock at Nonquitt, 1981

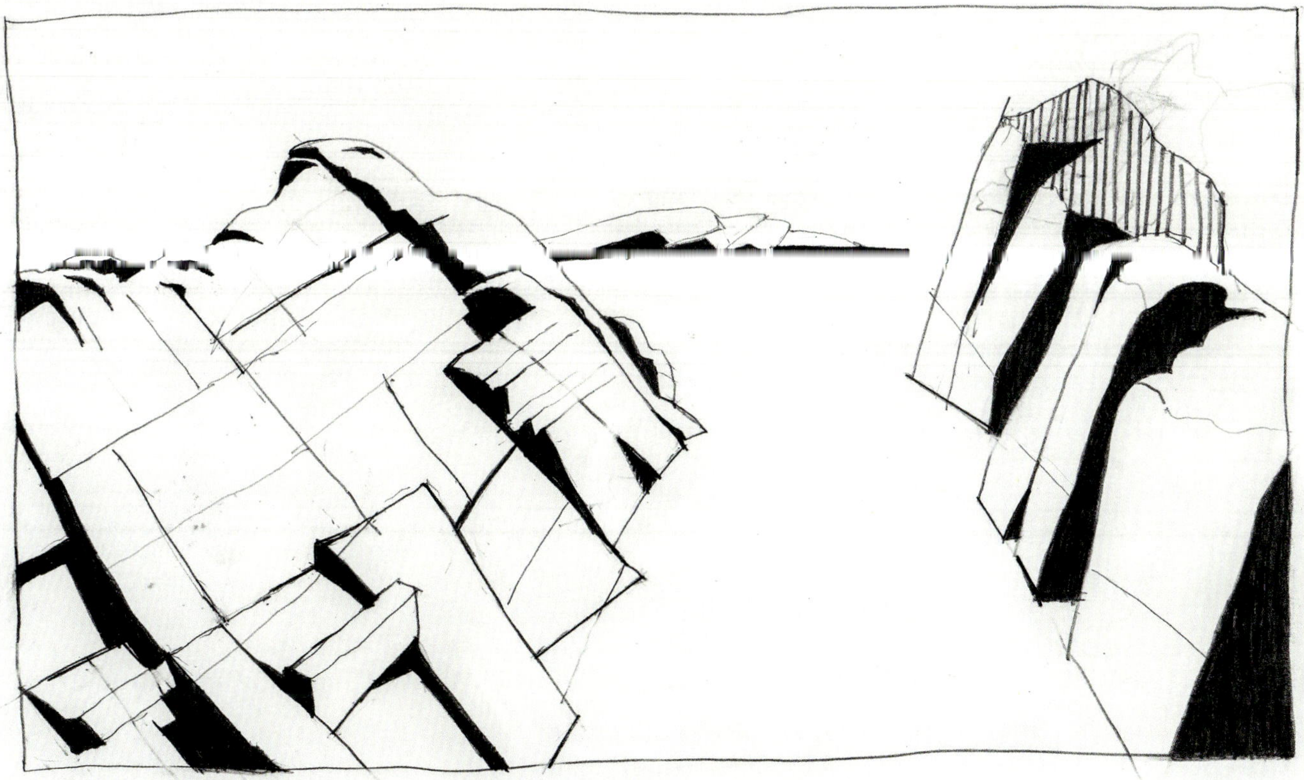

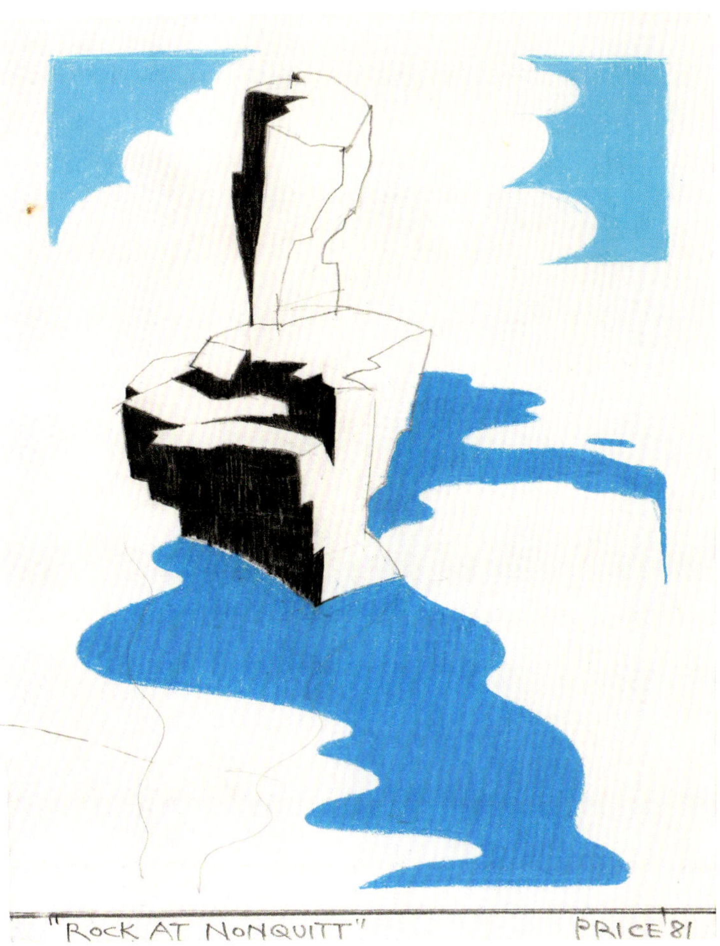
"ROCK AT NONQUITT"
PRICE '81

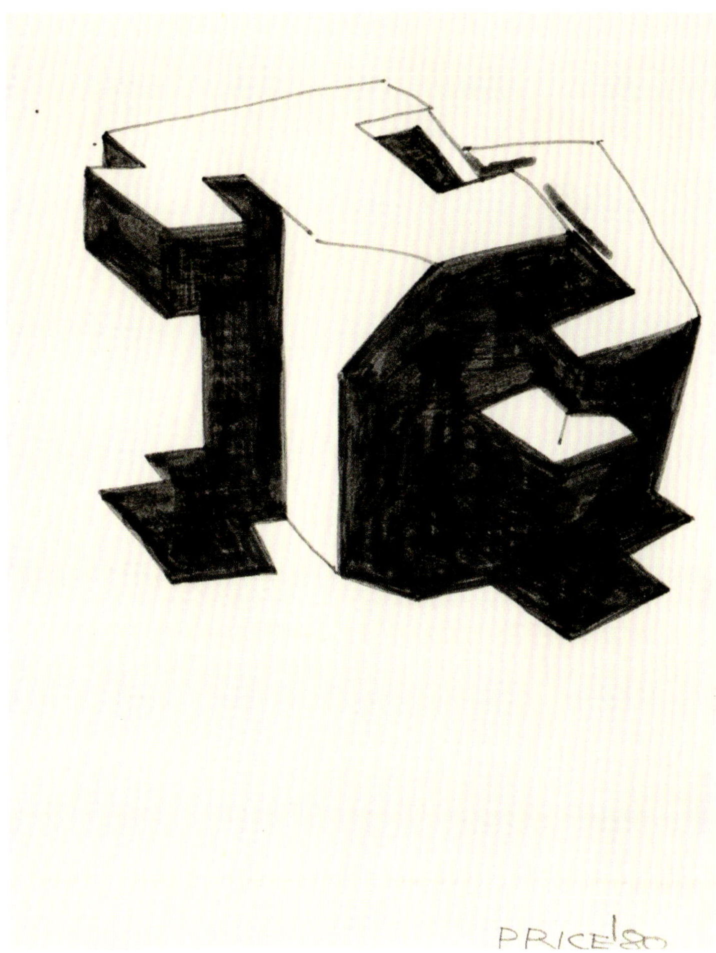
PRICE '80

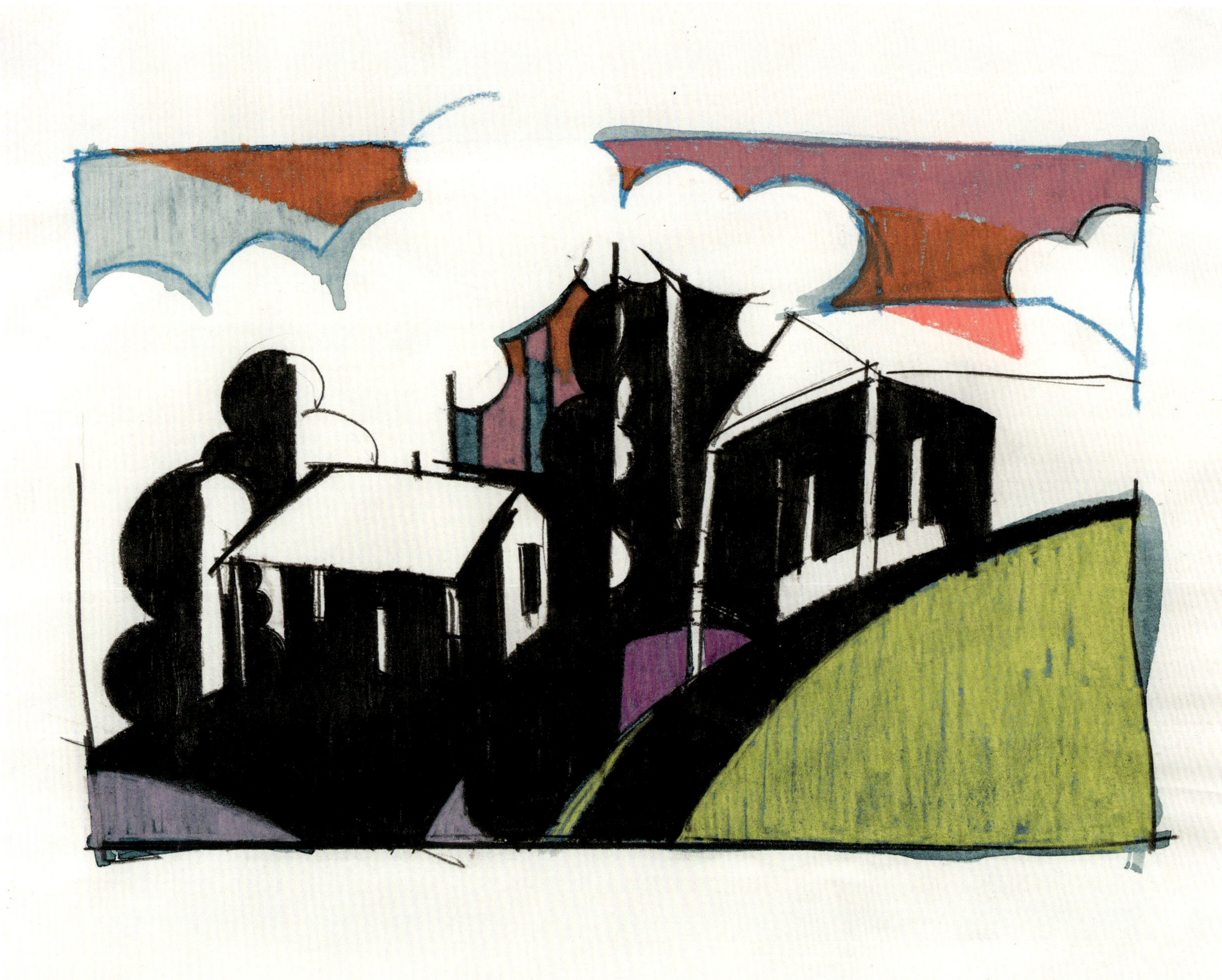

Untitled, 1981

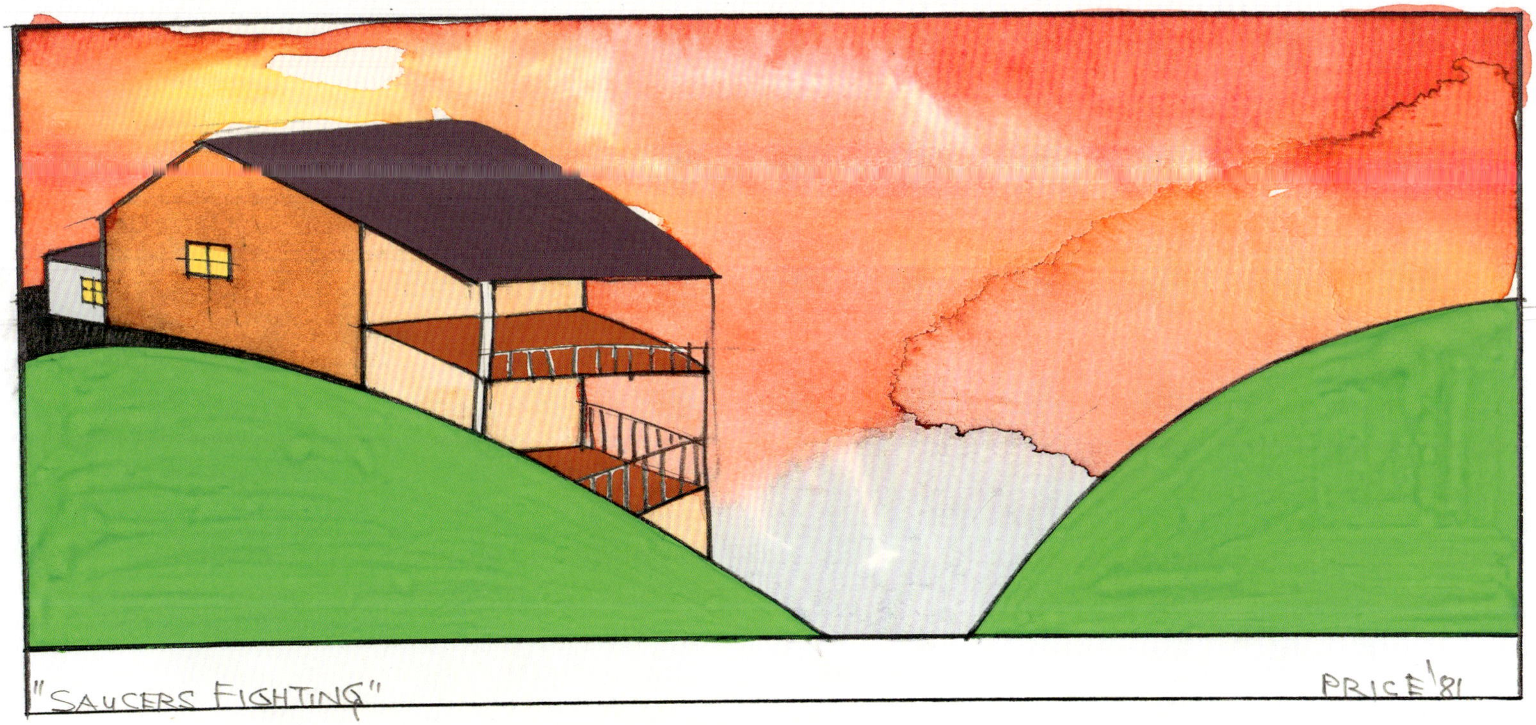

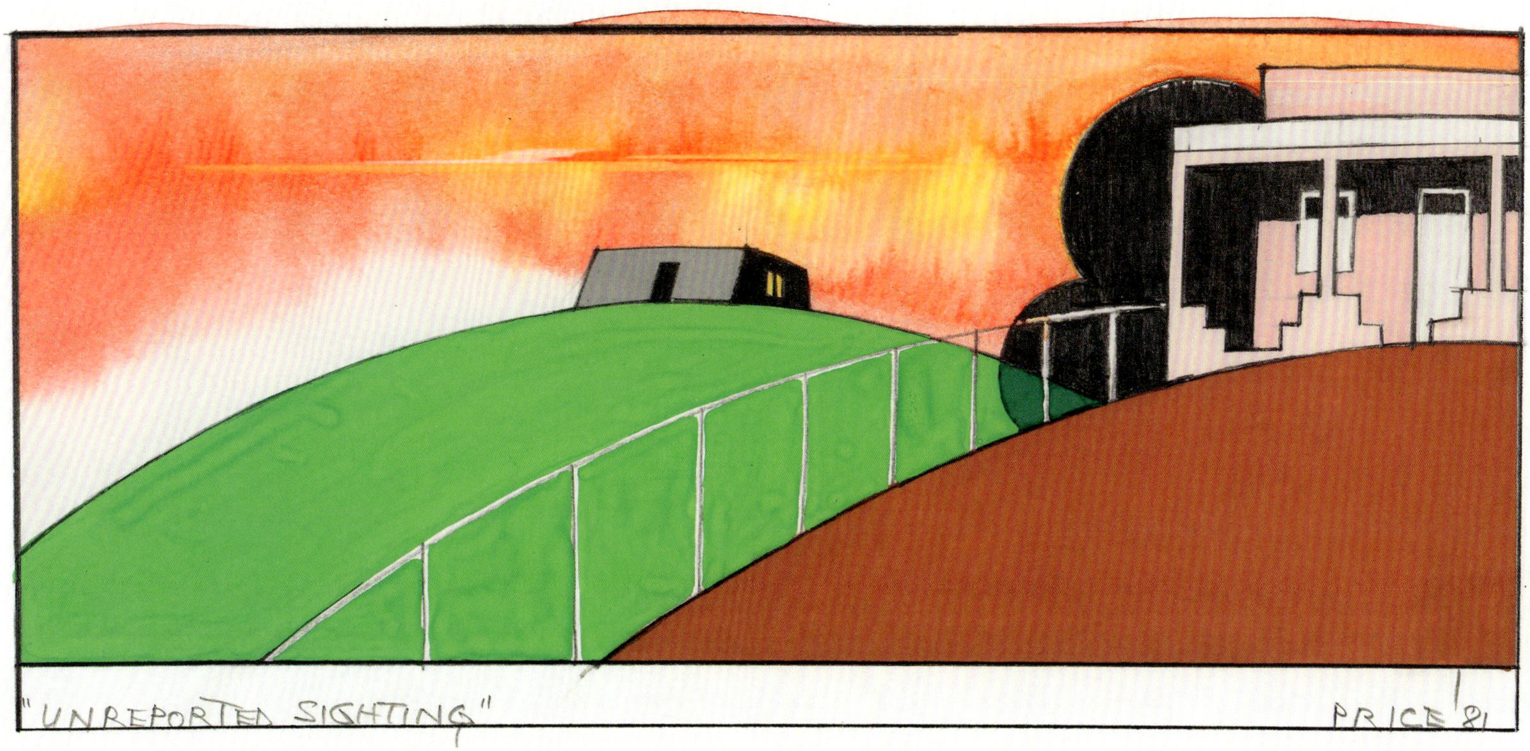

Saucers Fighting, 1981
Unreported Sighting, 1981

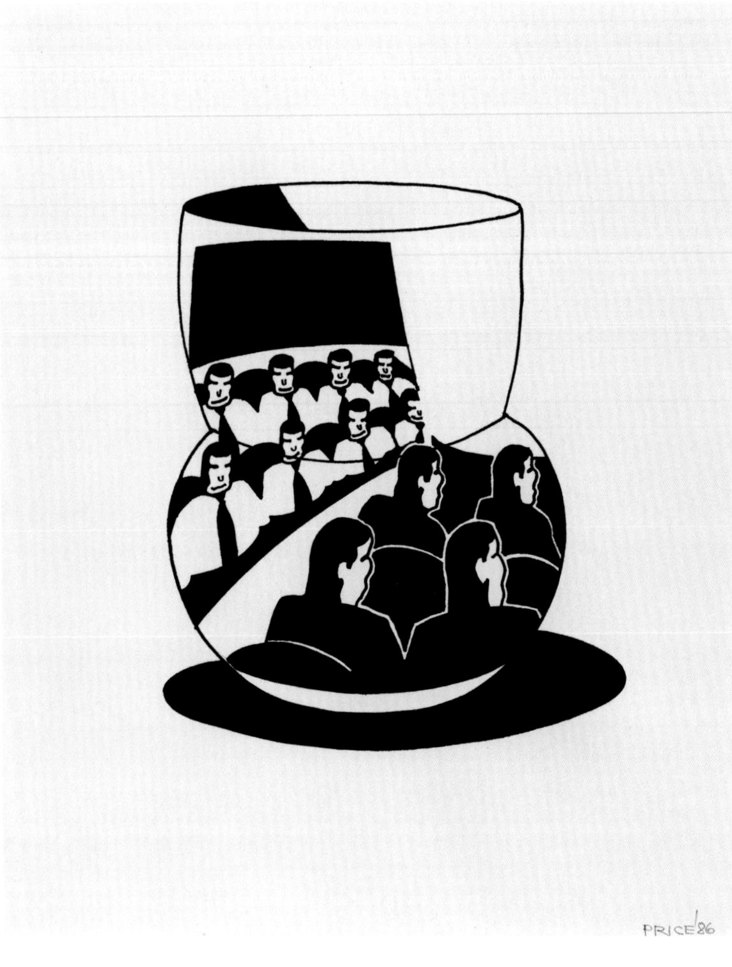

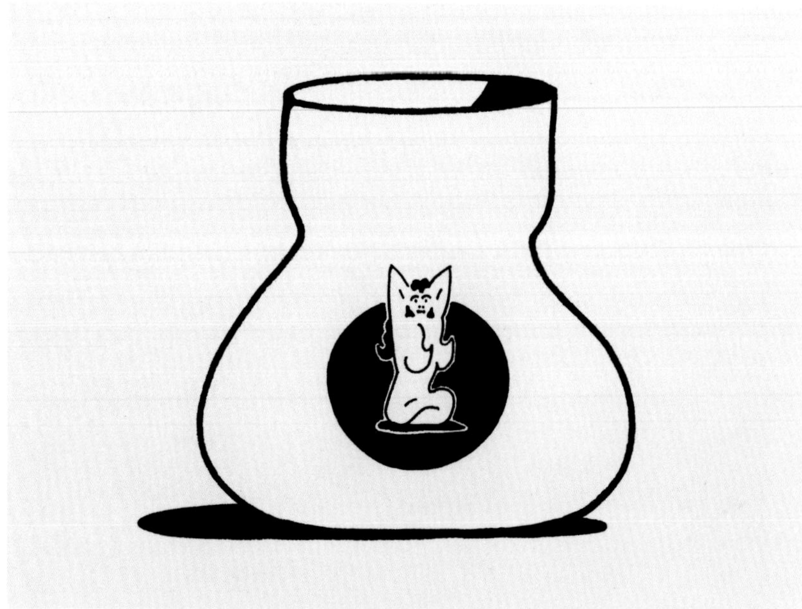

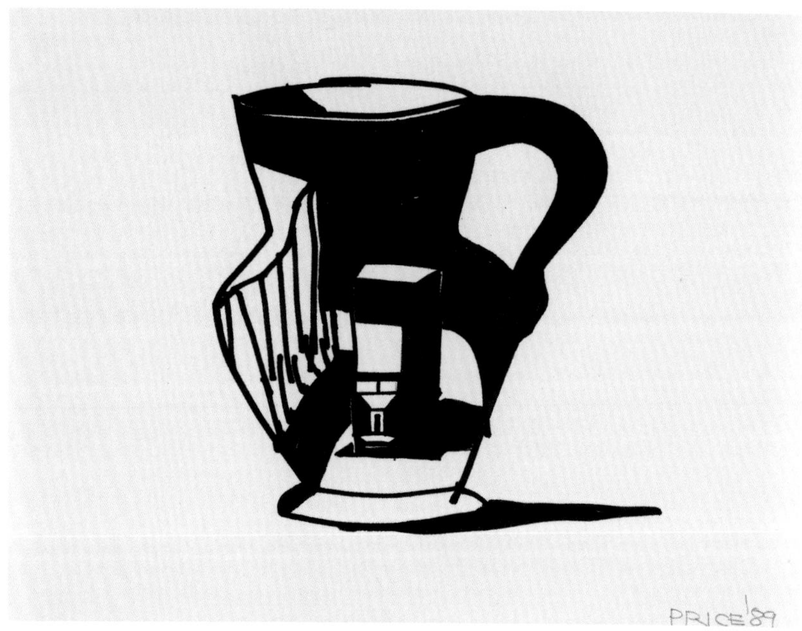

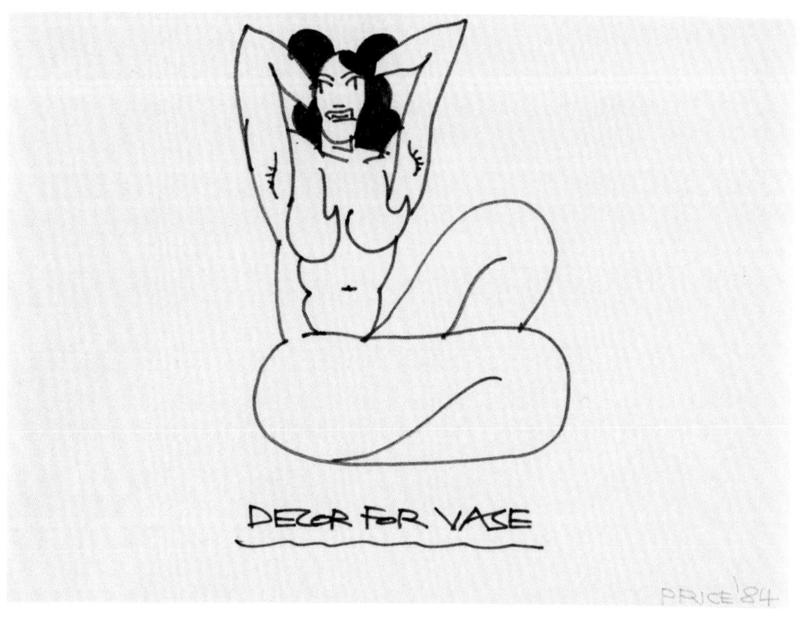

CLOCKWISE FROM TOP LEFT:
Untitled, 1986
Untitled, 1989
Untitled, 1989
Decor for Vase, 1984

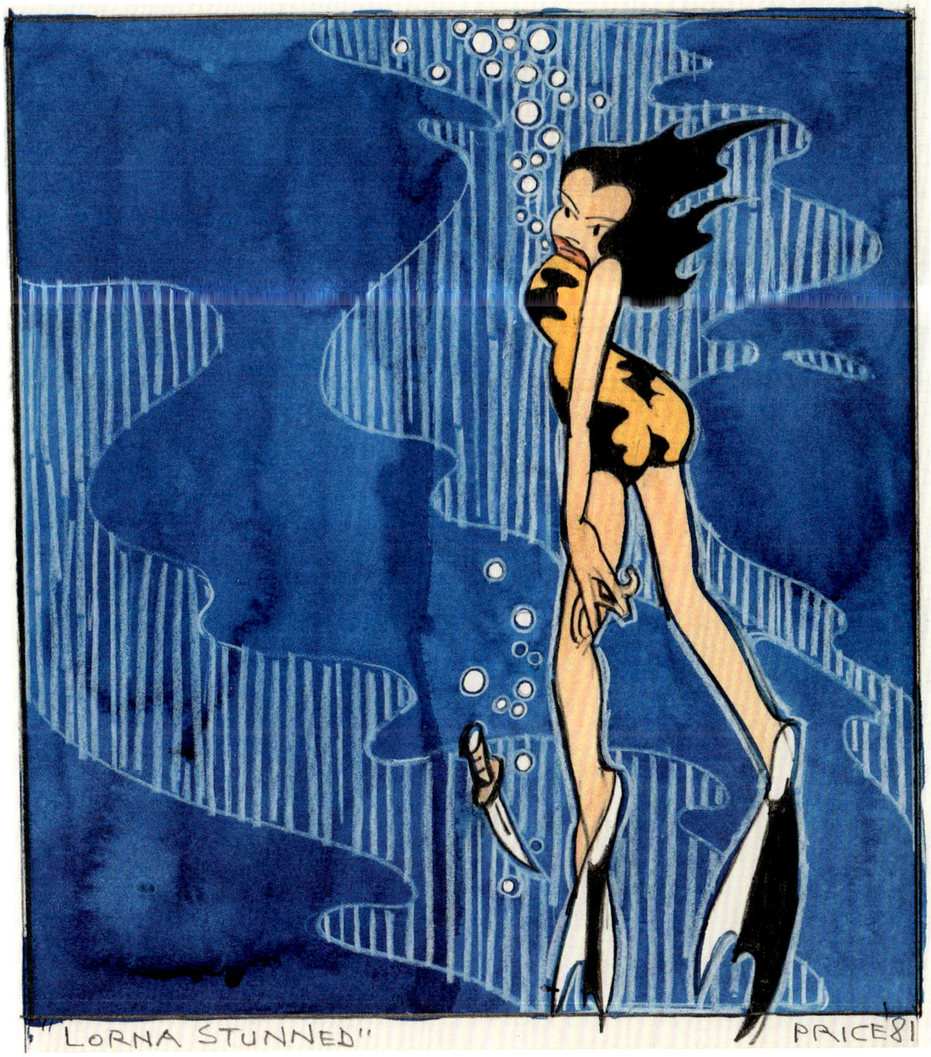

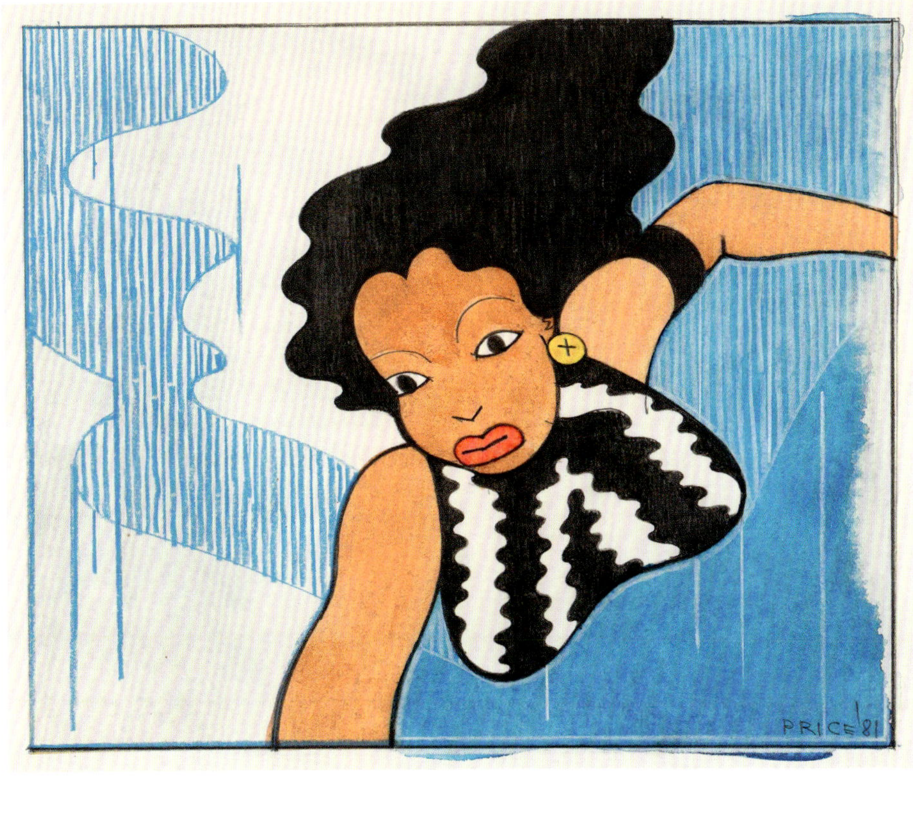

Lorna Stunned, 1981
Lorna Diving, 1981

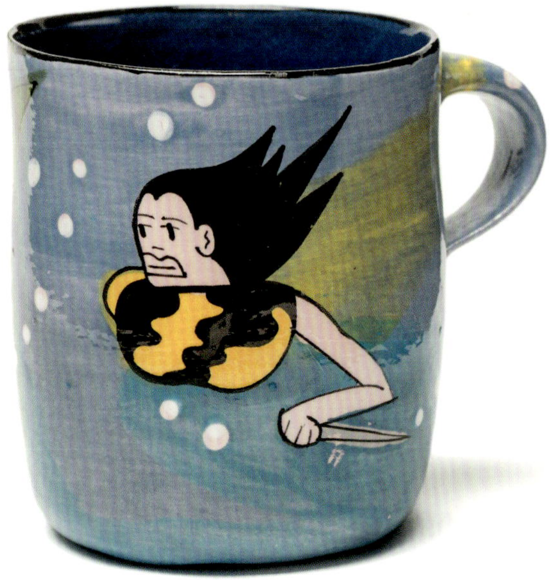

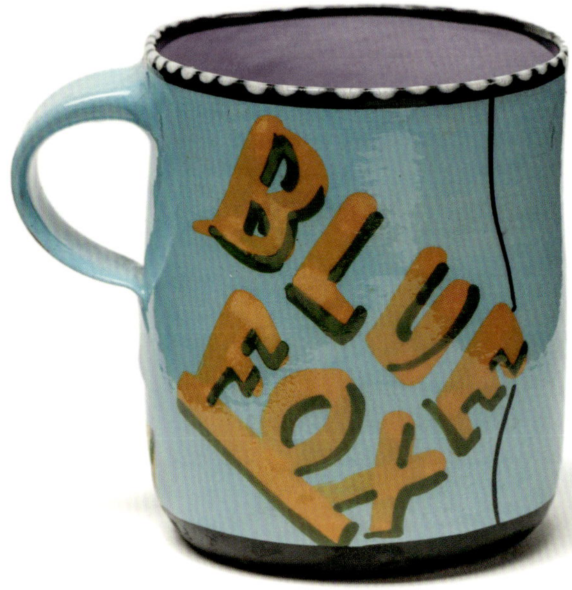

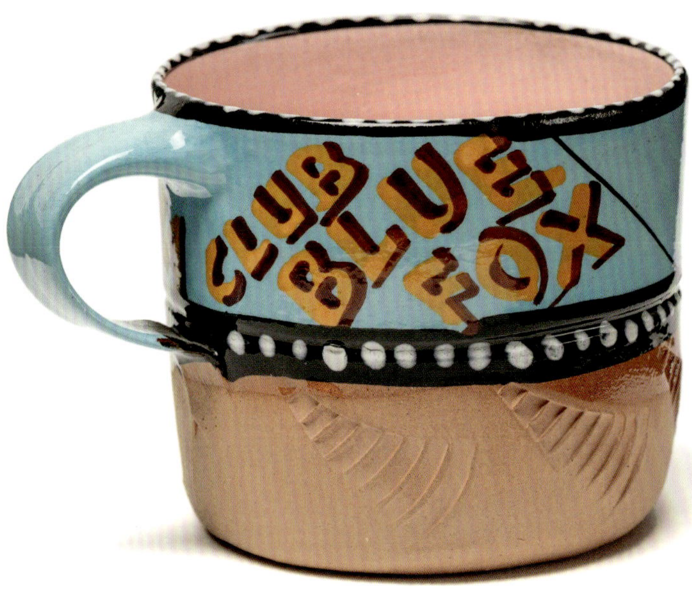

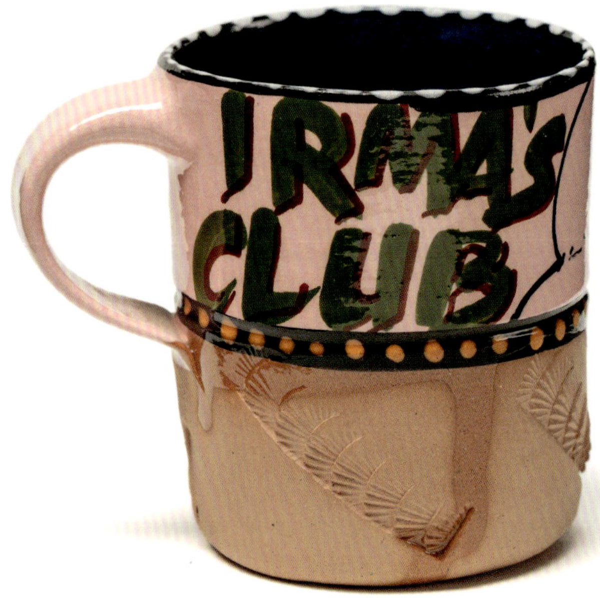

ALL WORKS:
Untitled, 1982

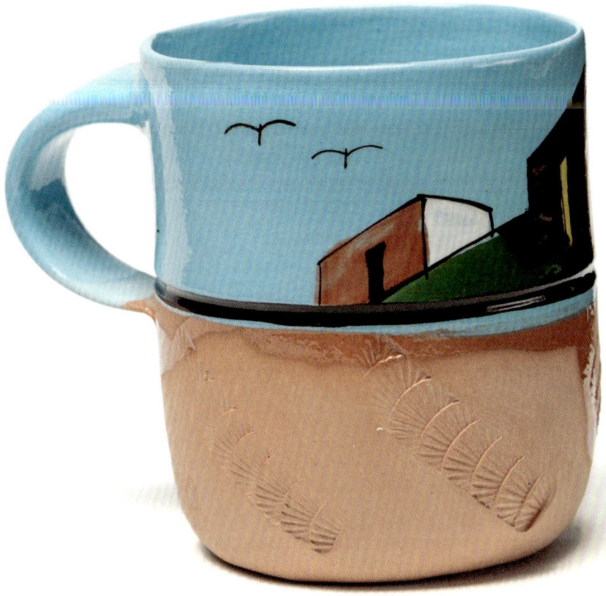

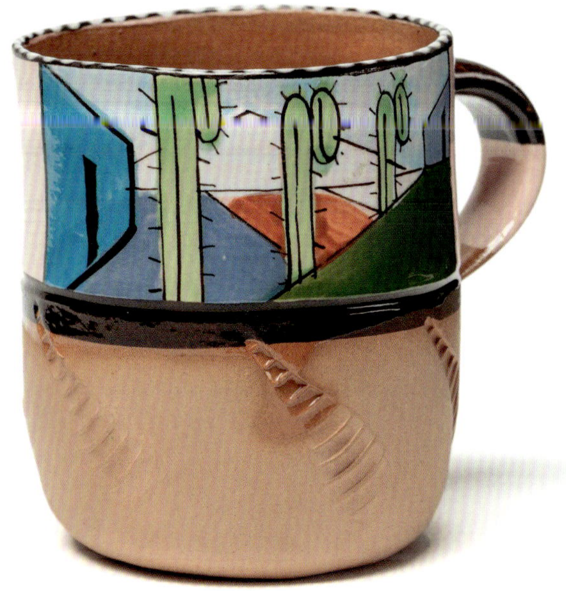

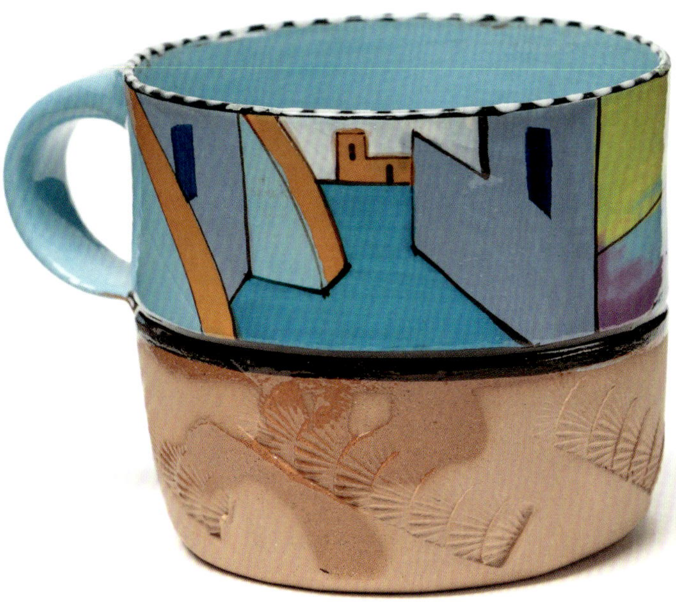

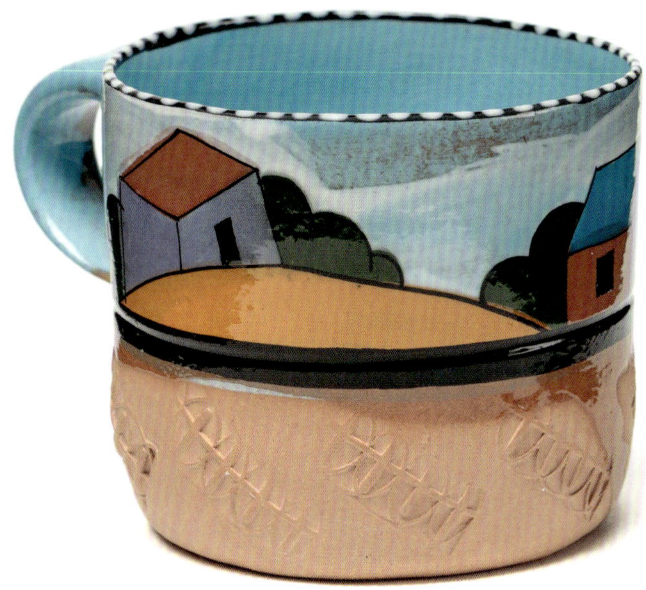

ALL WORKS:
Untitled, 1972–77

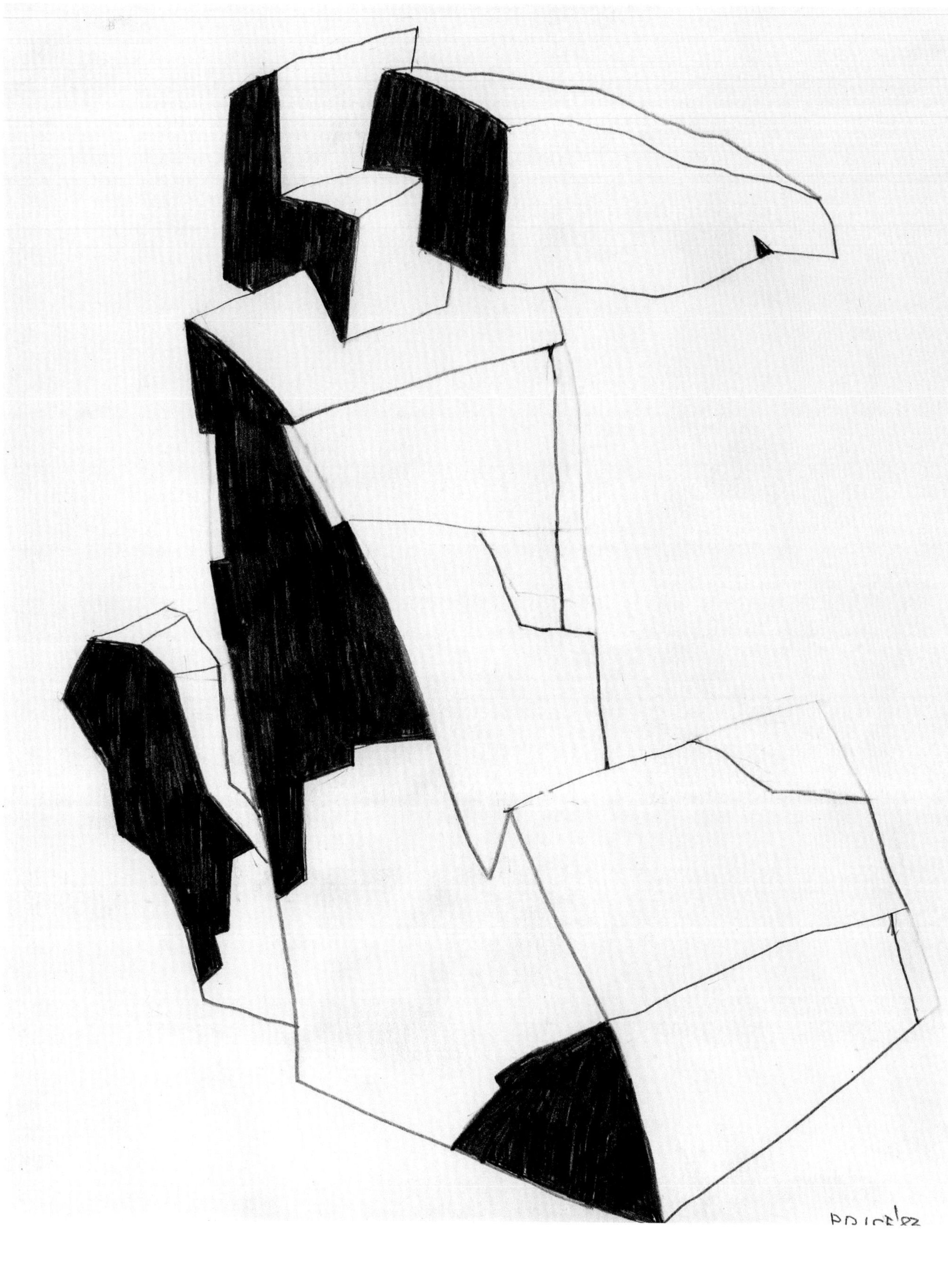

Untitled, 1983

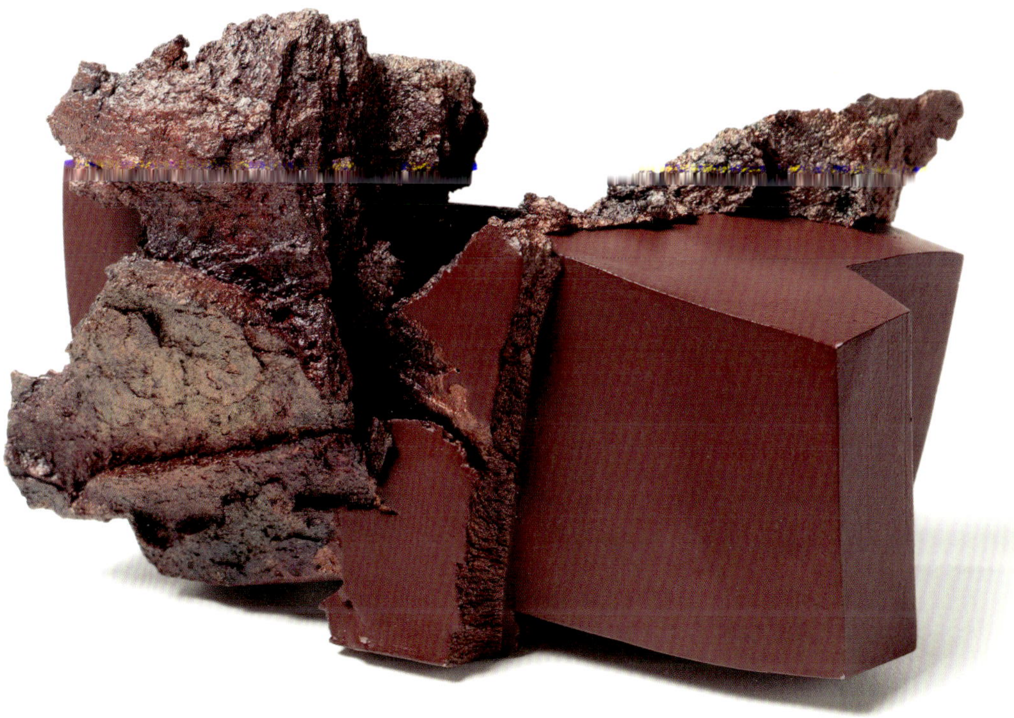

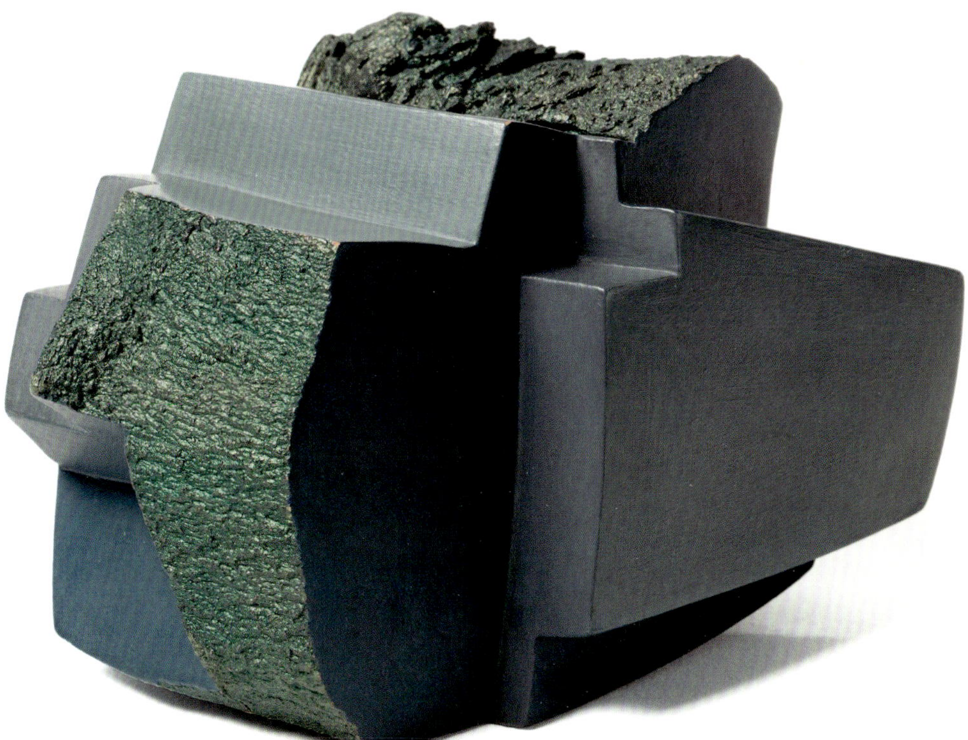

Padanaram, 1983
Untitled, 1983

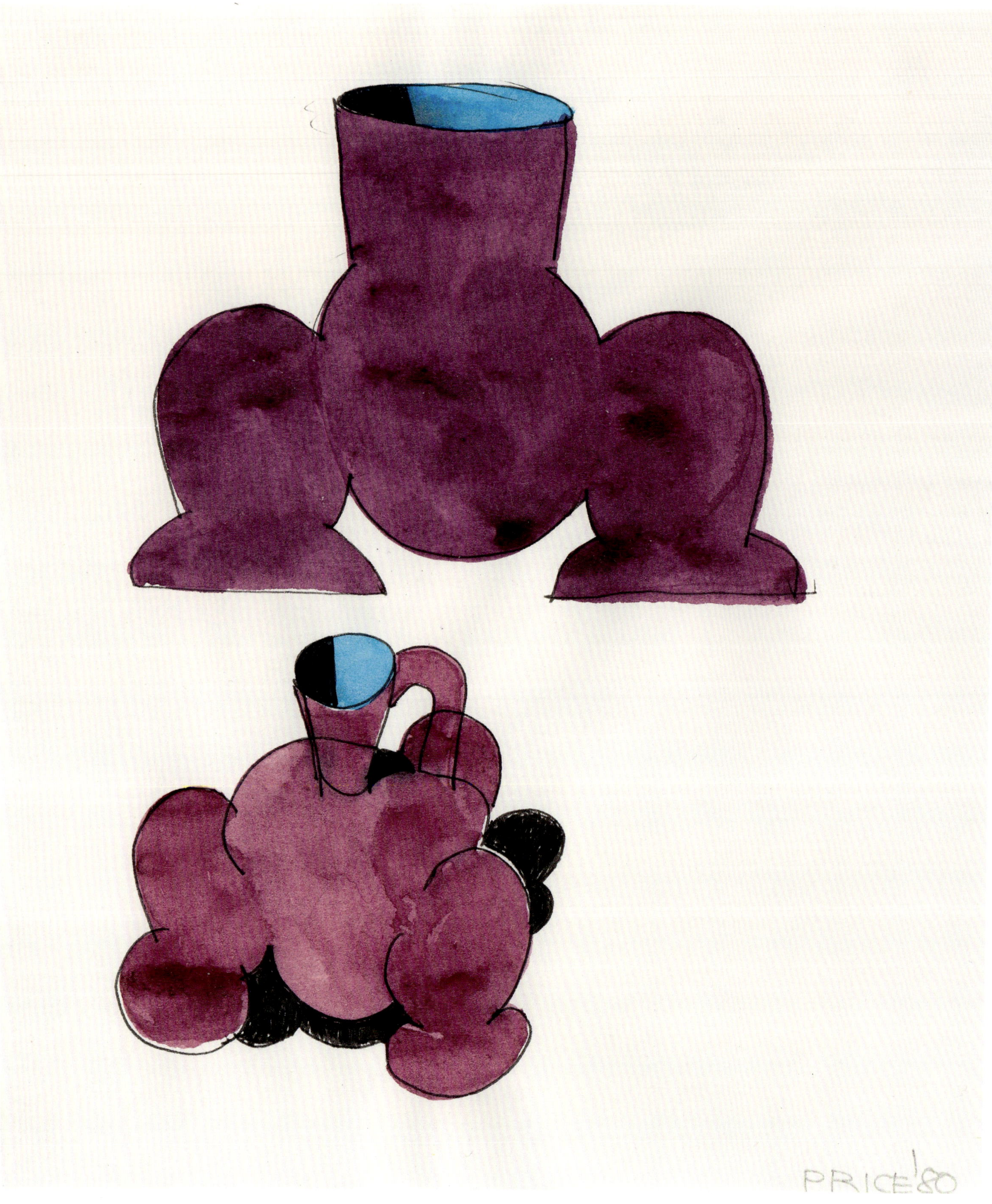

Untitled, 1980

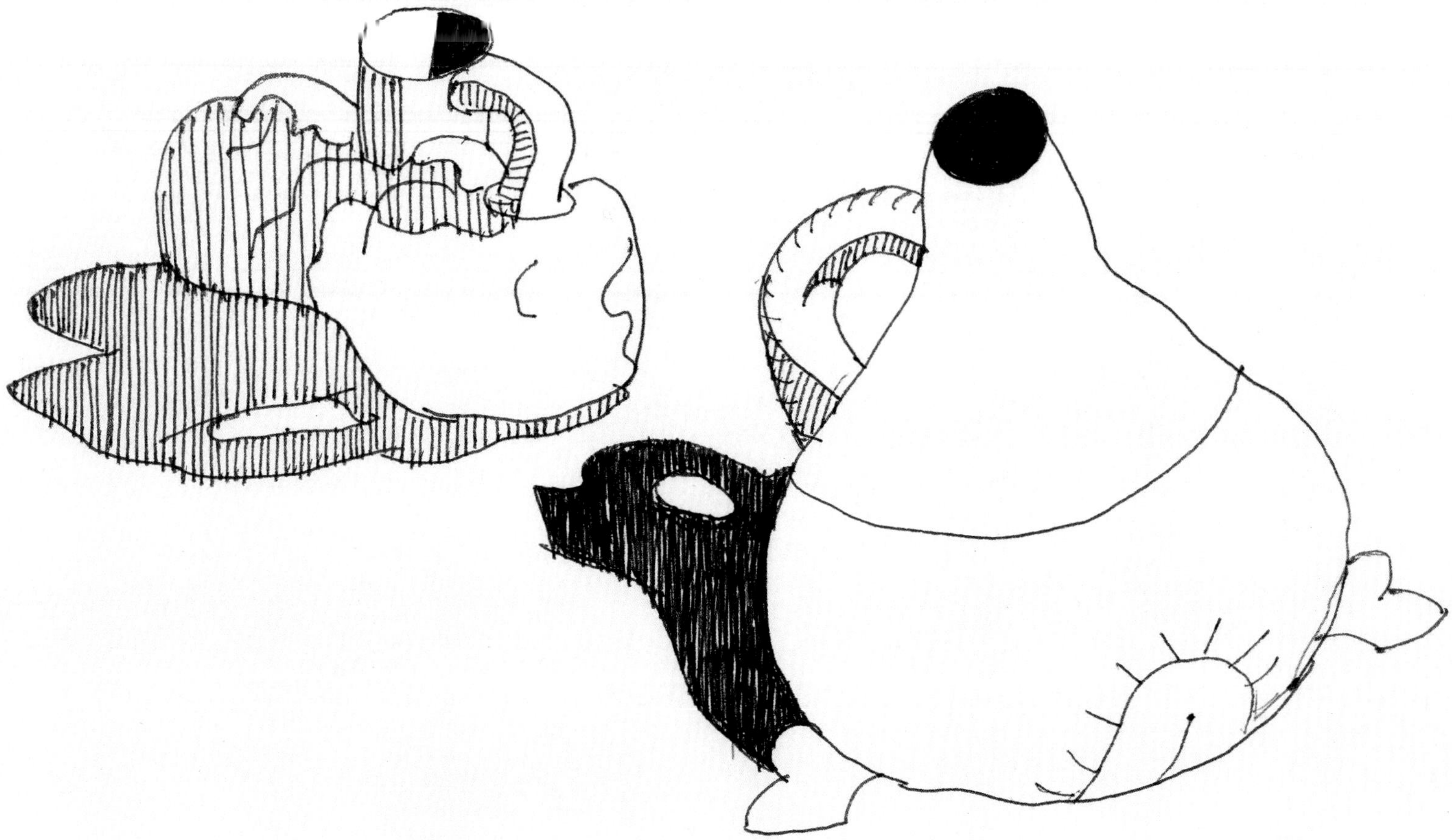

Untitled, 1986

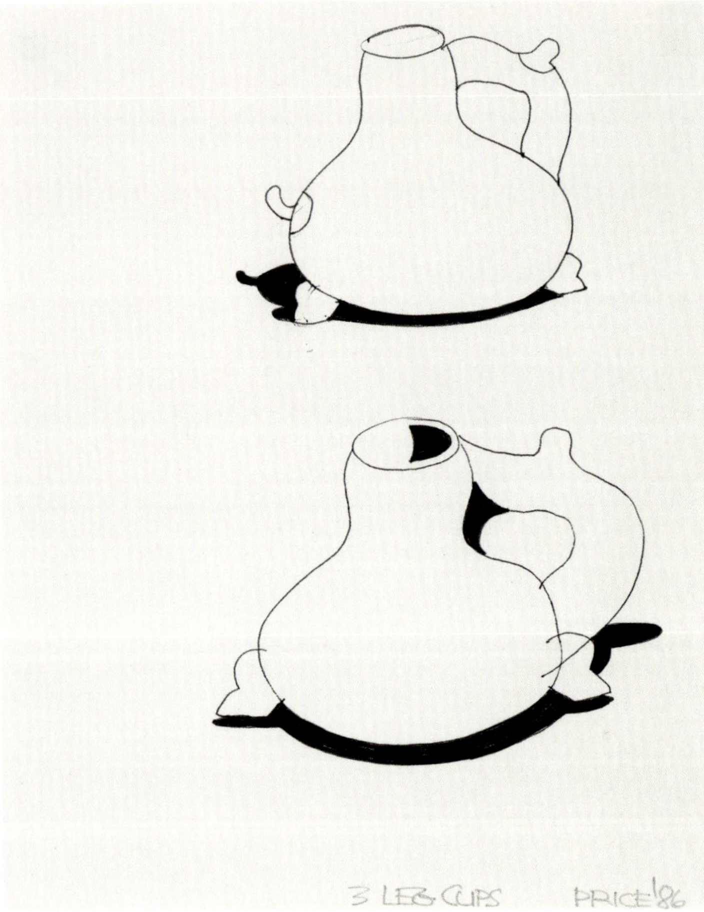

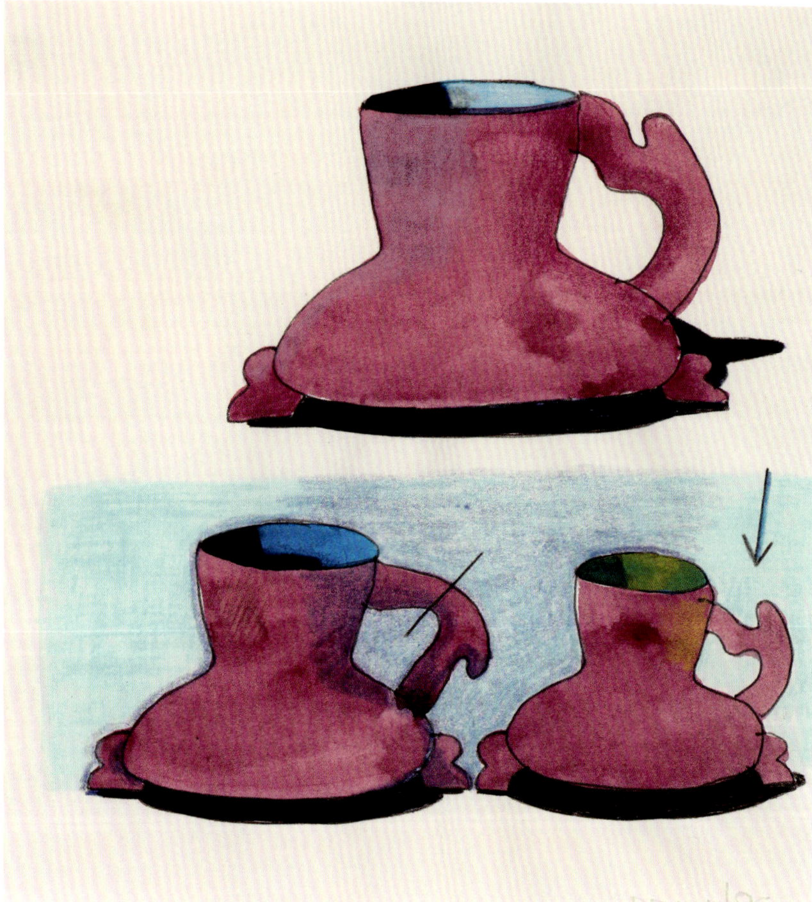

BOTH WORKS:
Untitled, 1986

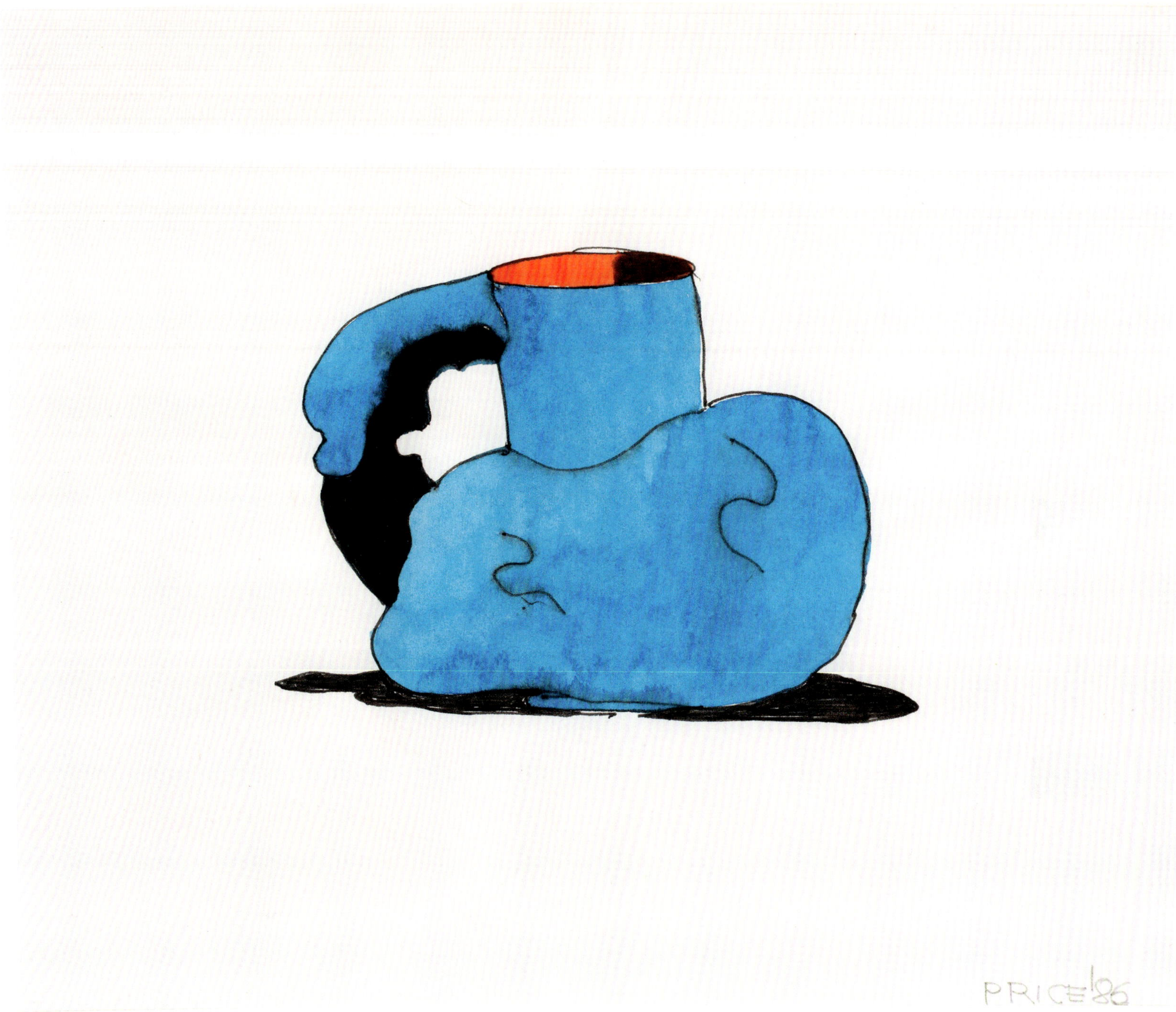

Untitled, 1986

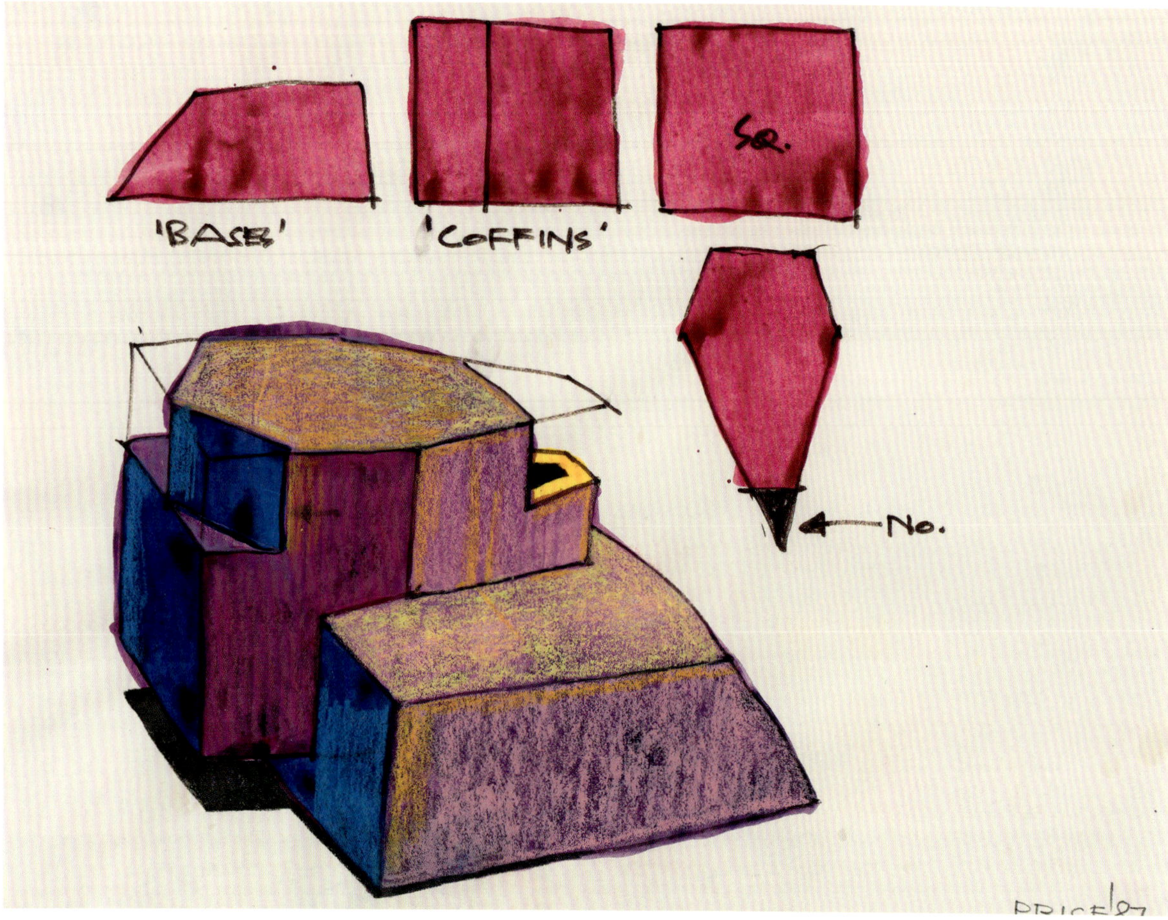

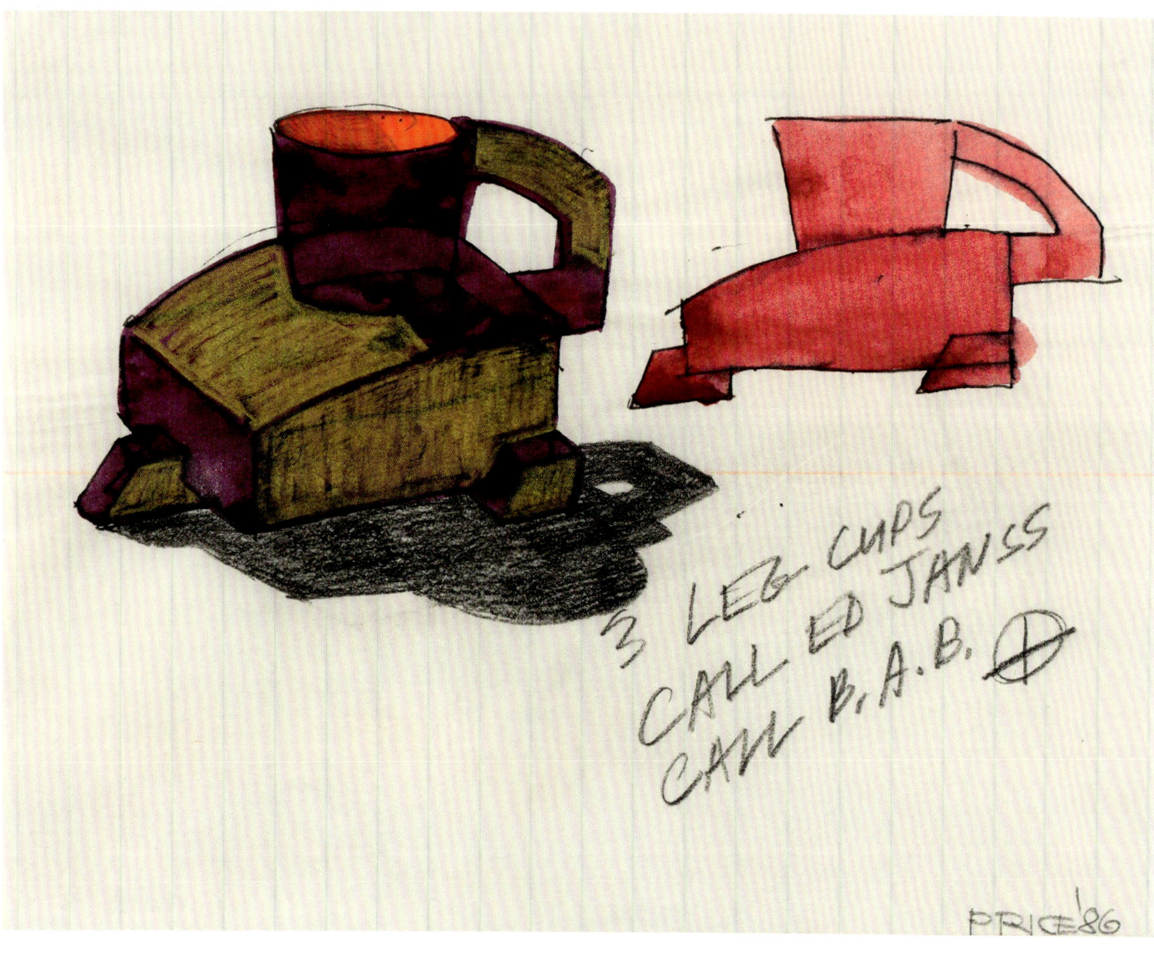

Untitled, 1987
Untitled, 1986

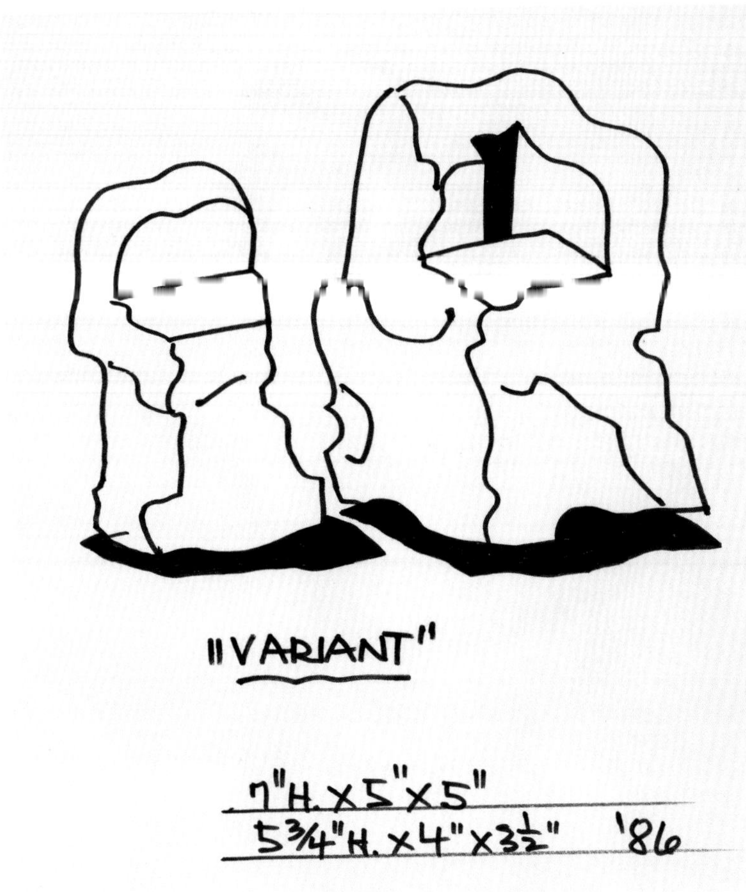

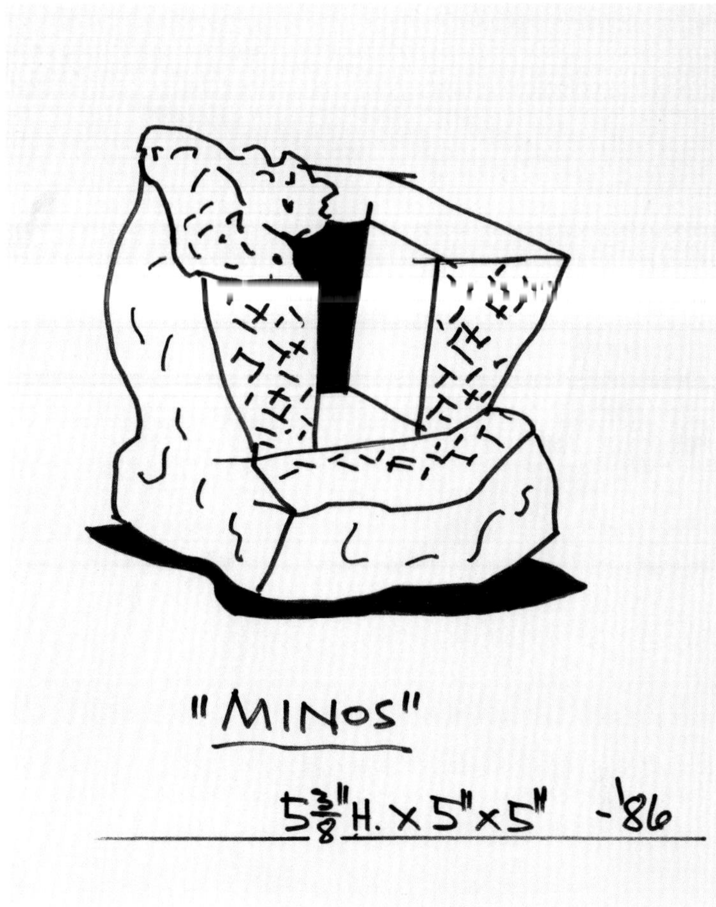

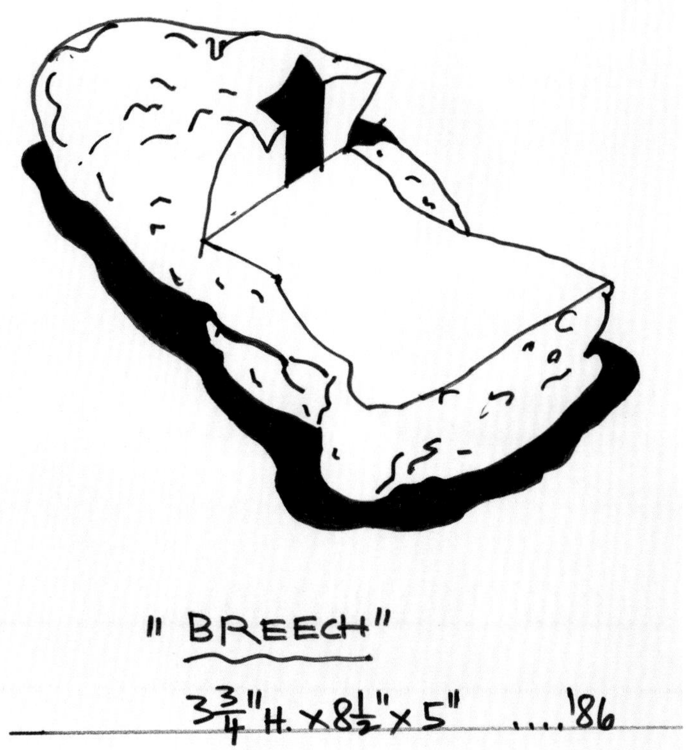

CLOCKWISE FROM TOP LEFT:
Variant, no date
Minos, no date
Breech, no date

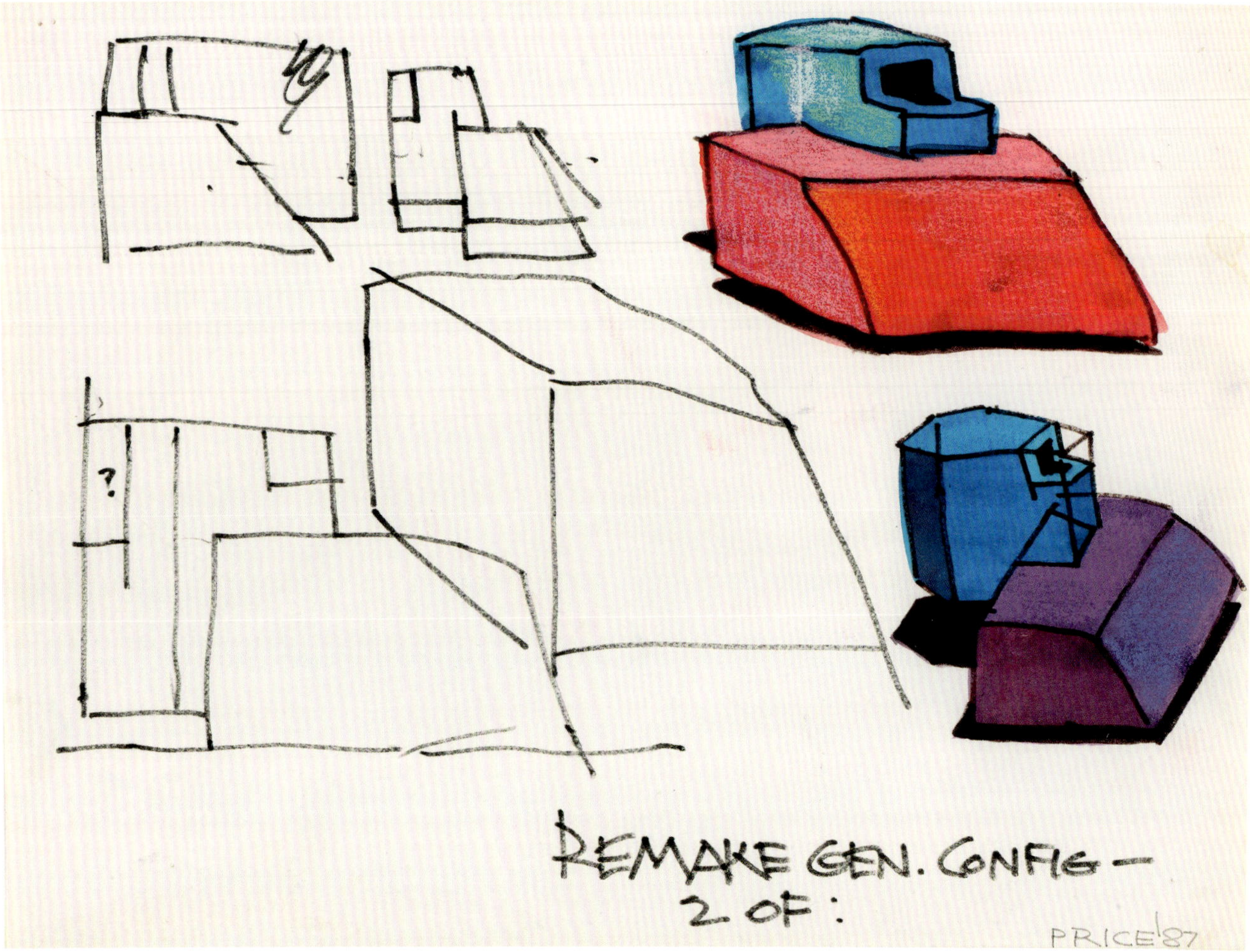

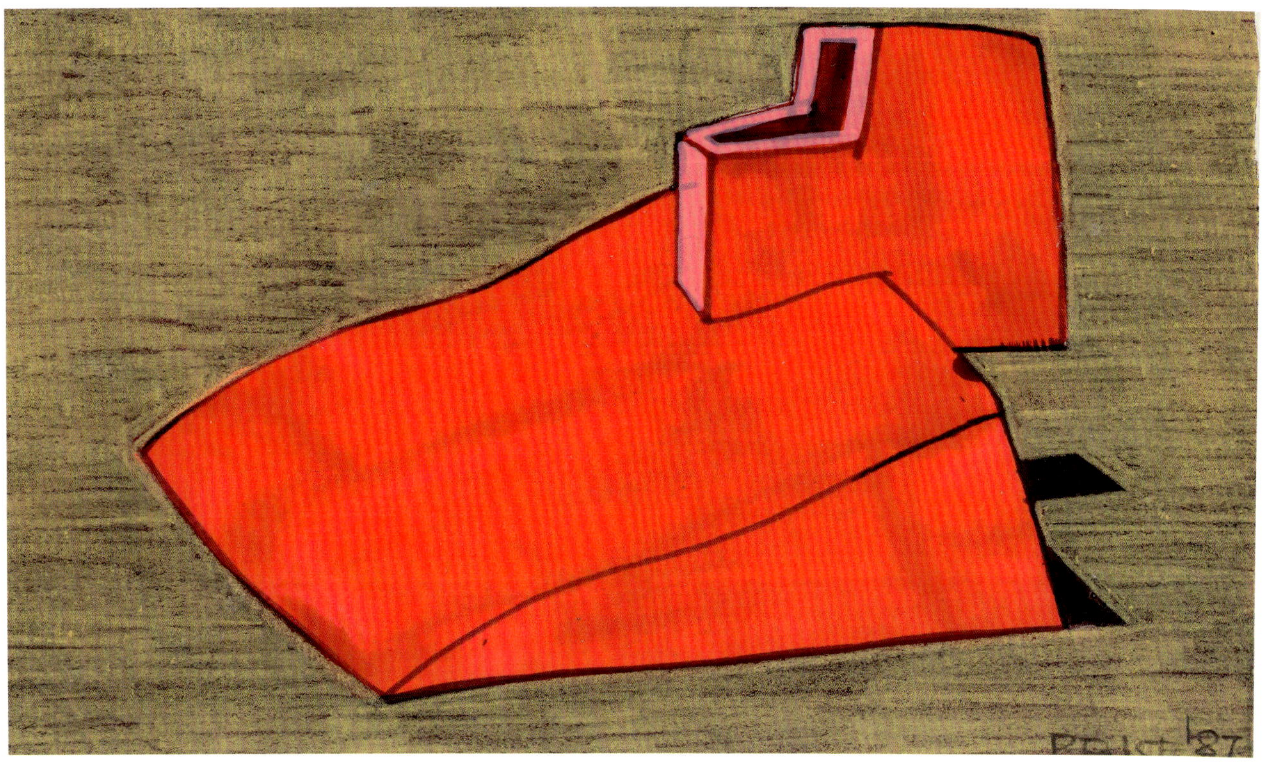

BOTH WORKS:
Untitled, 1987

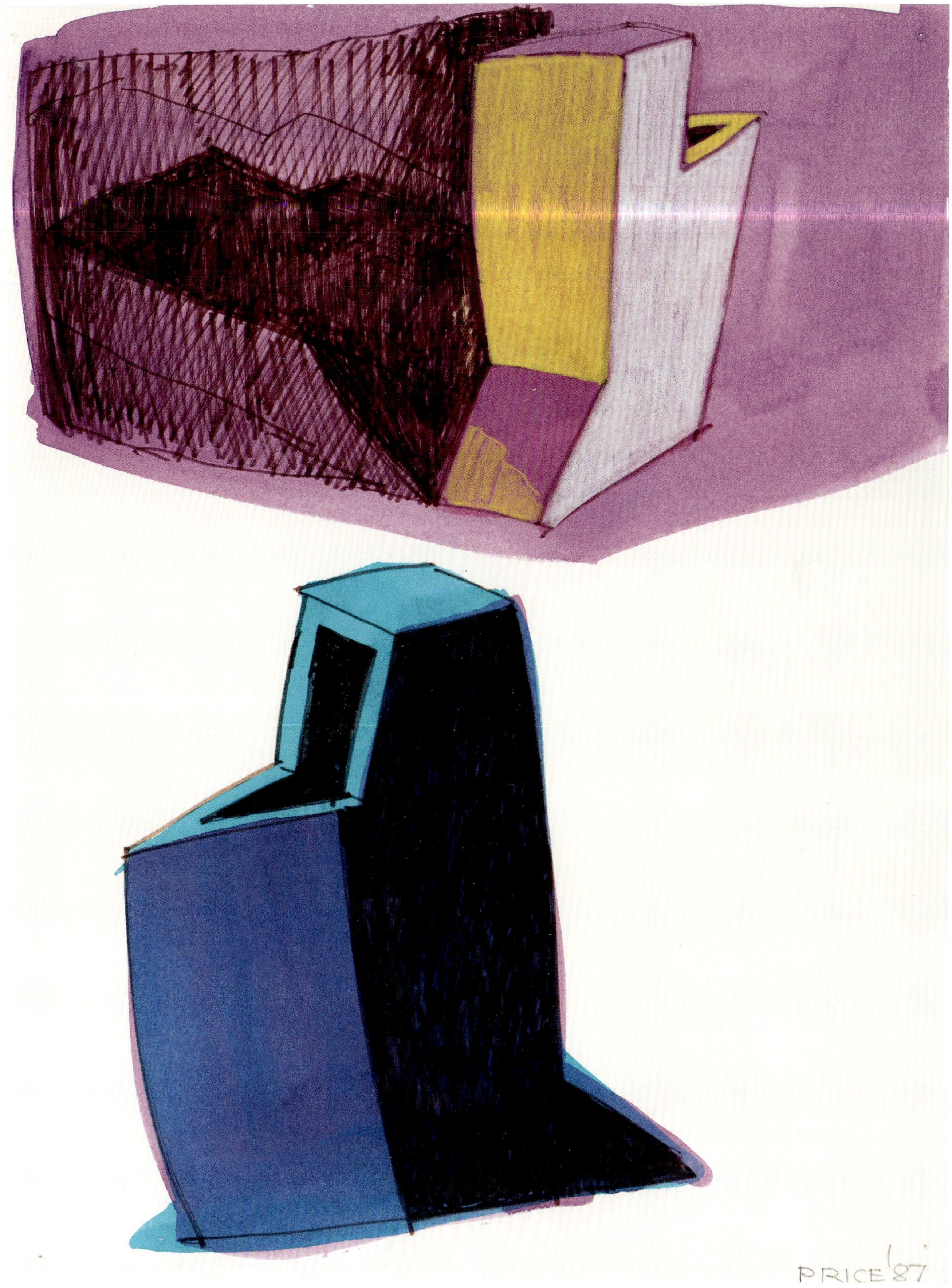

Untitled, 1987

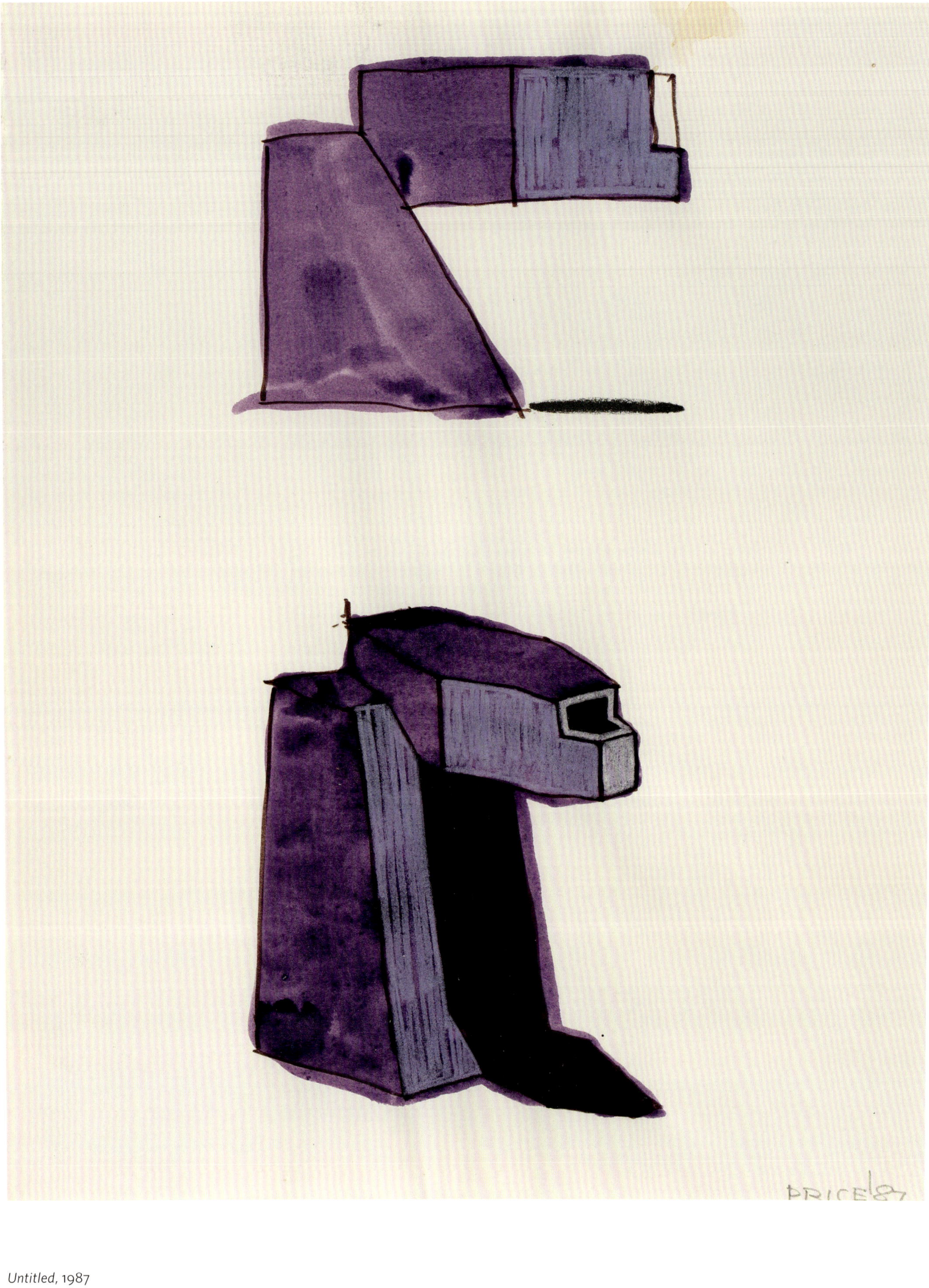

Untitled, 1987

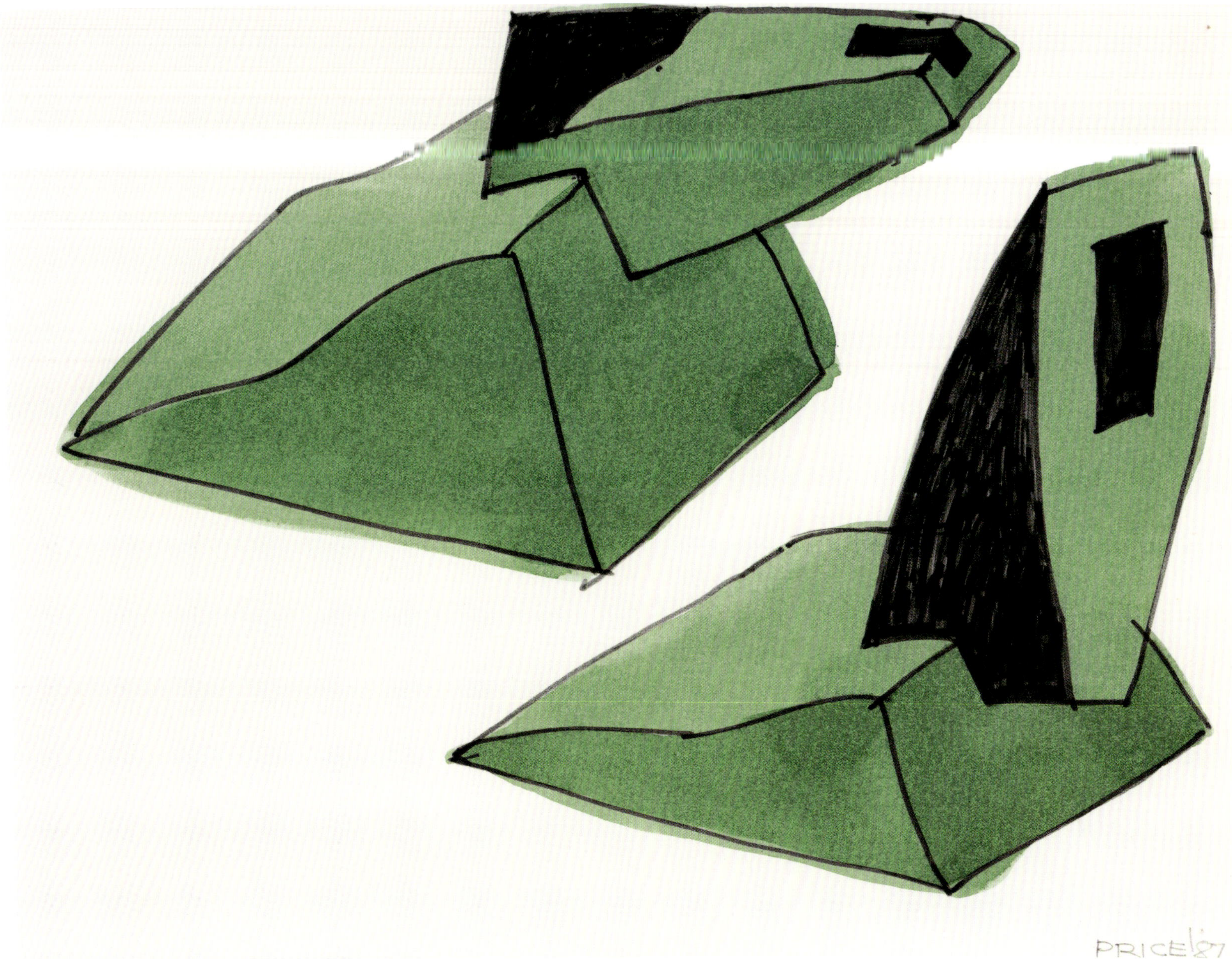

Untitled, 1987

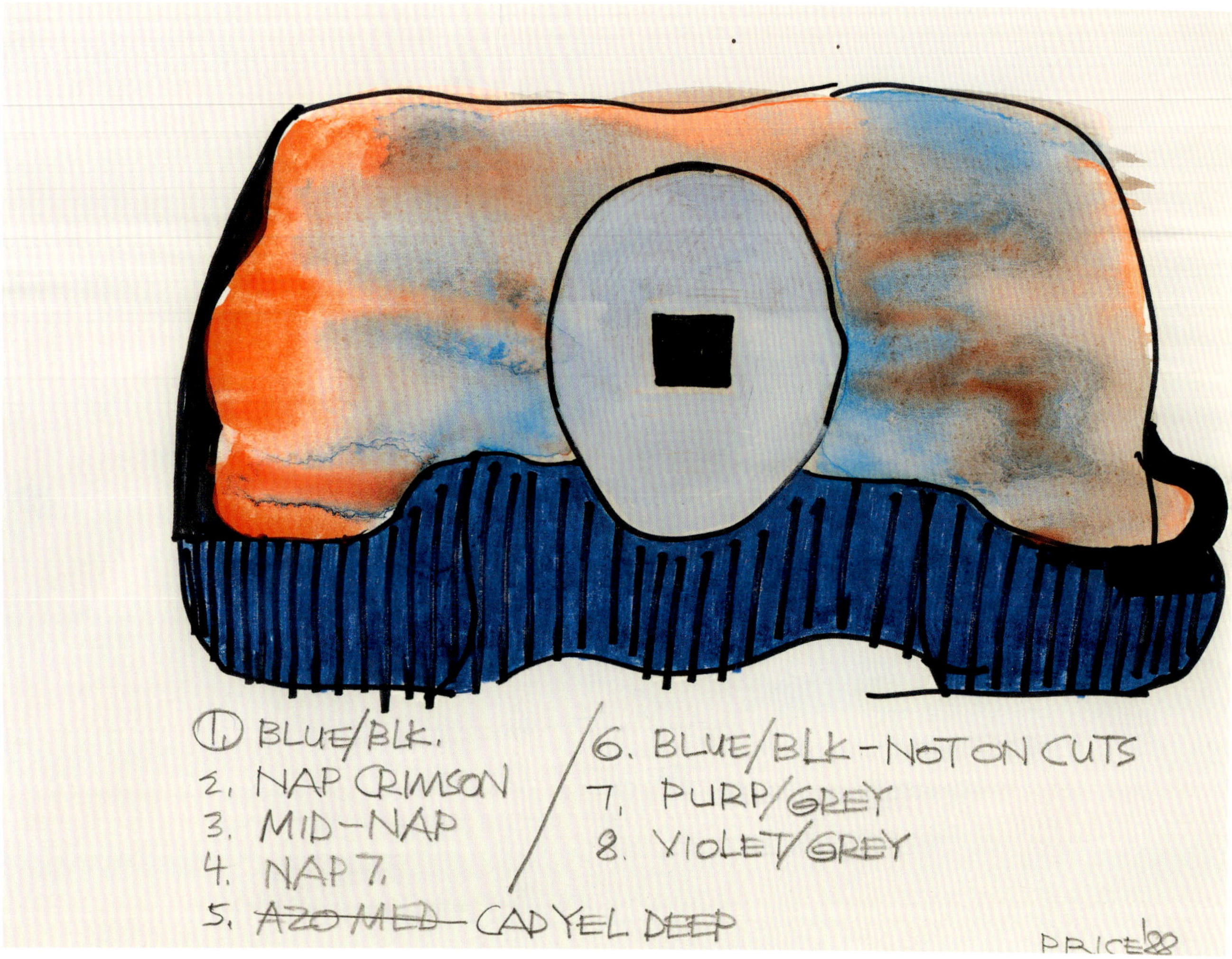

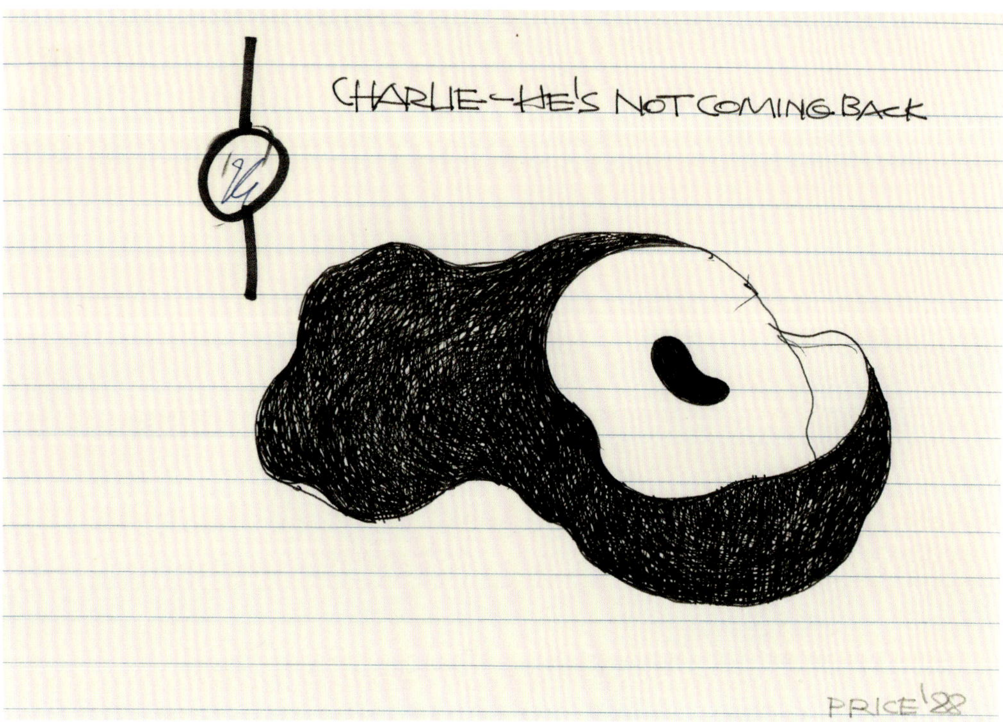

BOTH WORKS:
Untitled, 1988

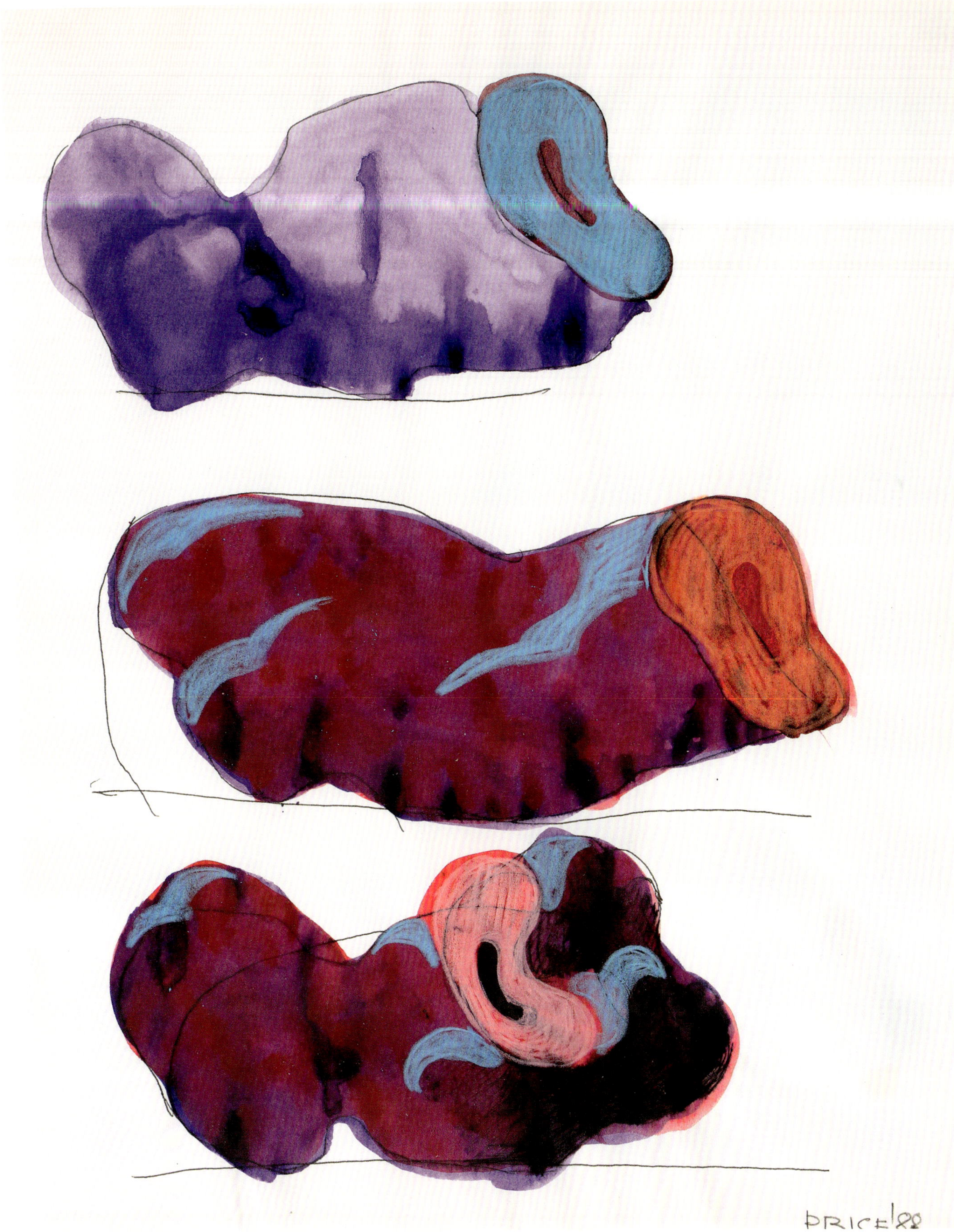

Untitled, 1988

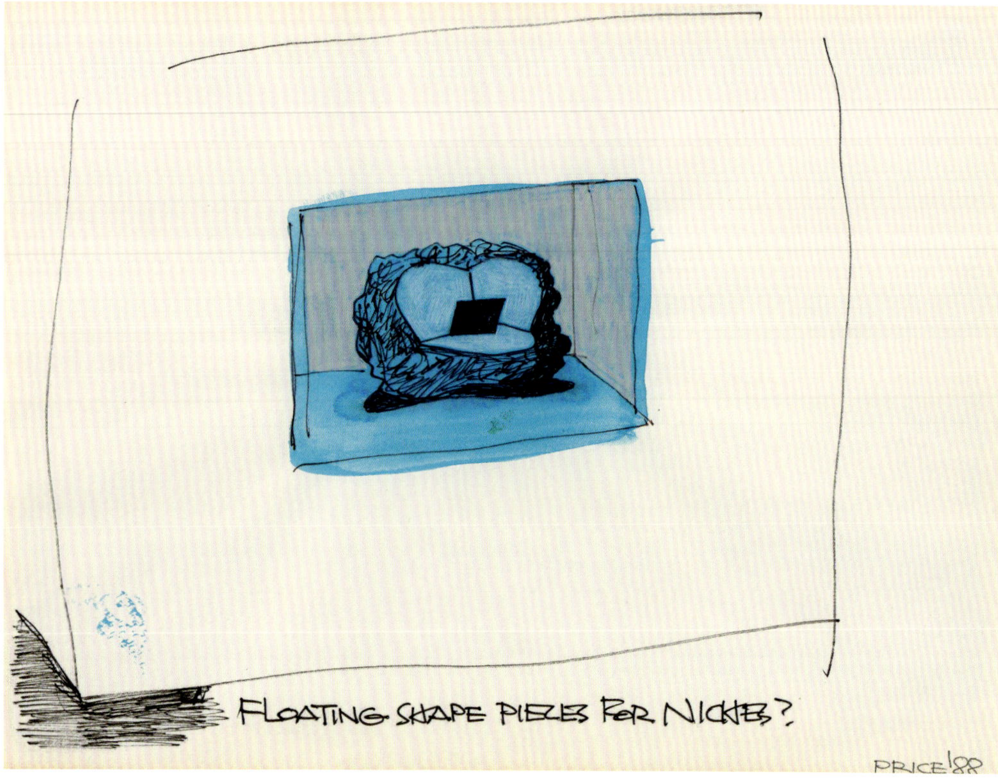

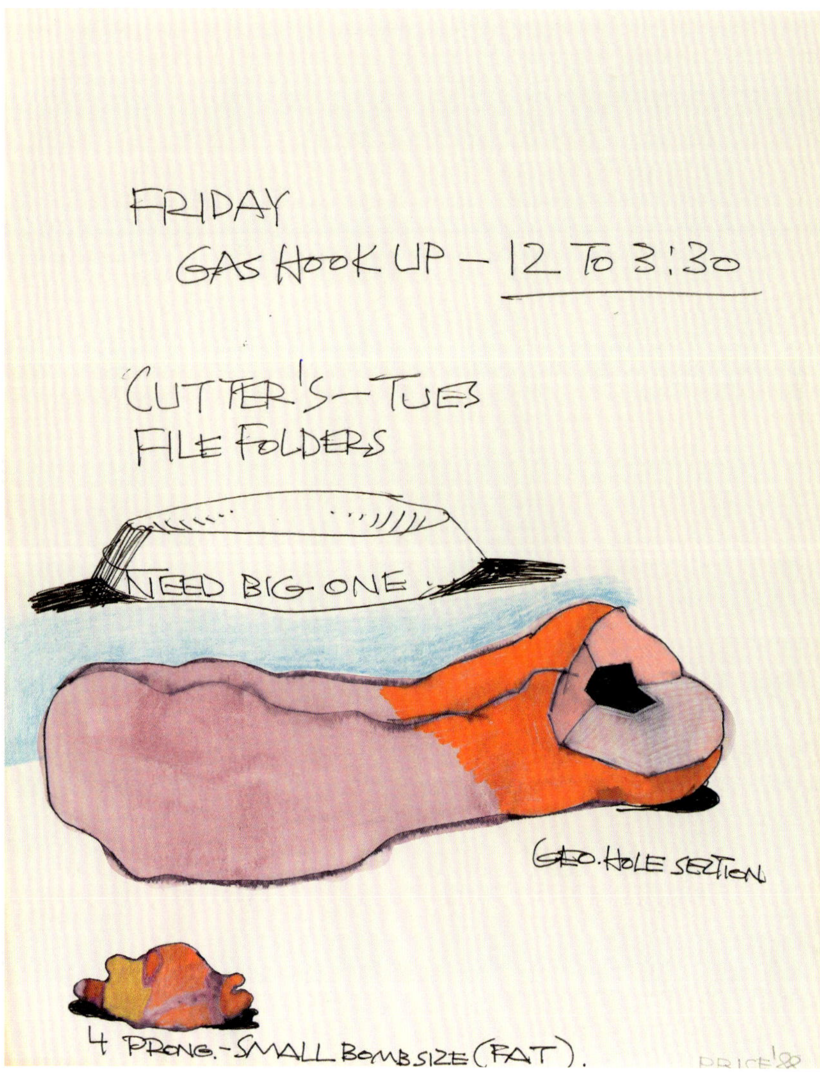

BOTH WORKS:
Untitled, 1988

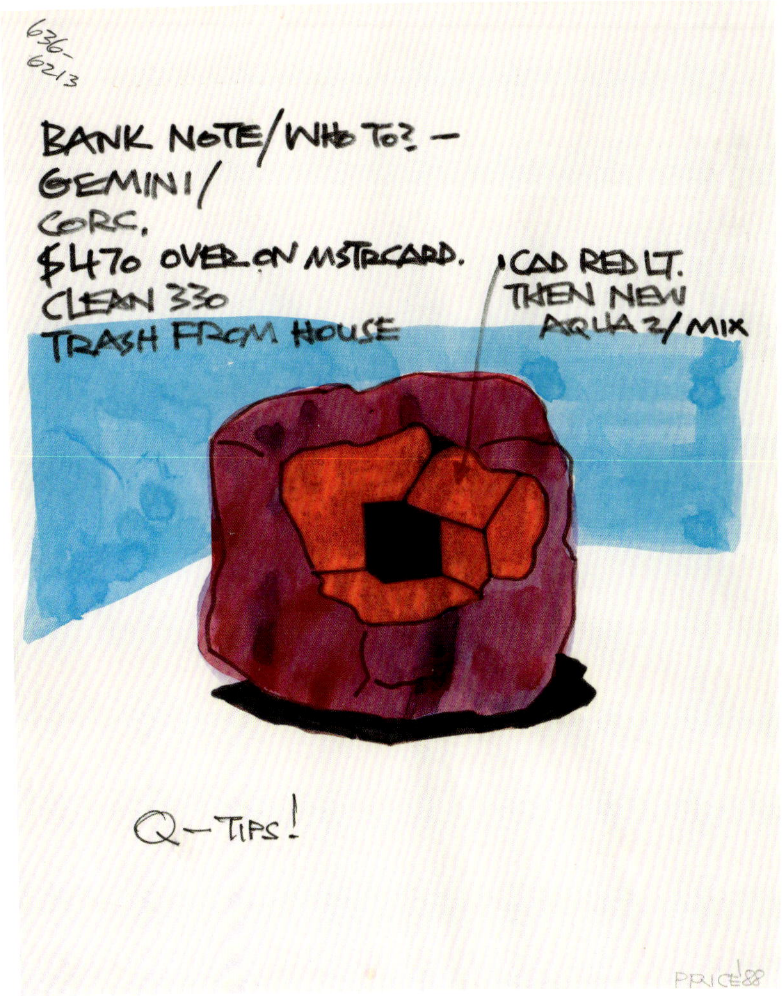

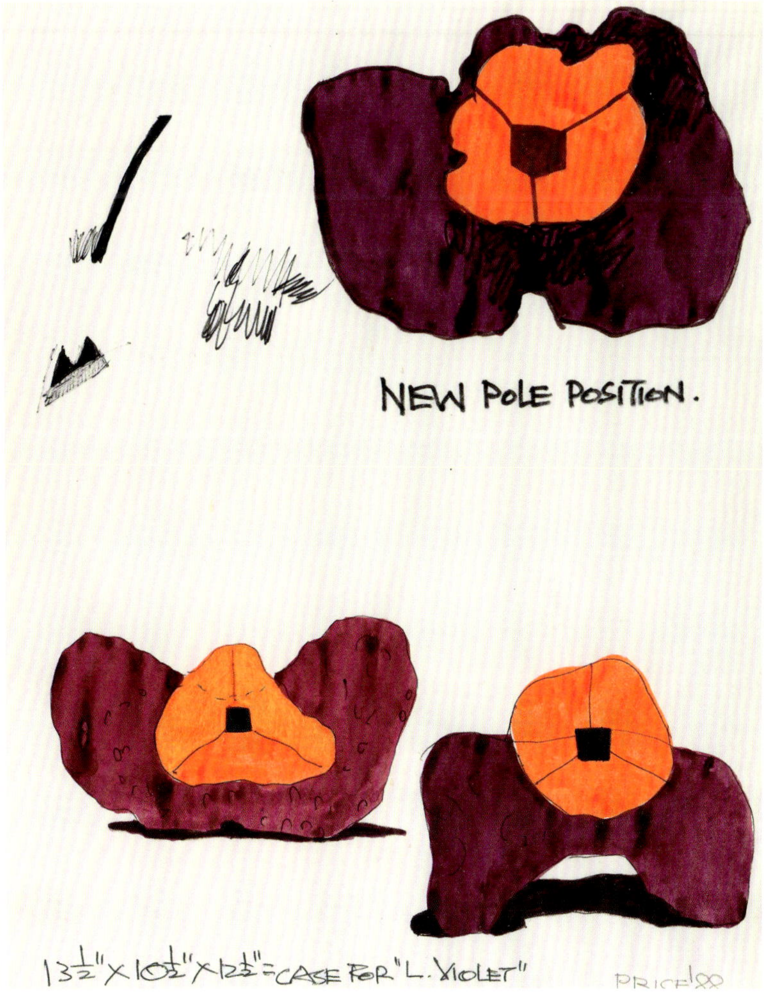

BOTH WORKS:
Untitled, 1988

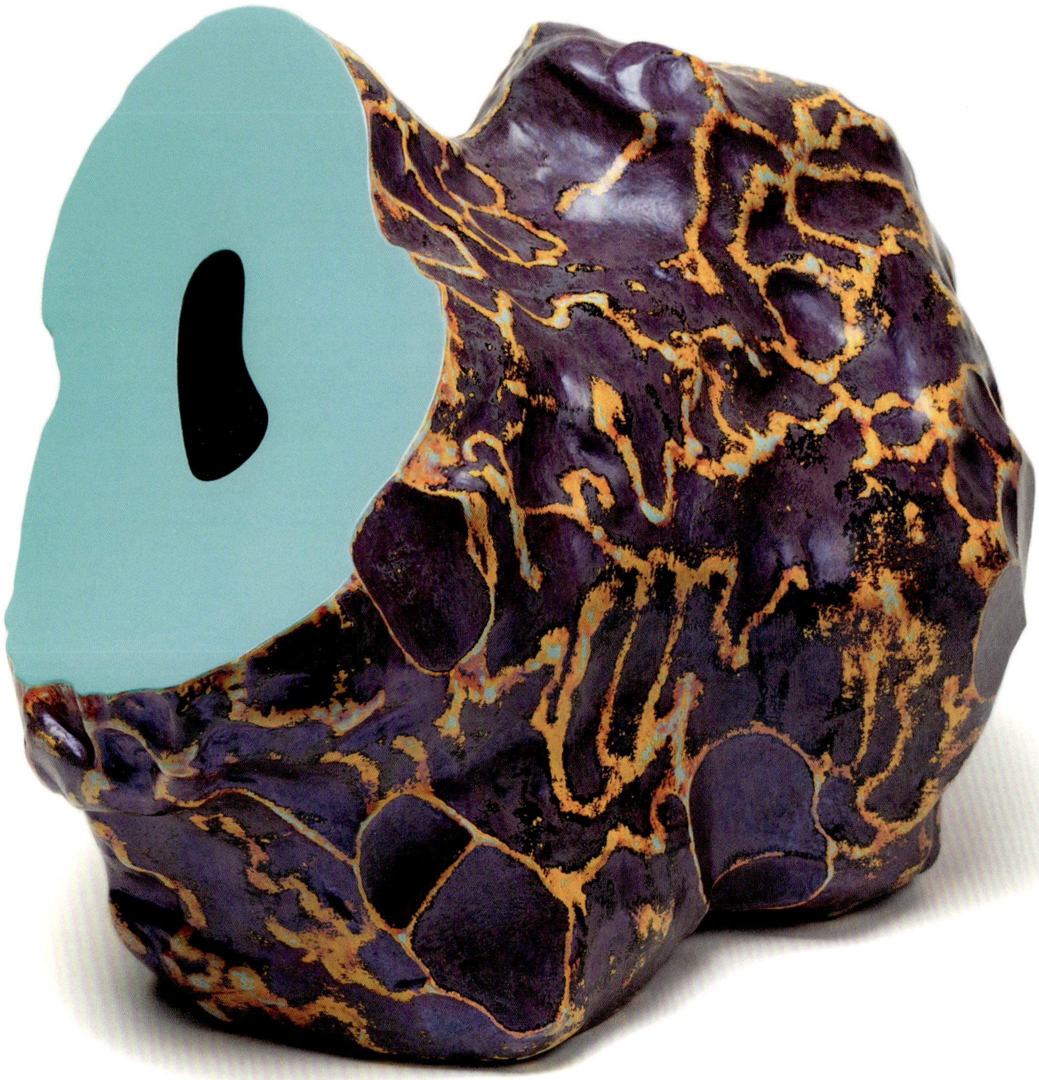

The Lug, 1988

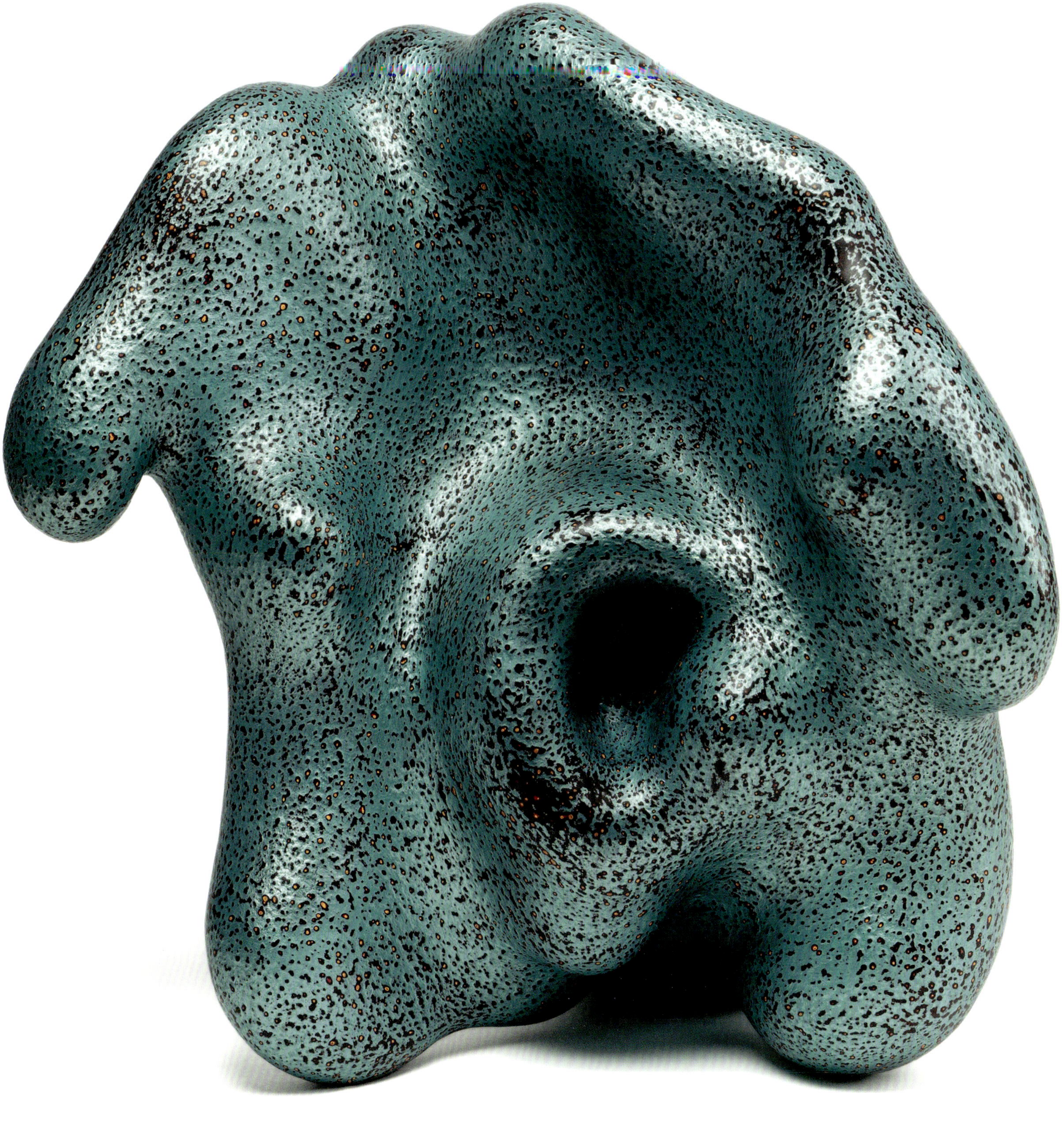

Ghosted, 1998

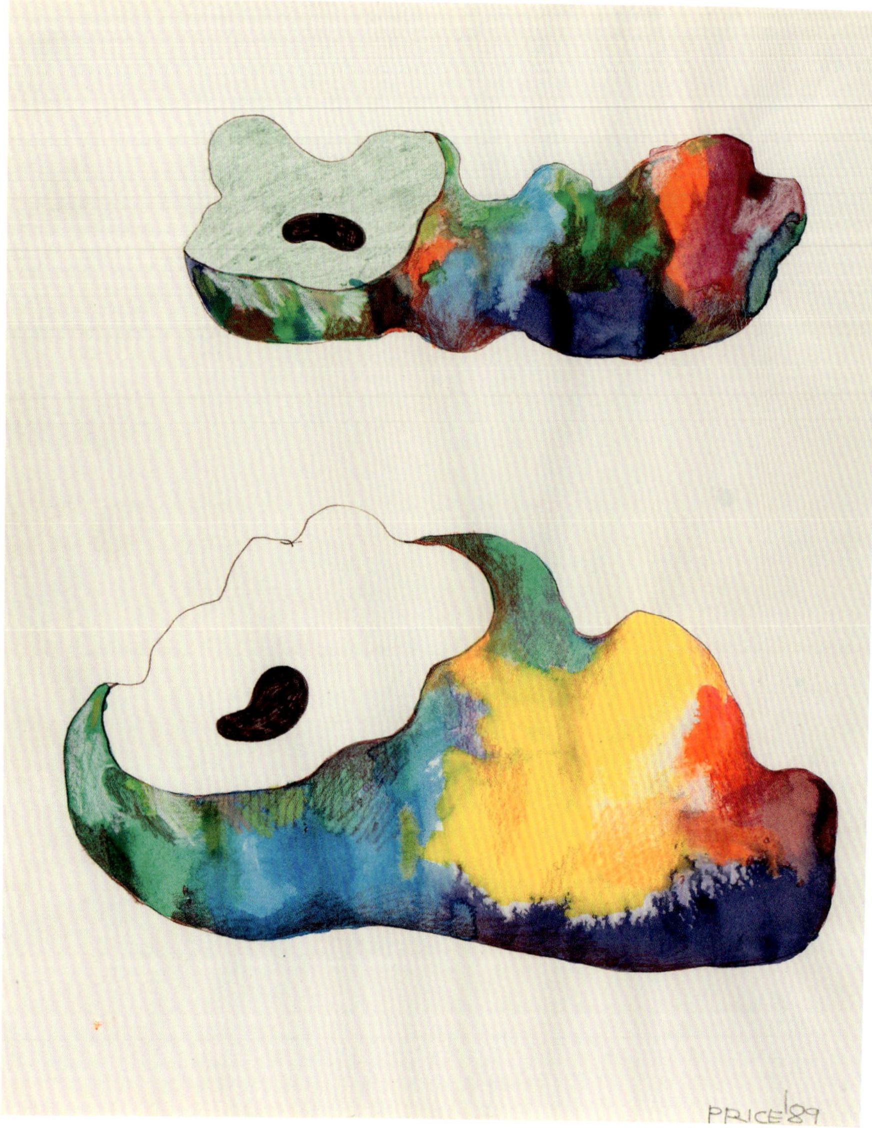
PRICE '89

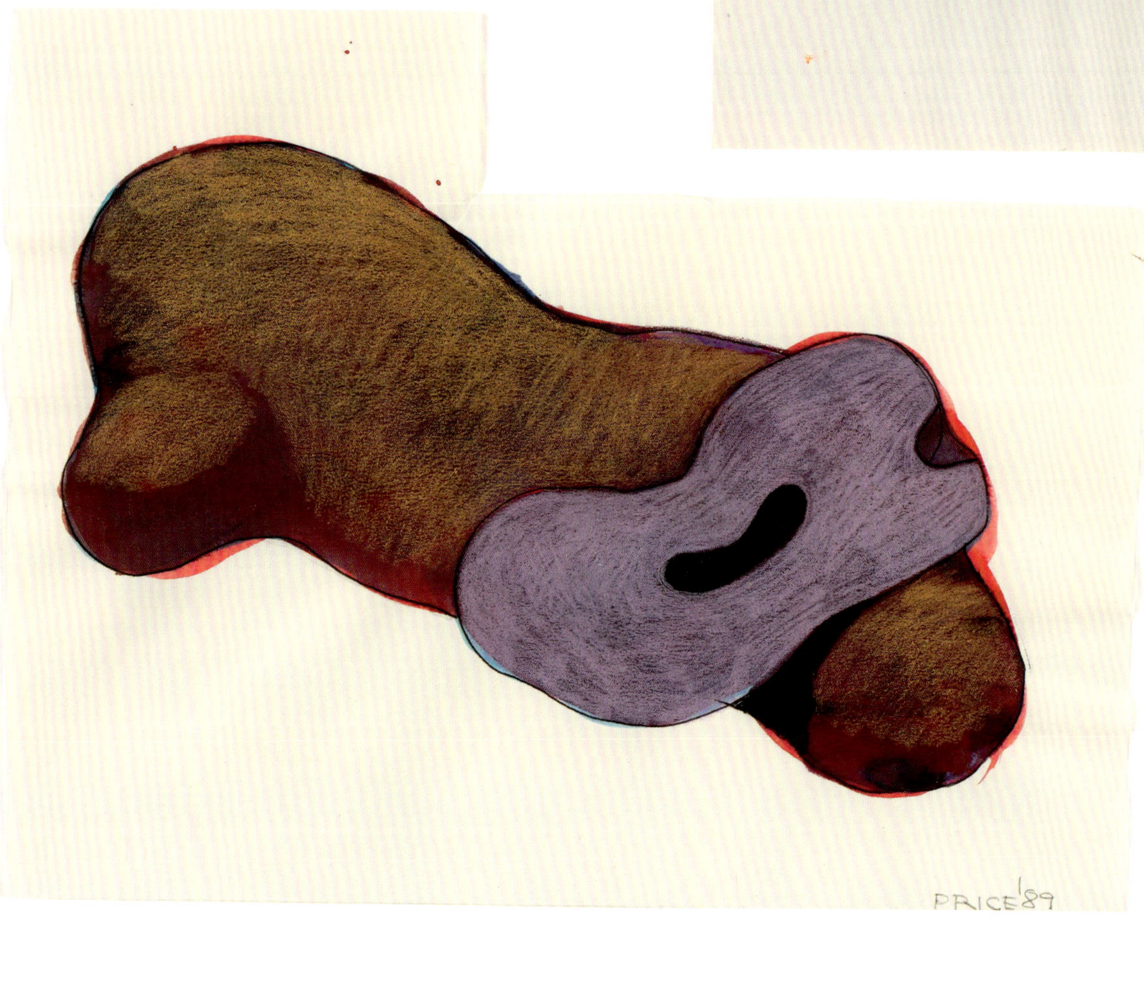
PRICE '89

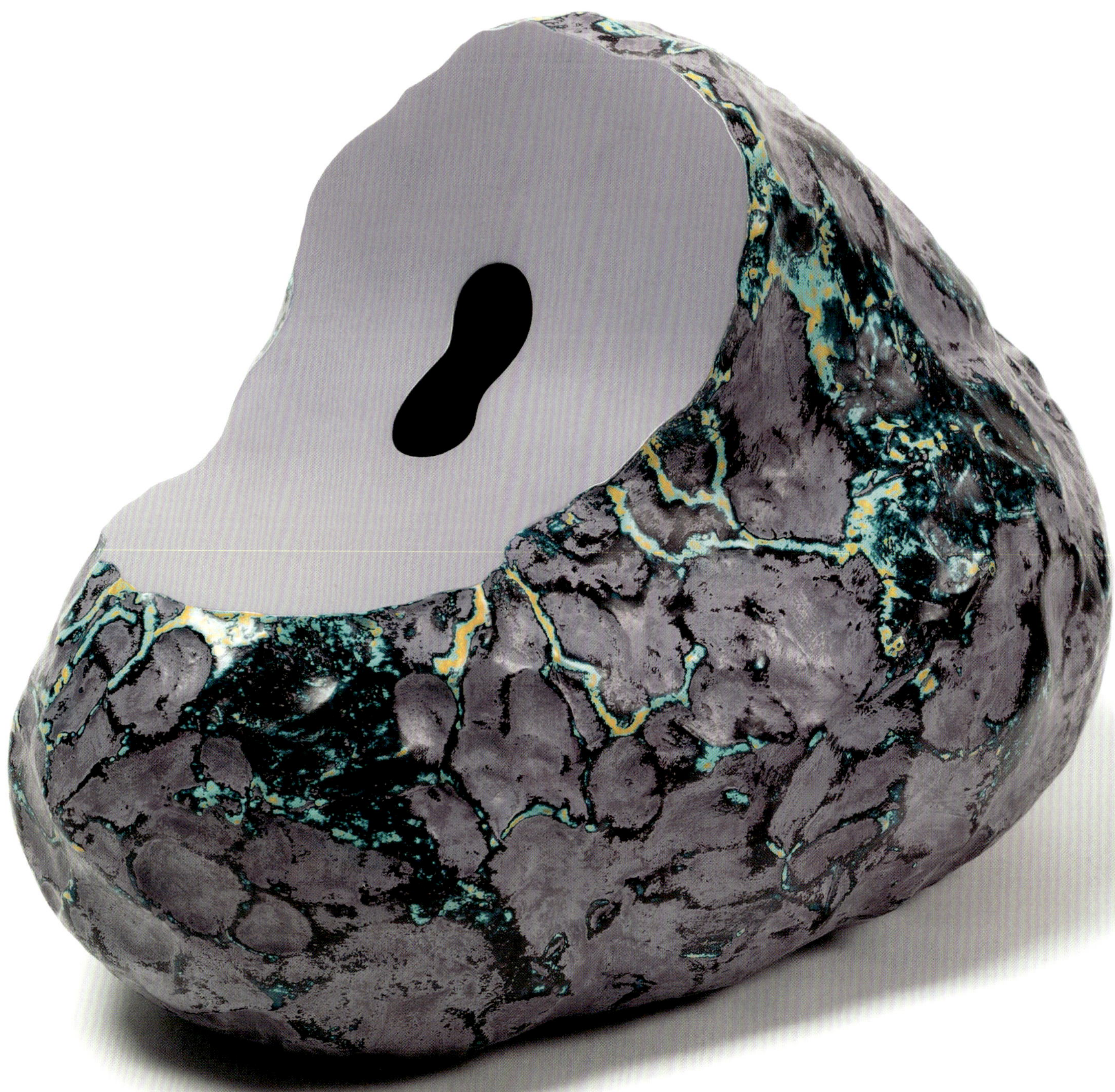

Color Sample, 1989
OPPOSITE, BOTH WORKS:
Untitled, 1989

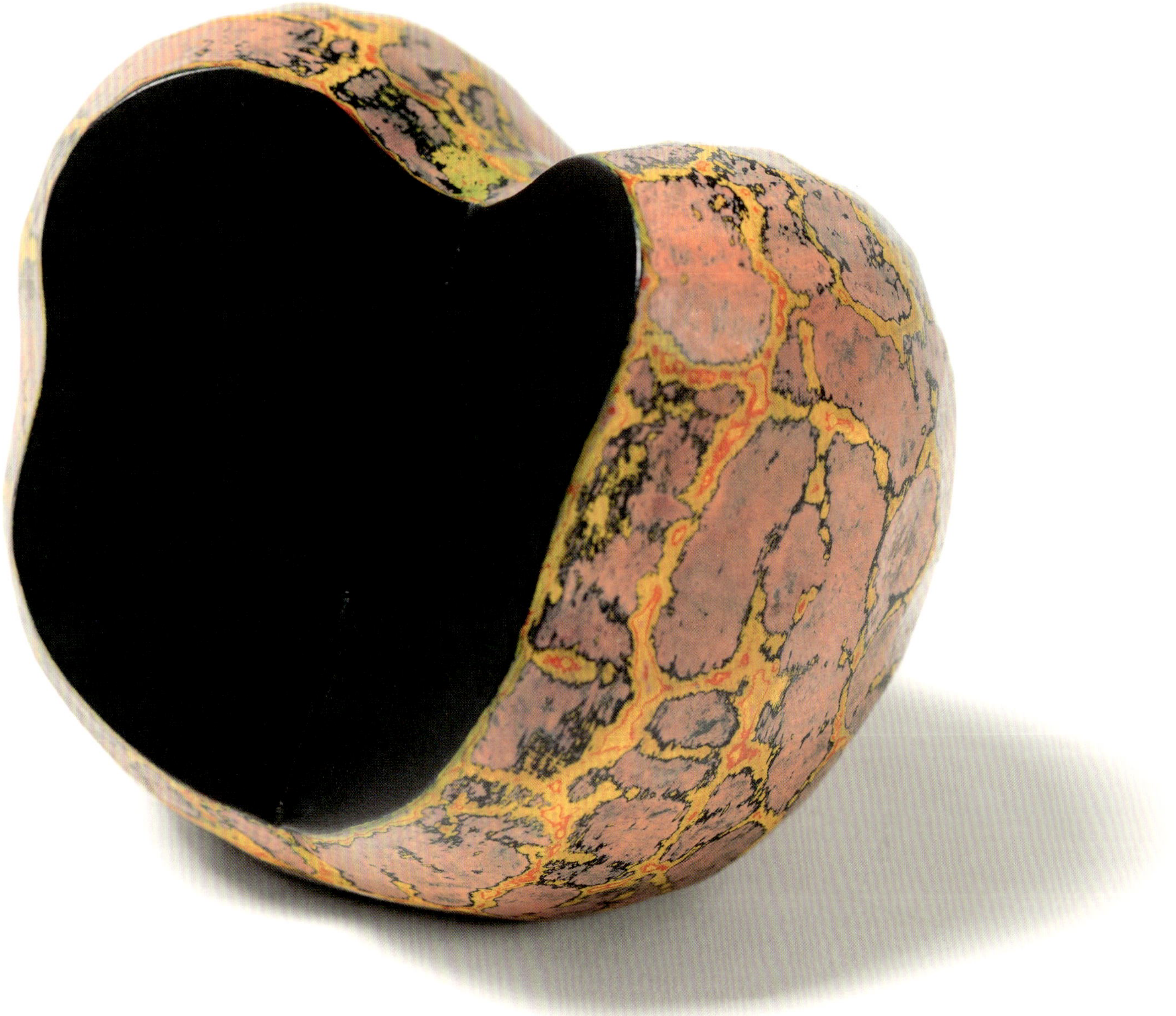

Untitled, c. 1990

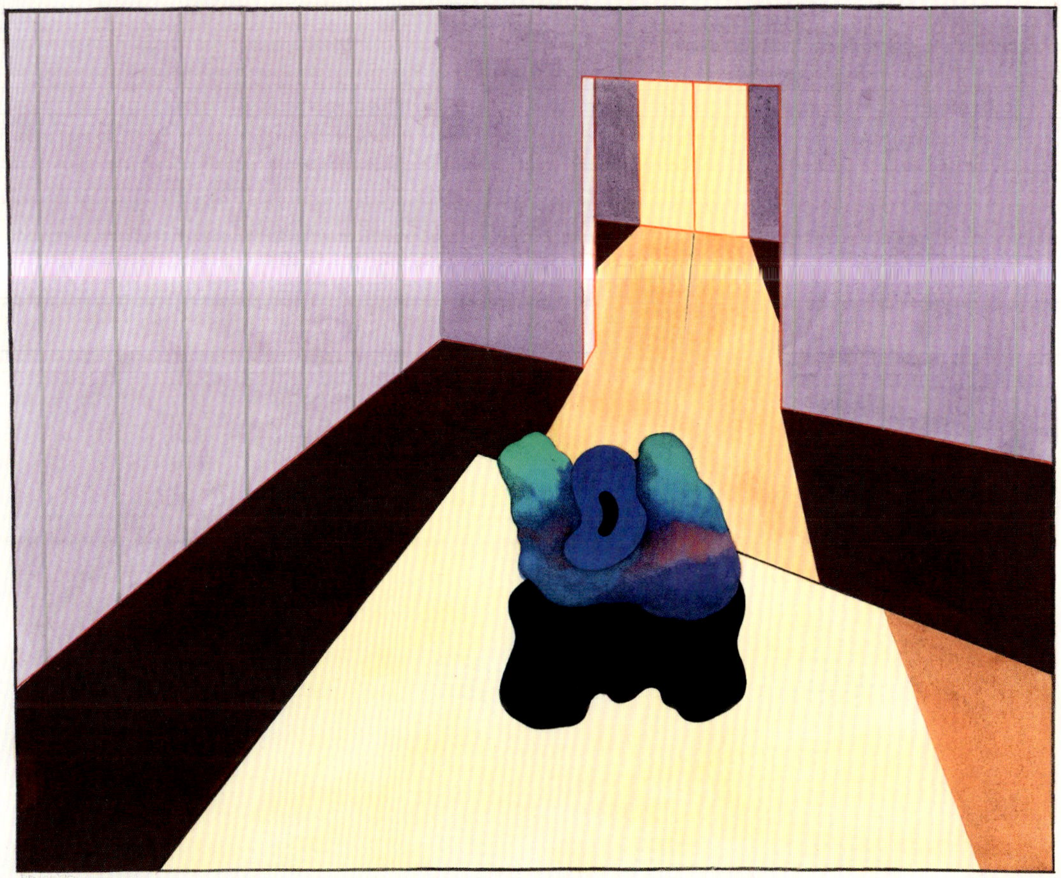

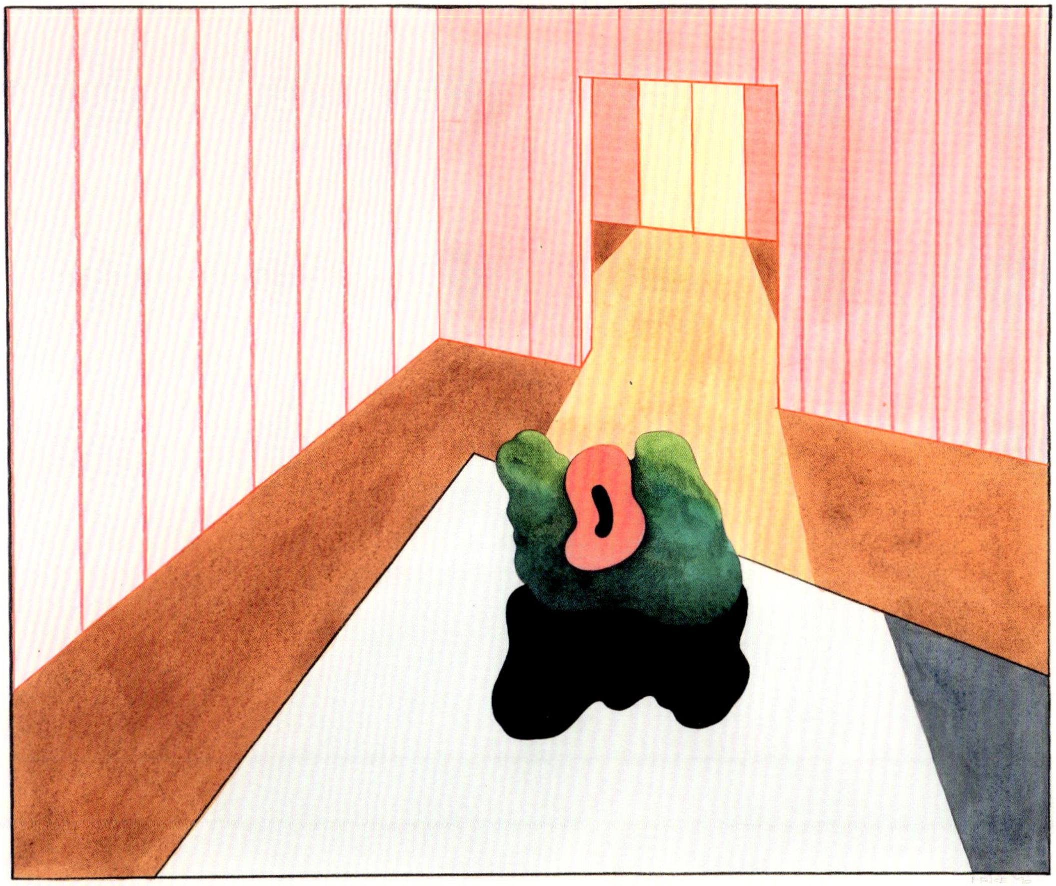

BOTH WORKS:
Untitled, 1990

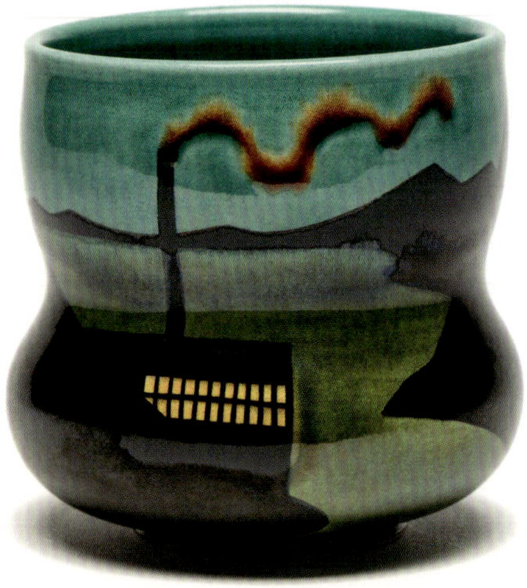

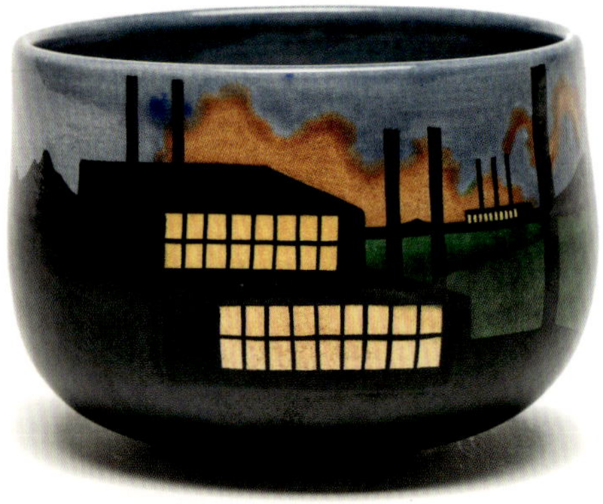

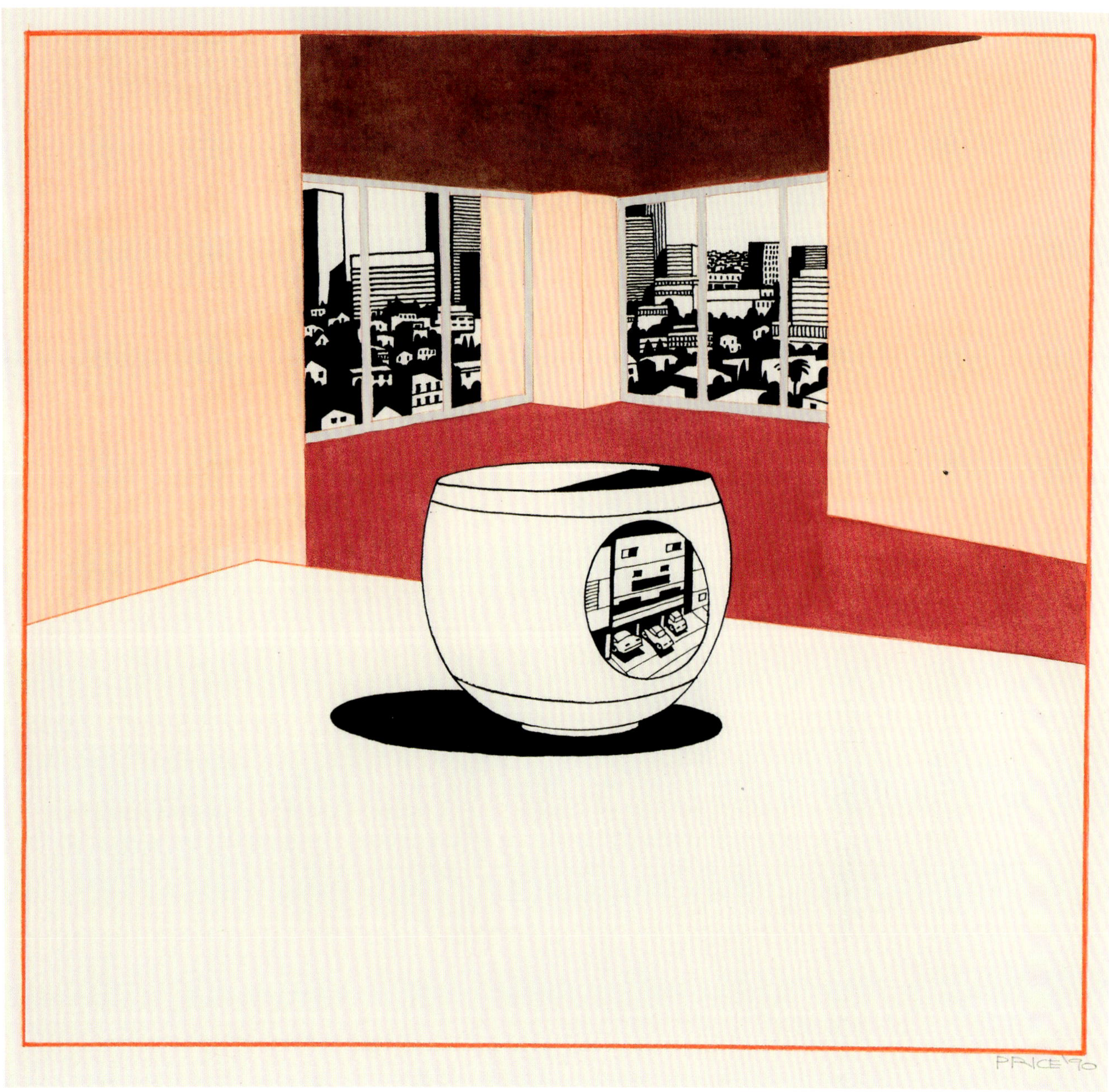

CLOCKWISE FROM TOP LEFT:
Untitled, 1993
Untitled, 1993
Untitled, 1990

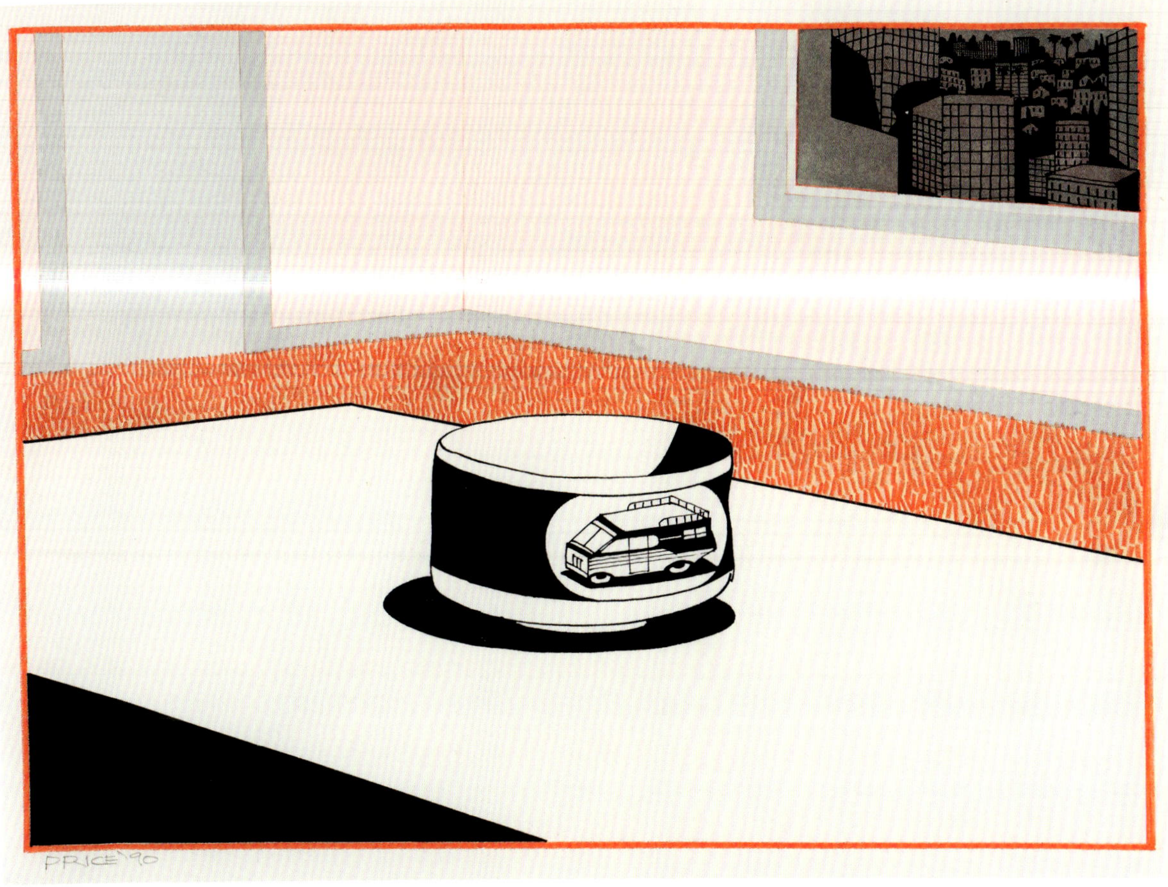

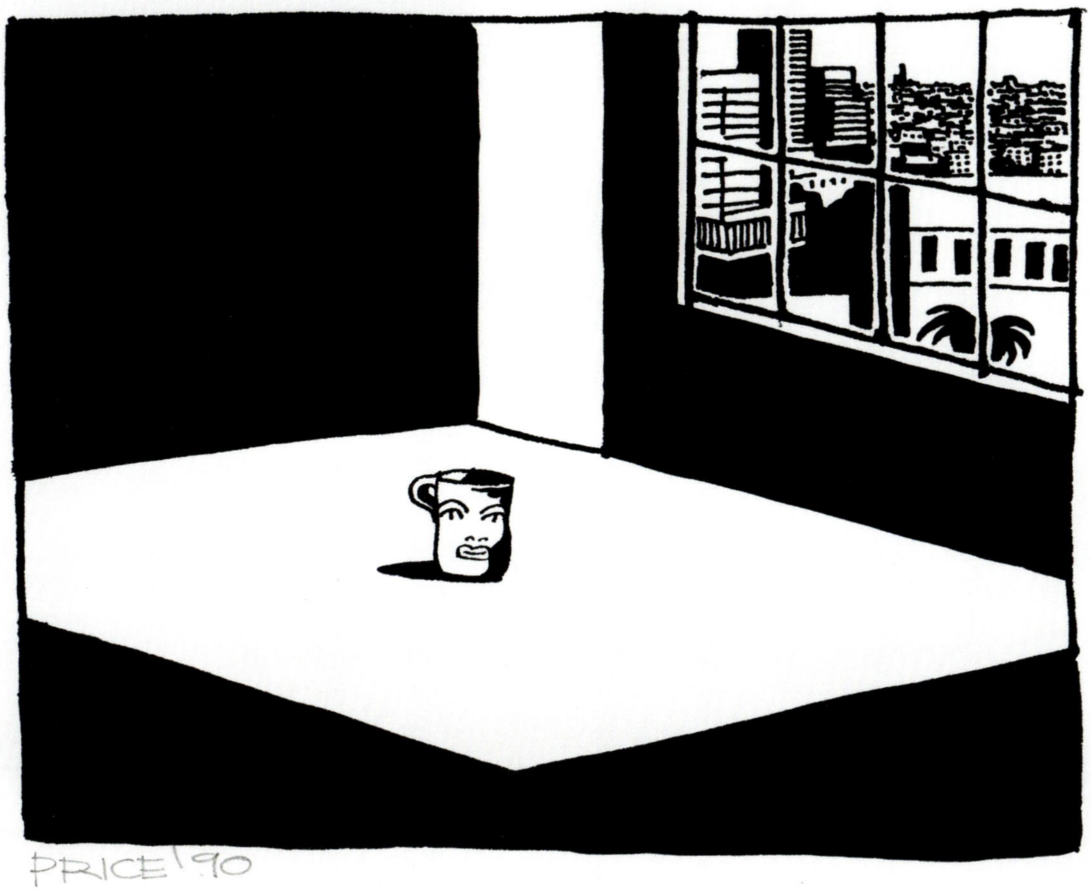

BOTH WORKS:
Untitled, 1990

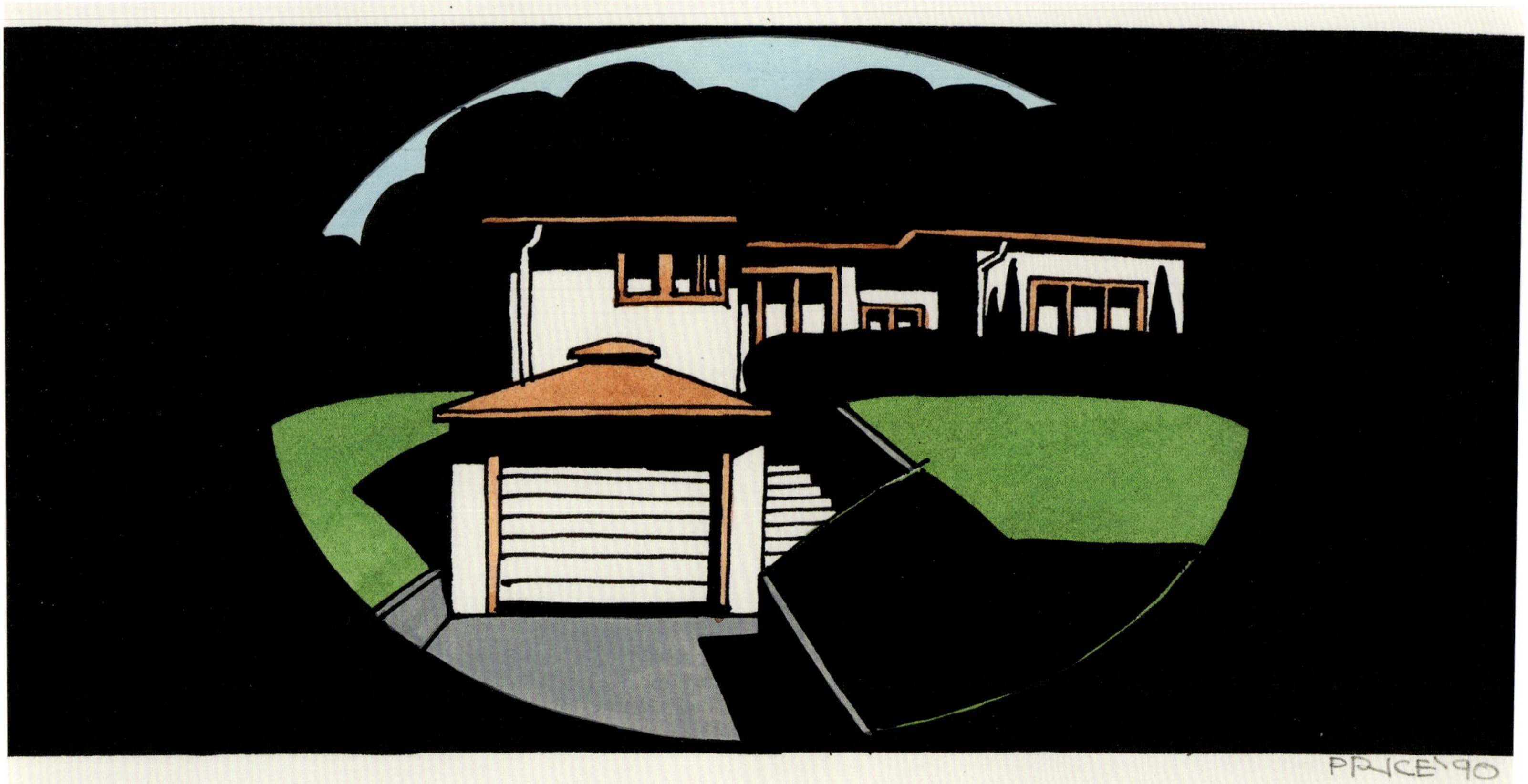

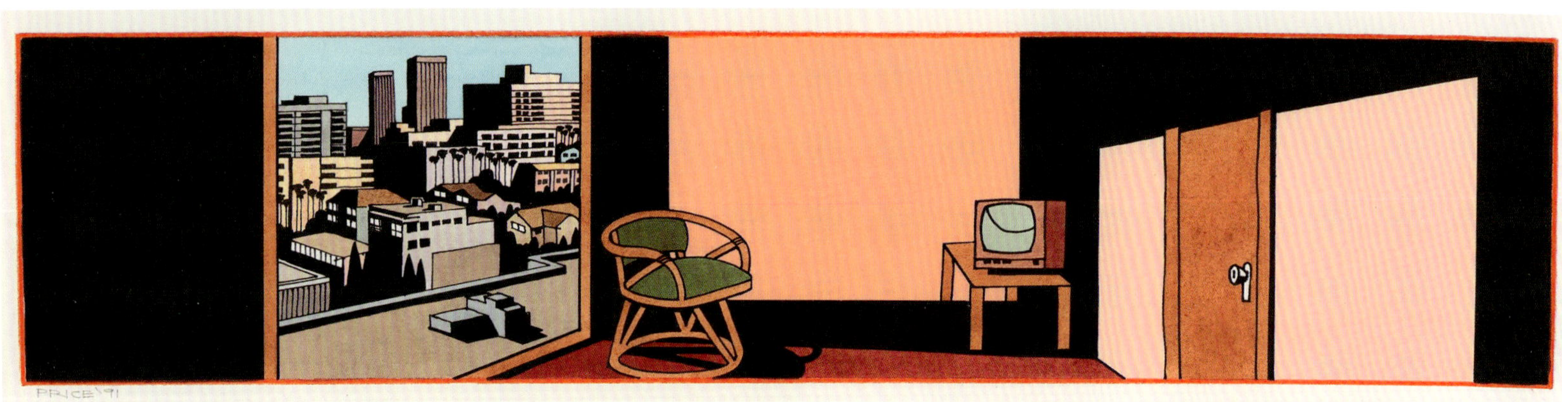

Untitled, 1990
Untitled, 1991

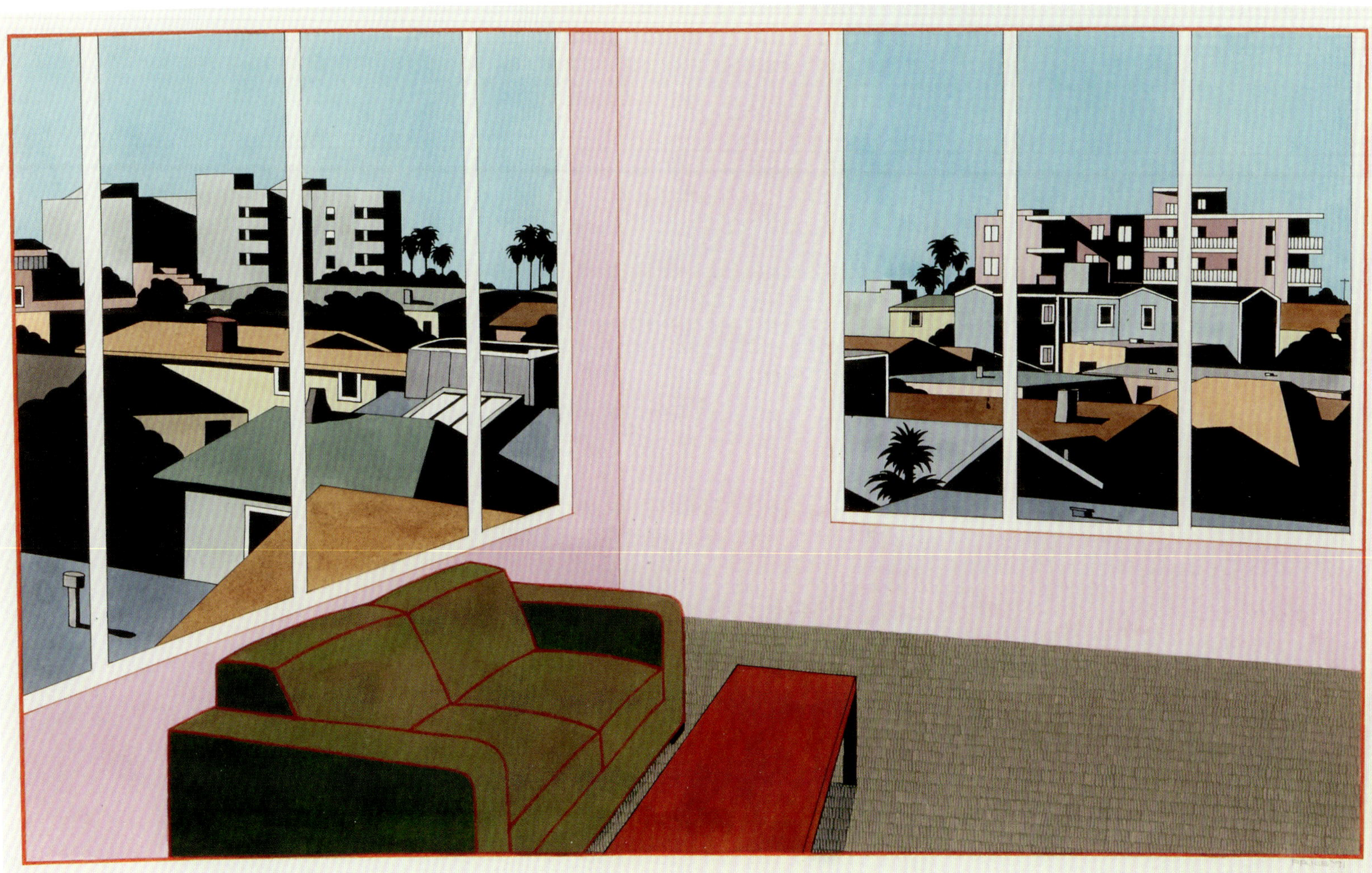

Untitled, 1991

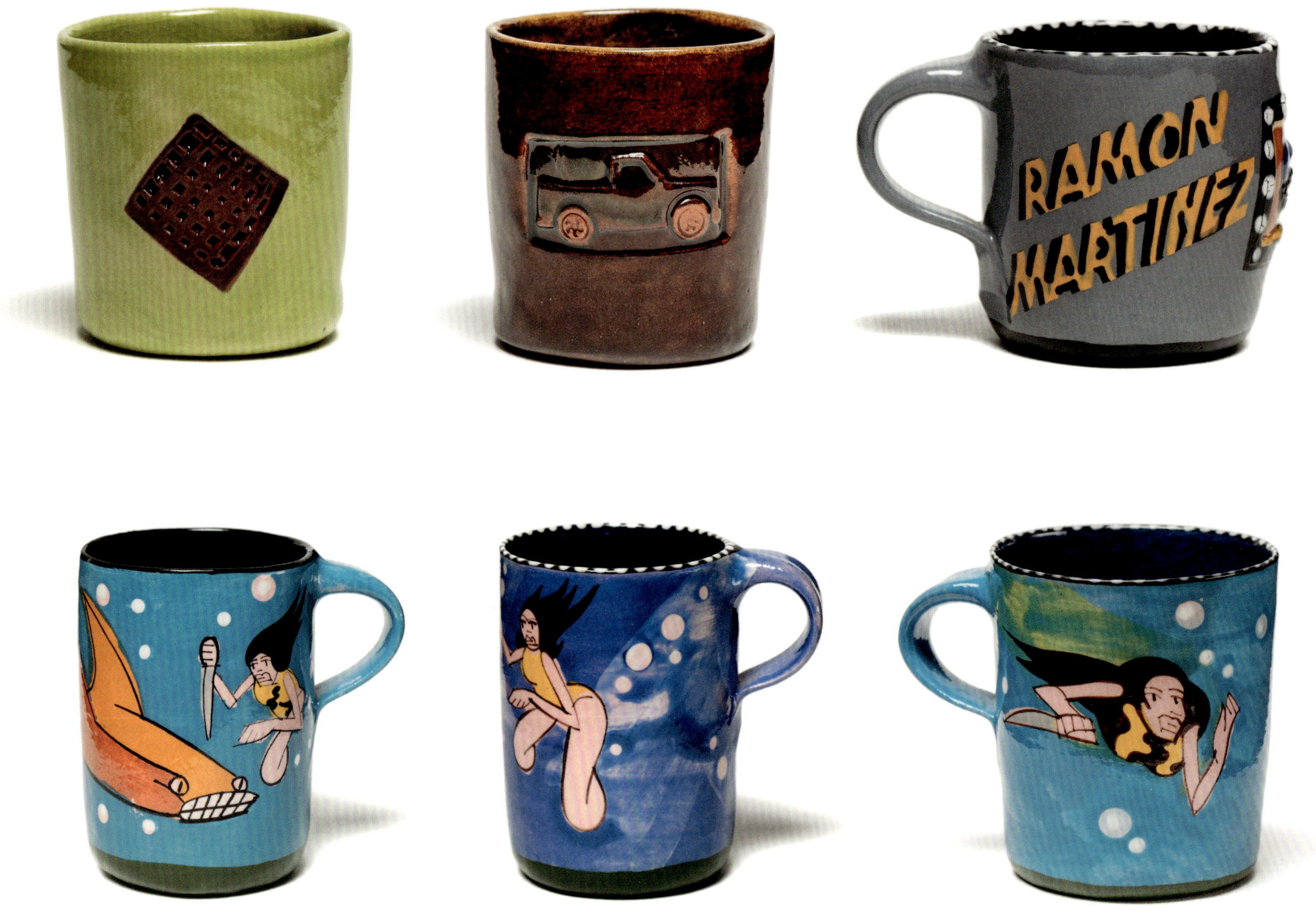

CLOCKWISE FROM TOP LEFT:
Untitled, 1972–77
Untitled, 1972–77
Untitled, 1992
Untitled, c. 1982
Untitled, c. 1982
Untitled, c. 1982

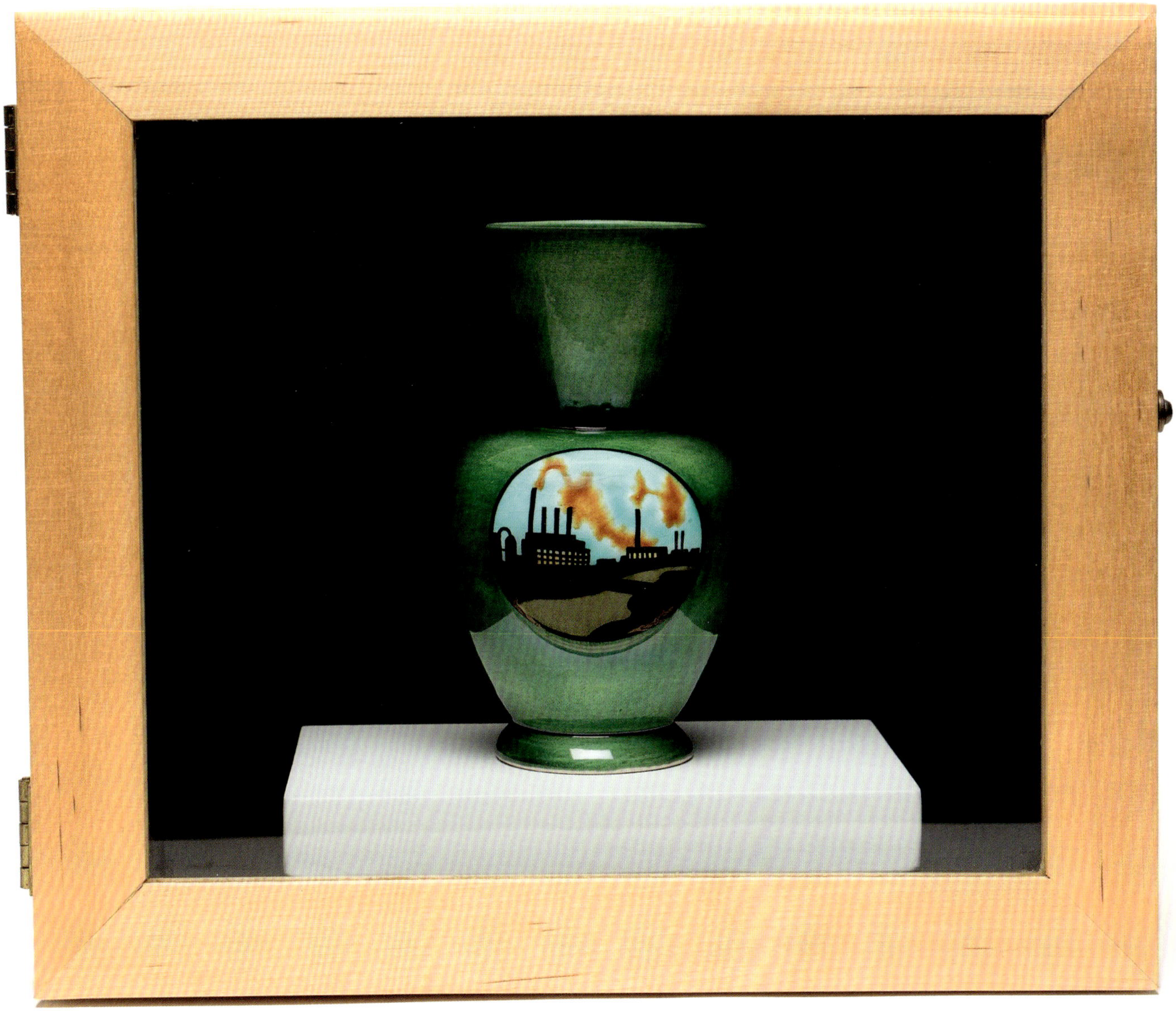

Untitled, c. 1993

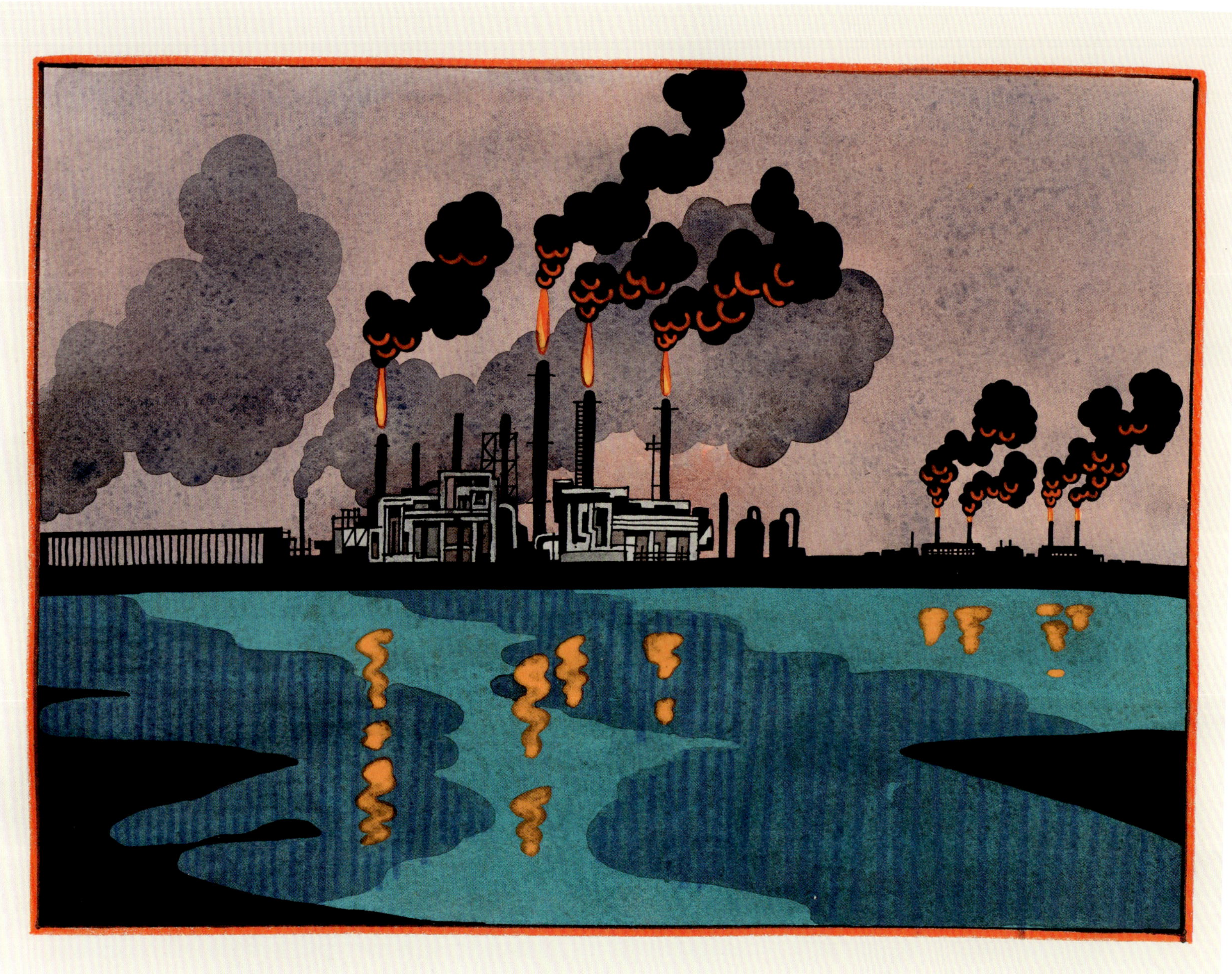

Untitled, 1993

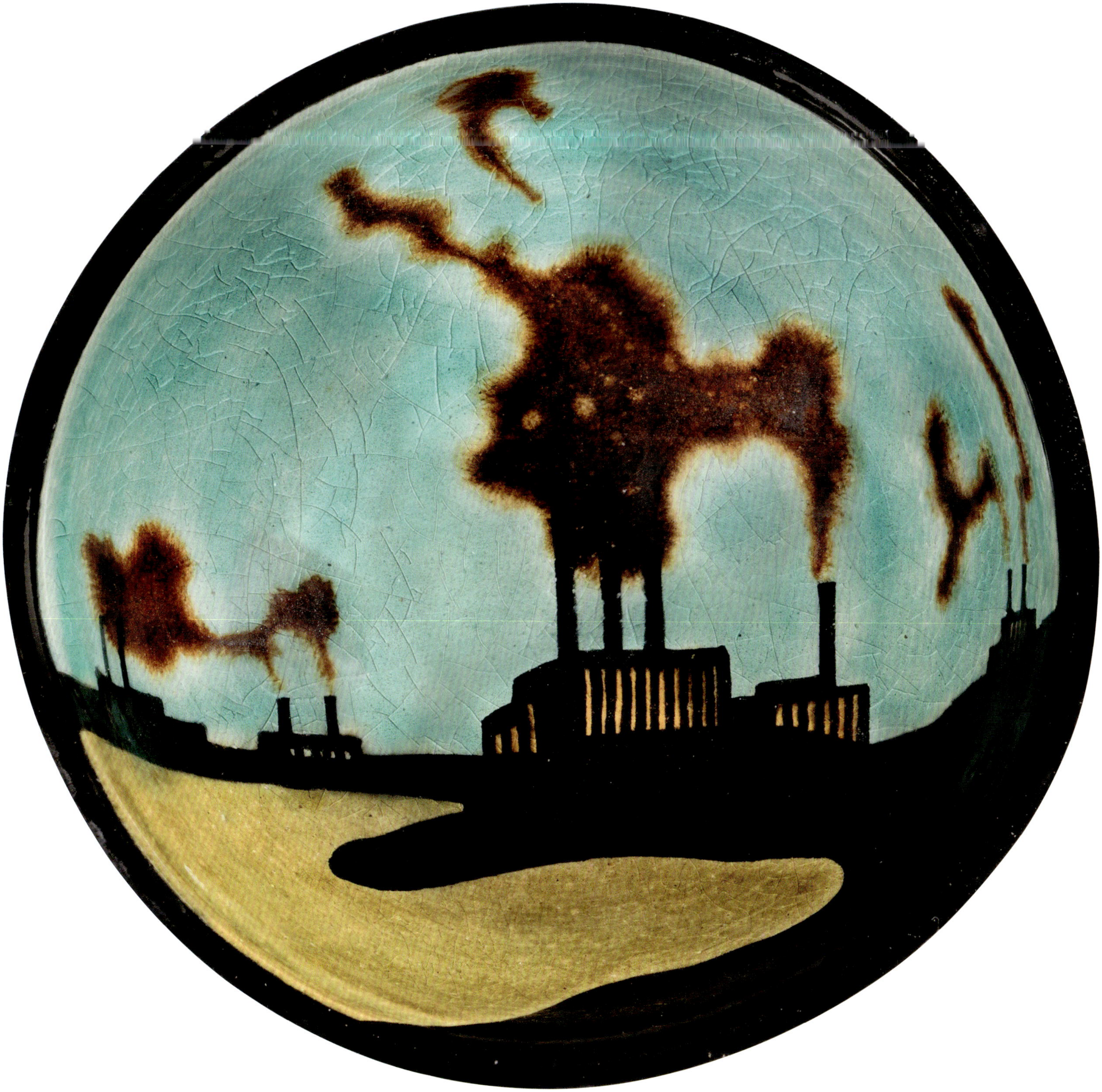

Untitled, 1993

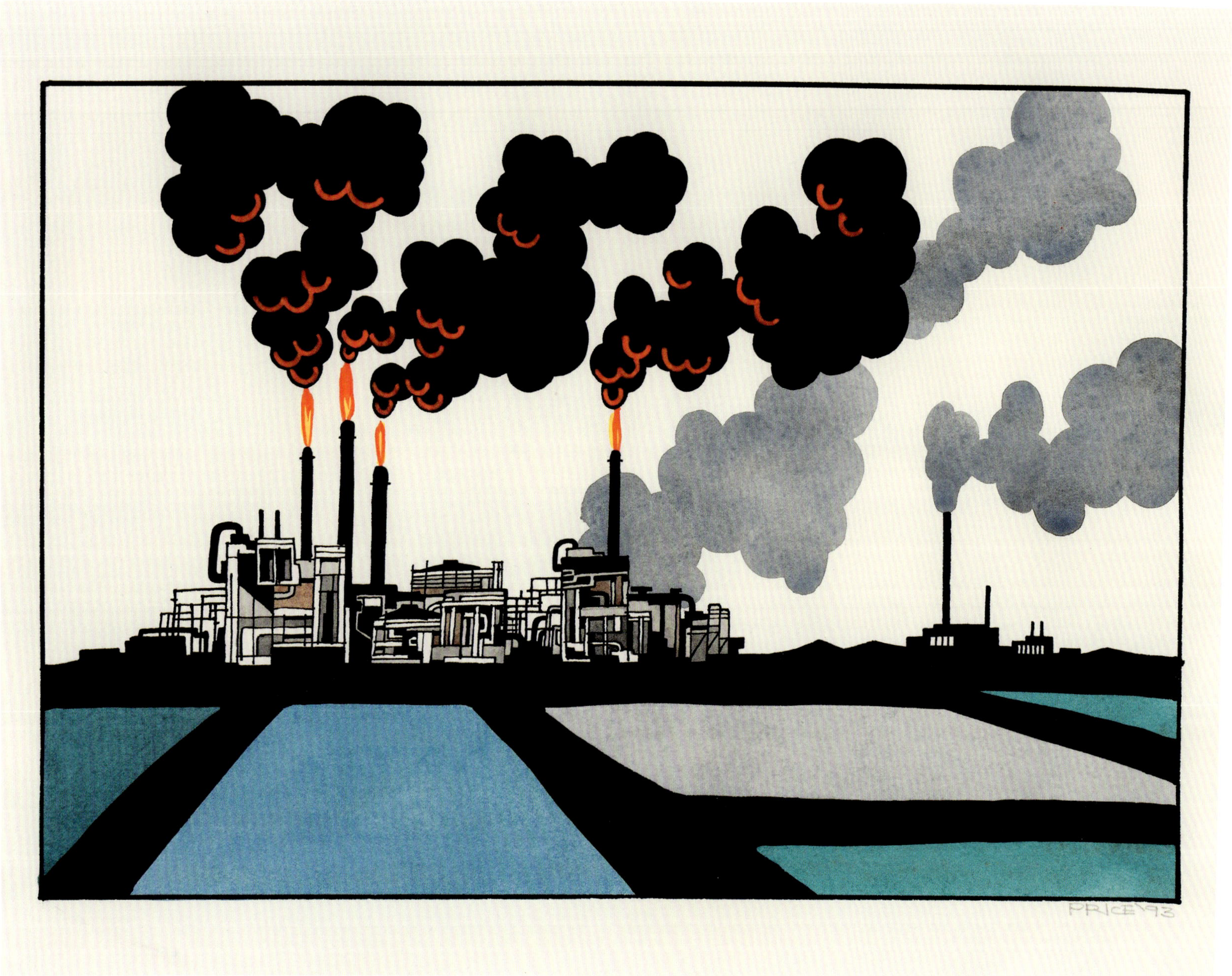

Untitled, 1993

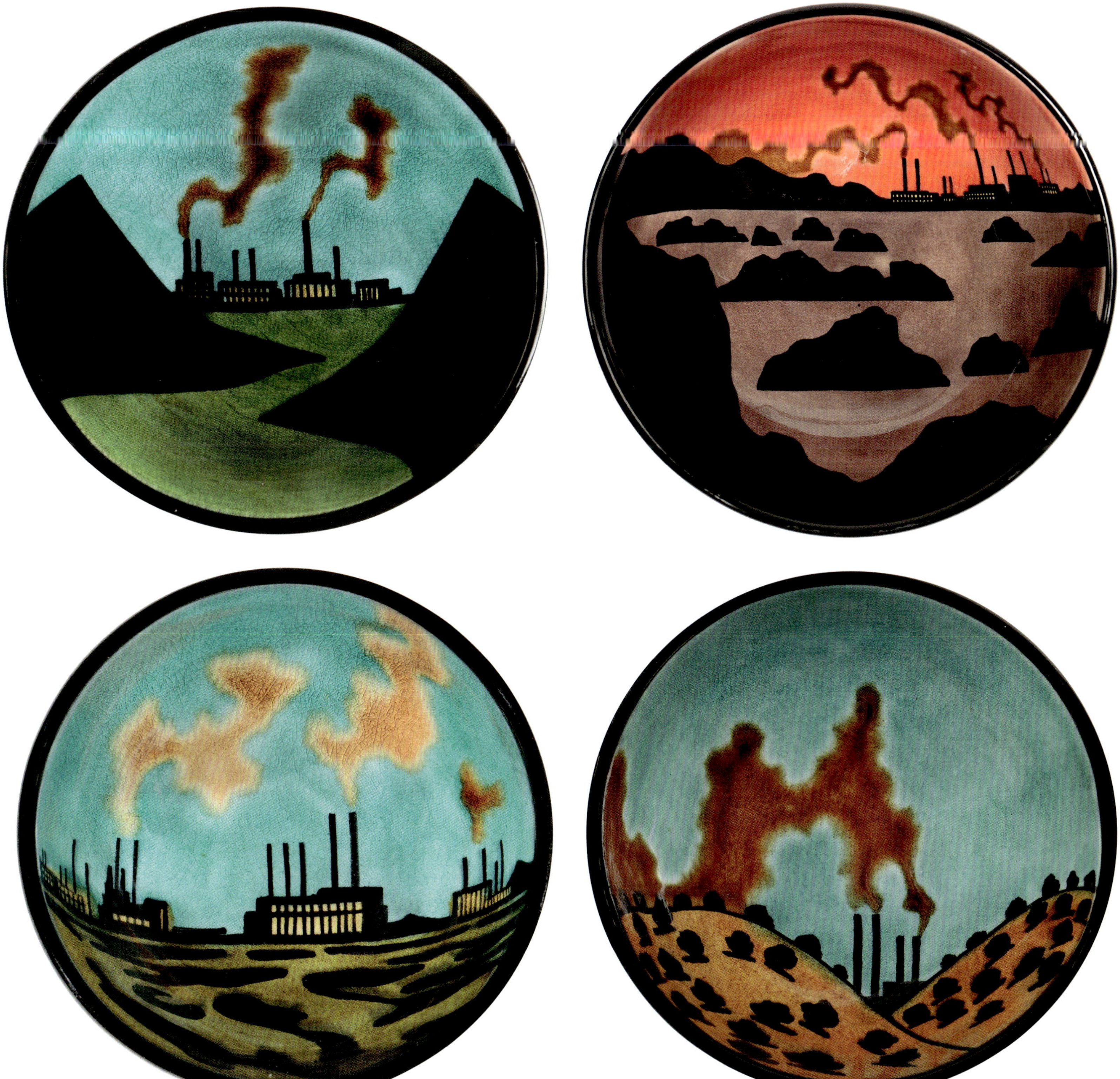

ALL WORKS:
Untitled, 1993

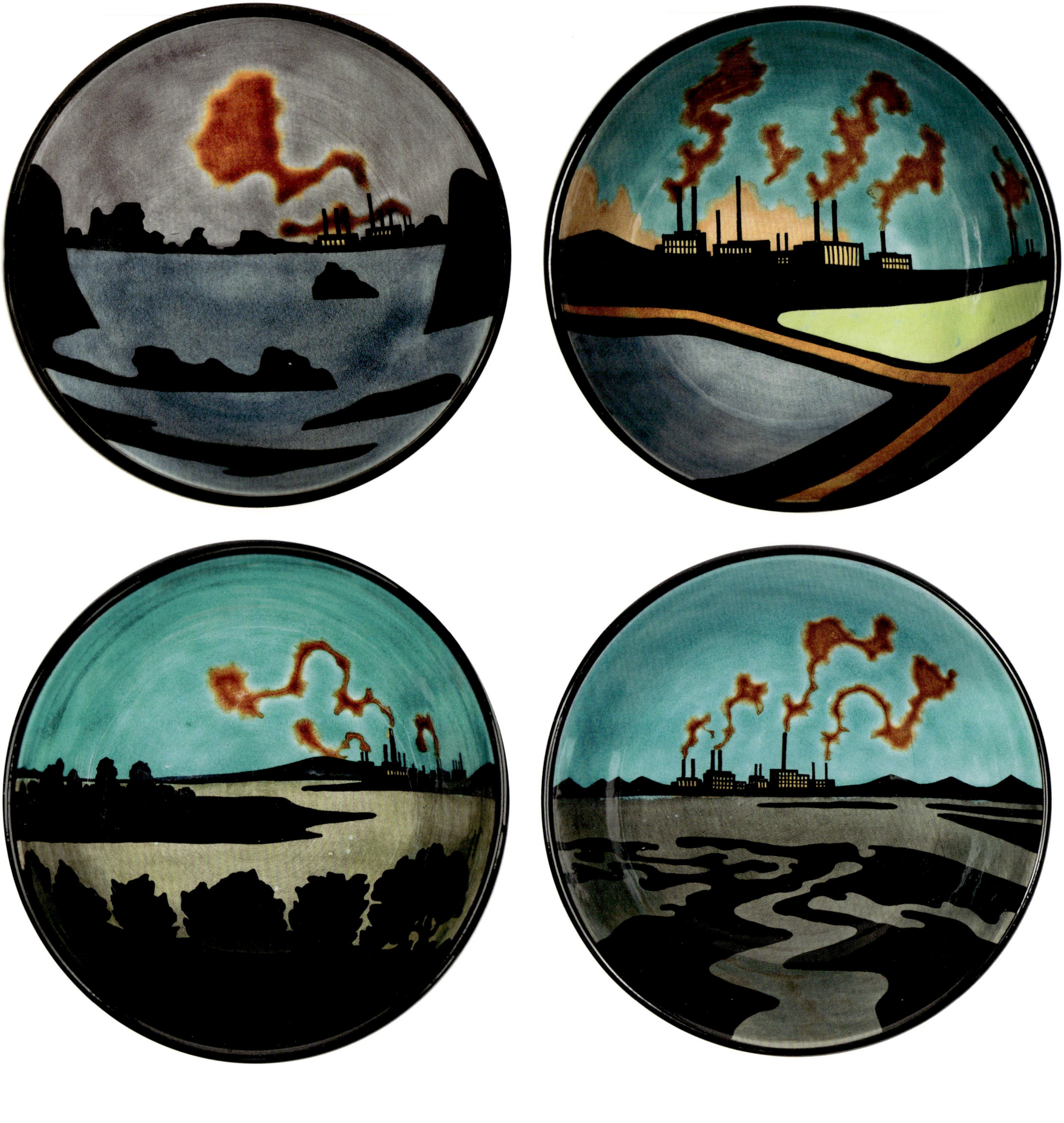

ALL WORKS:
Untitled, 1993

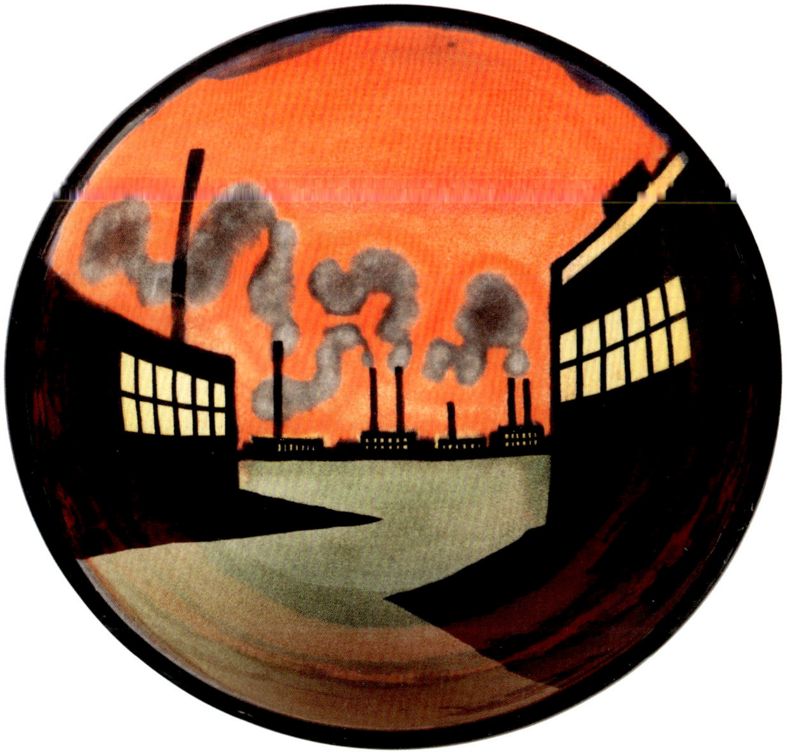

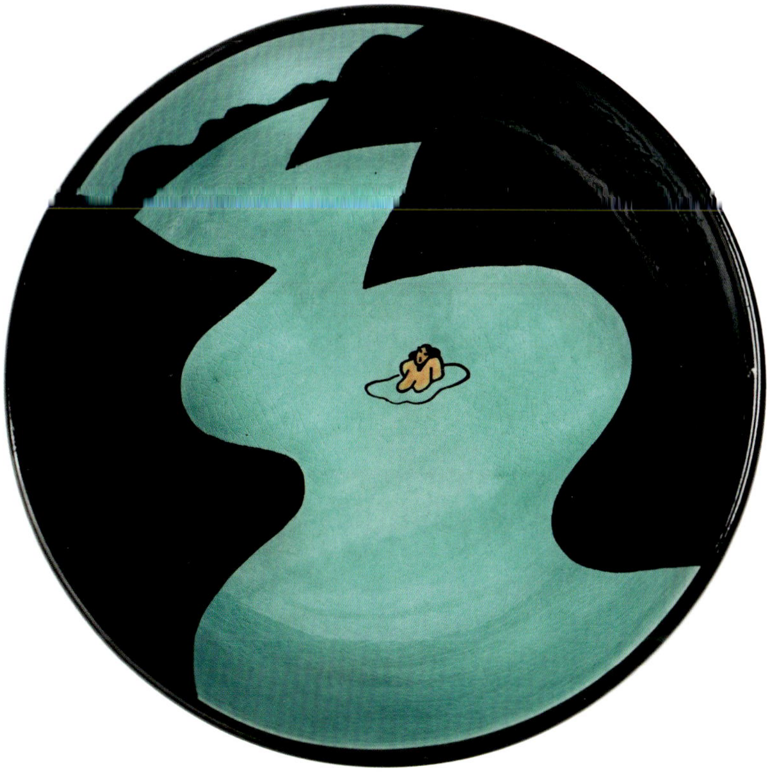

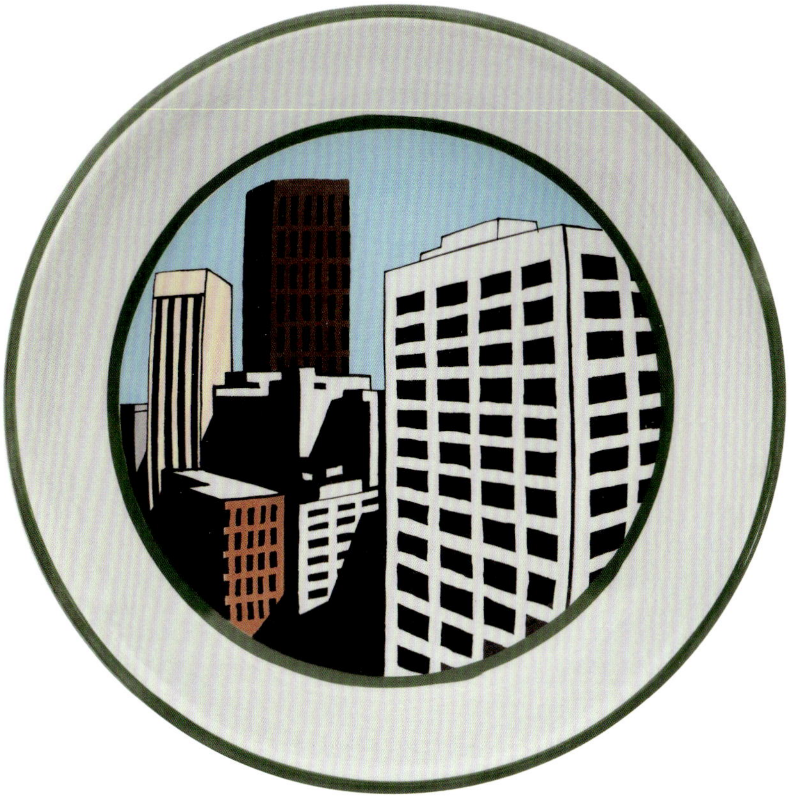

CLOCKWISE FROM TOP LEFT:
Untitled, 1993
Untitled, 1993
Untitled, 1991

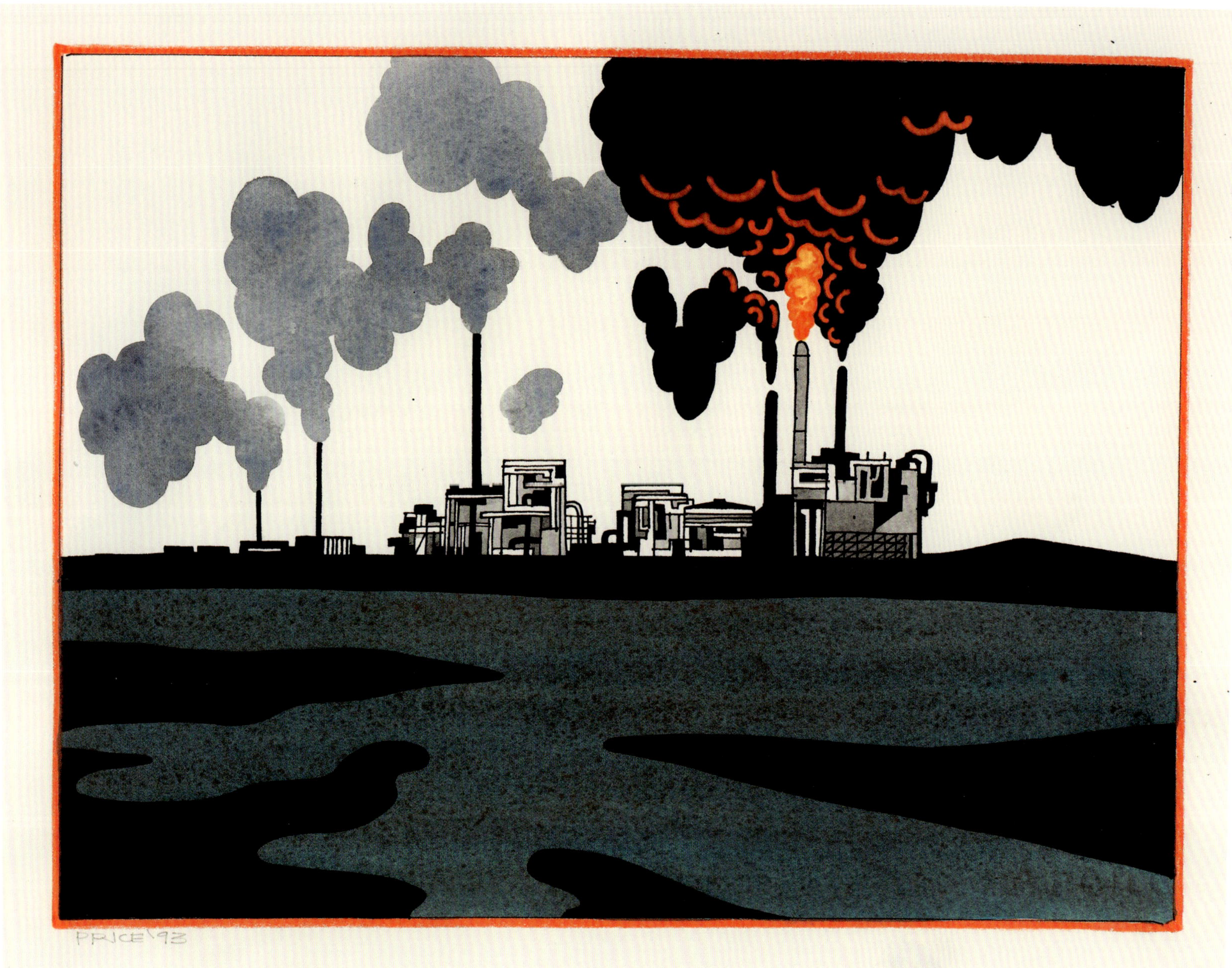

Untitled, 1993

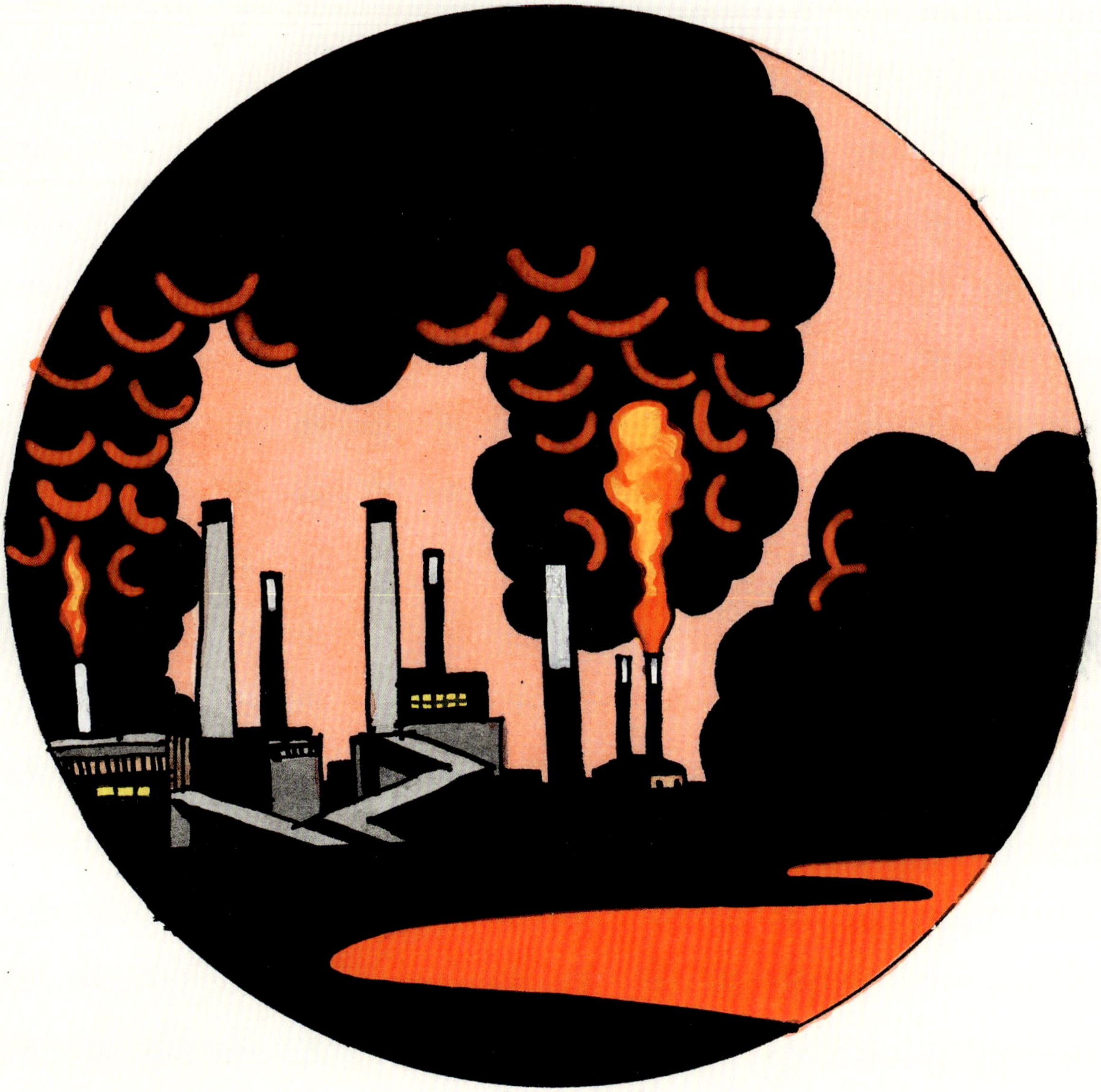

Untitled, 1993

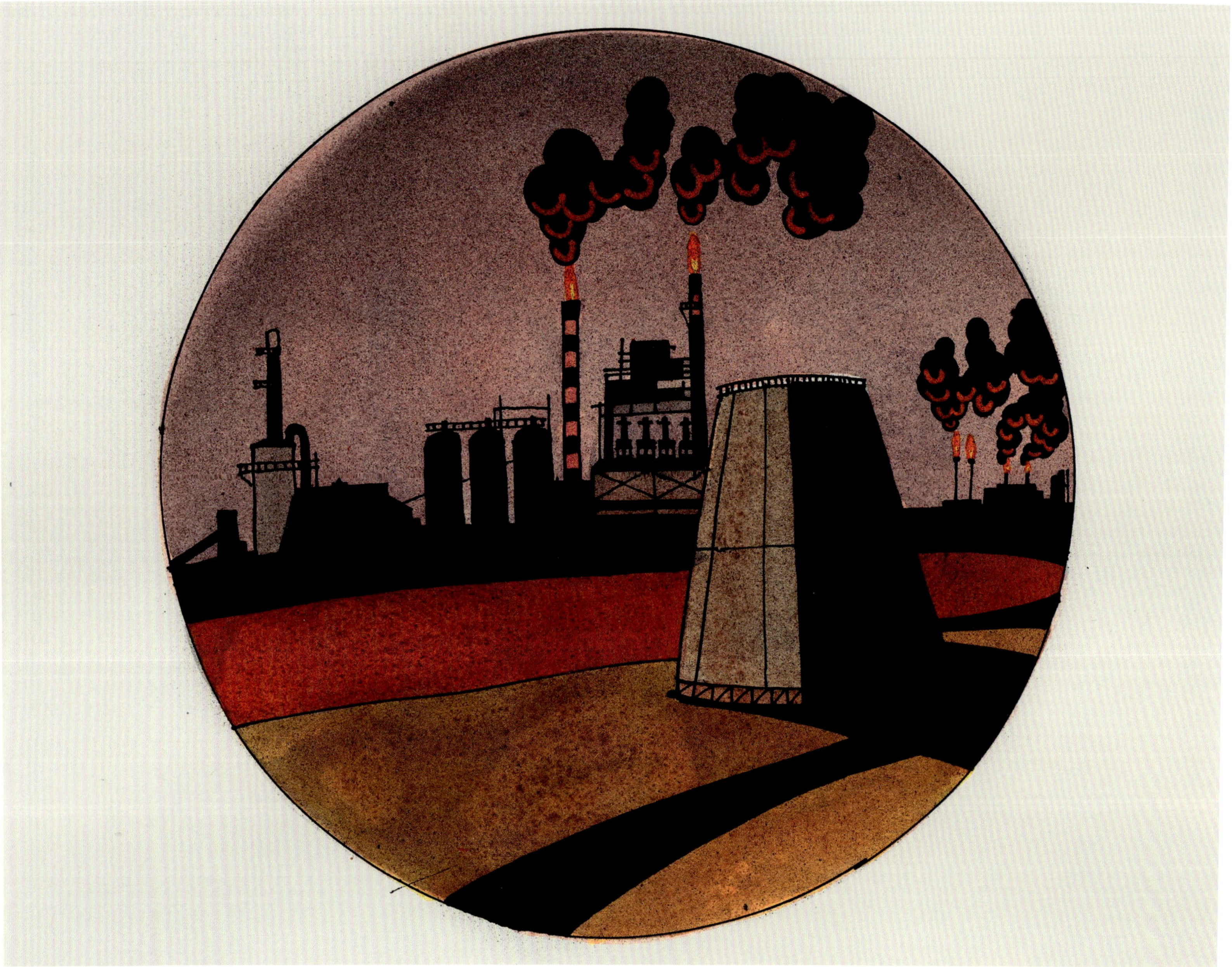

Untitled, 1993

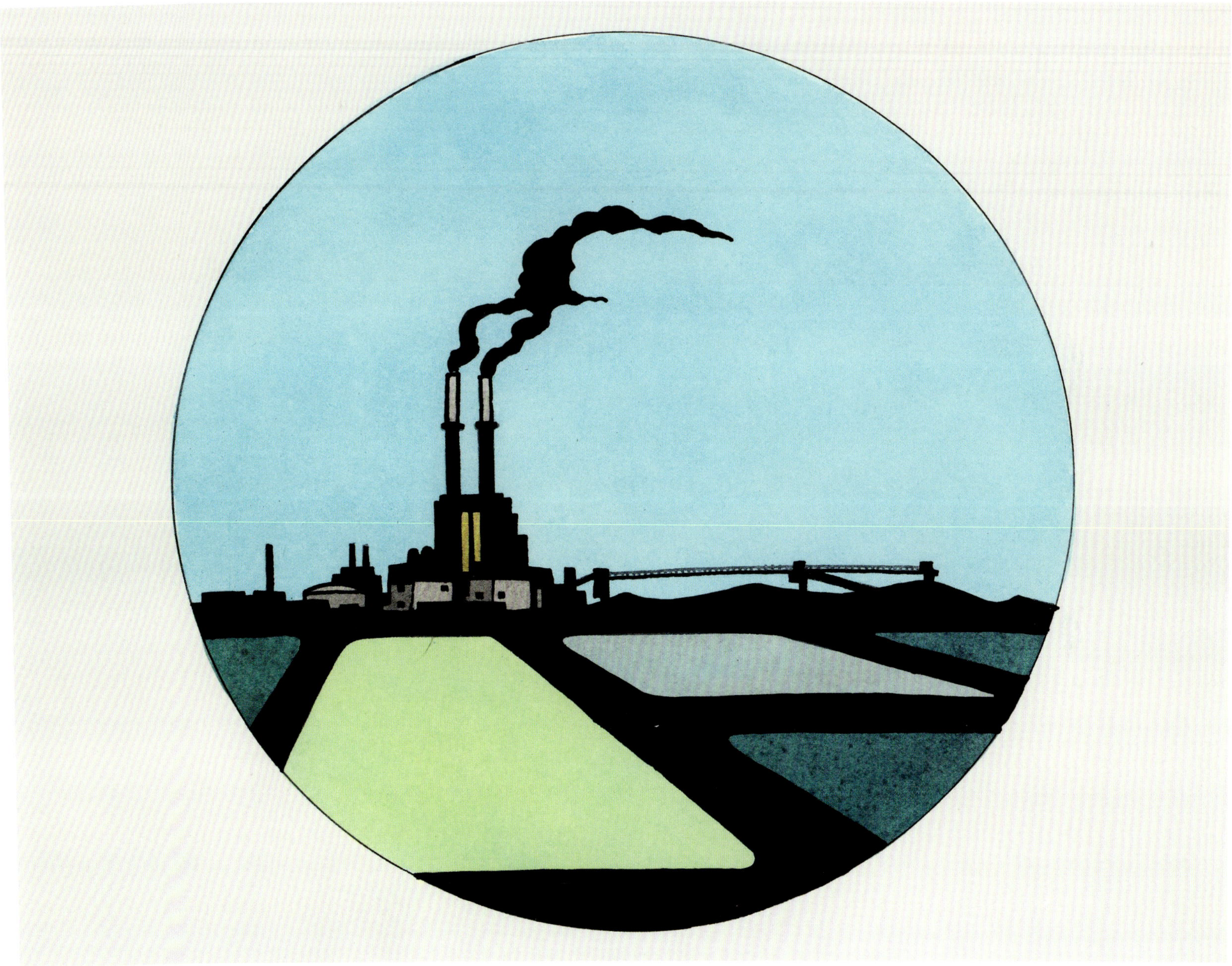

Untitled, 1993

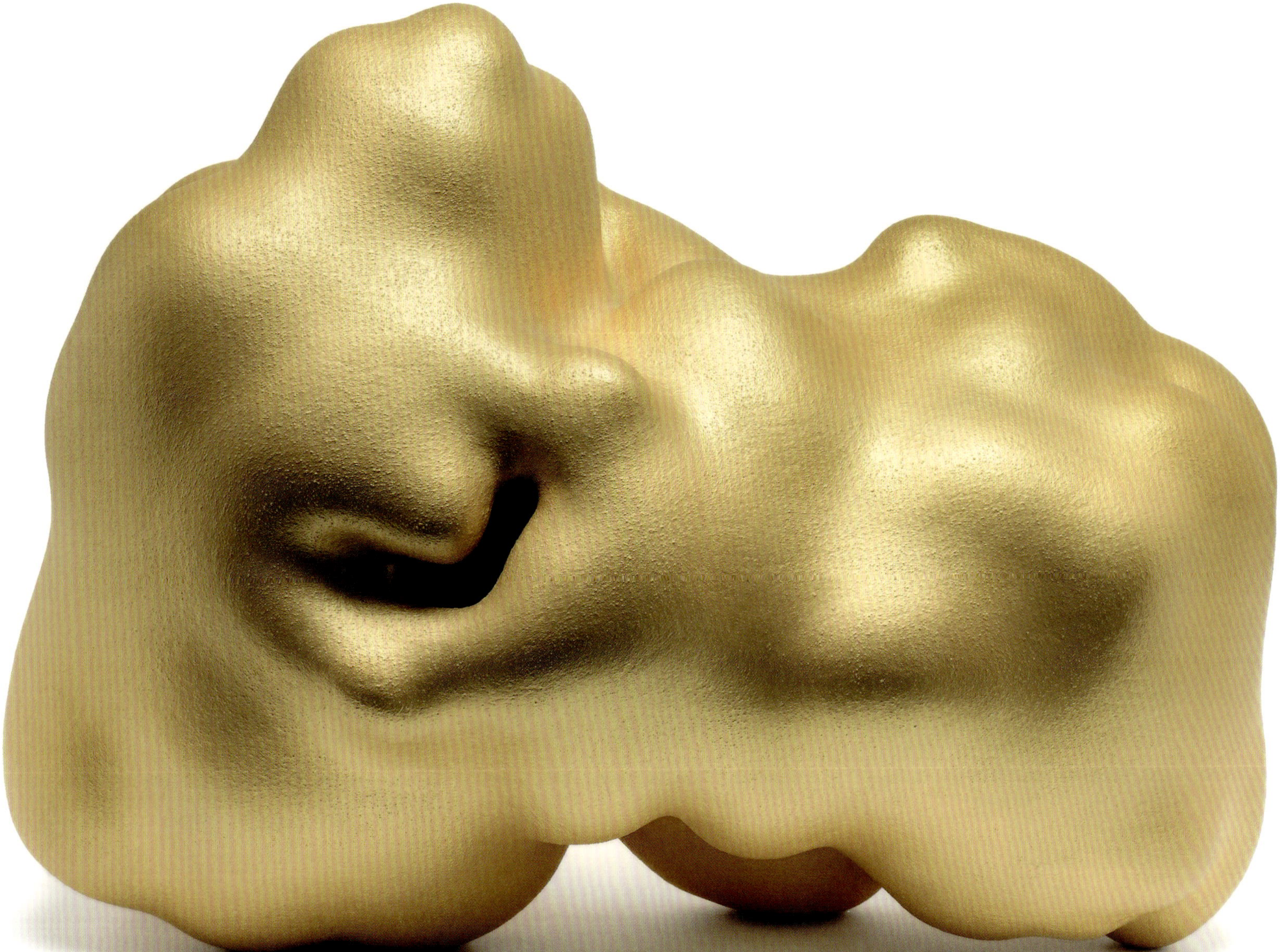

Bubbles, 1995

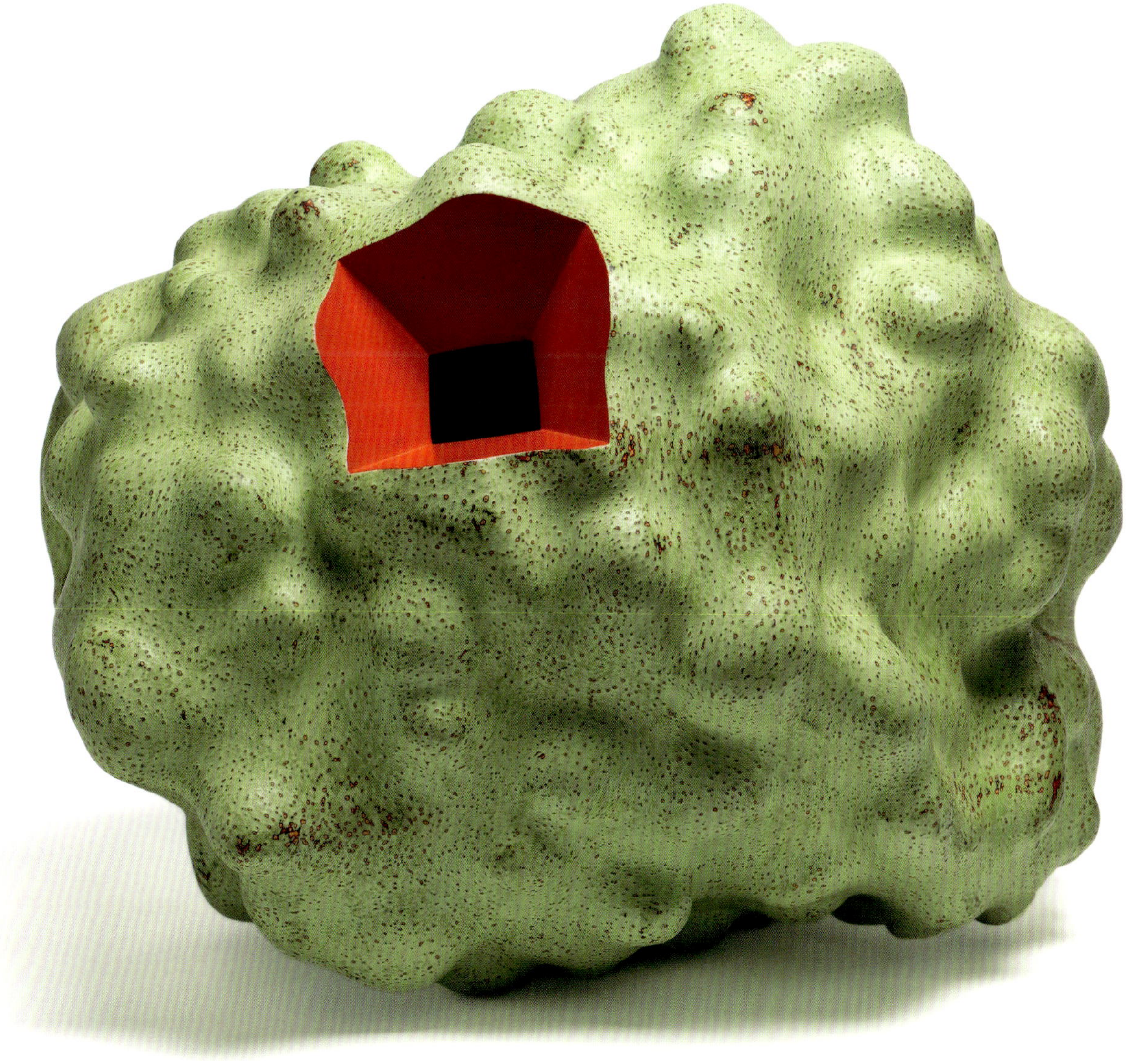

Pastel, 1995

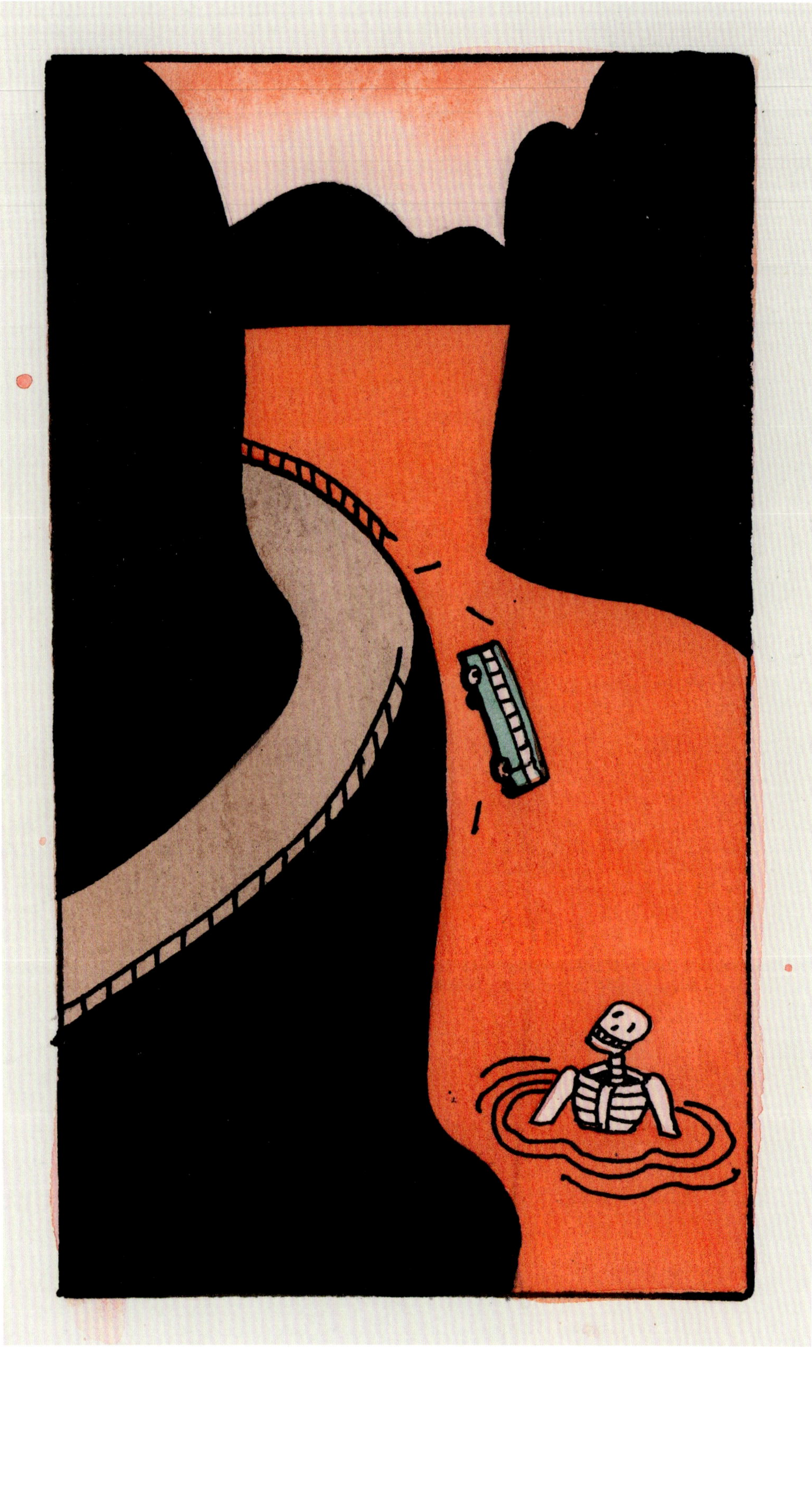

Untitled, 1997

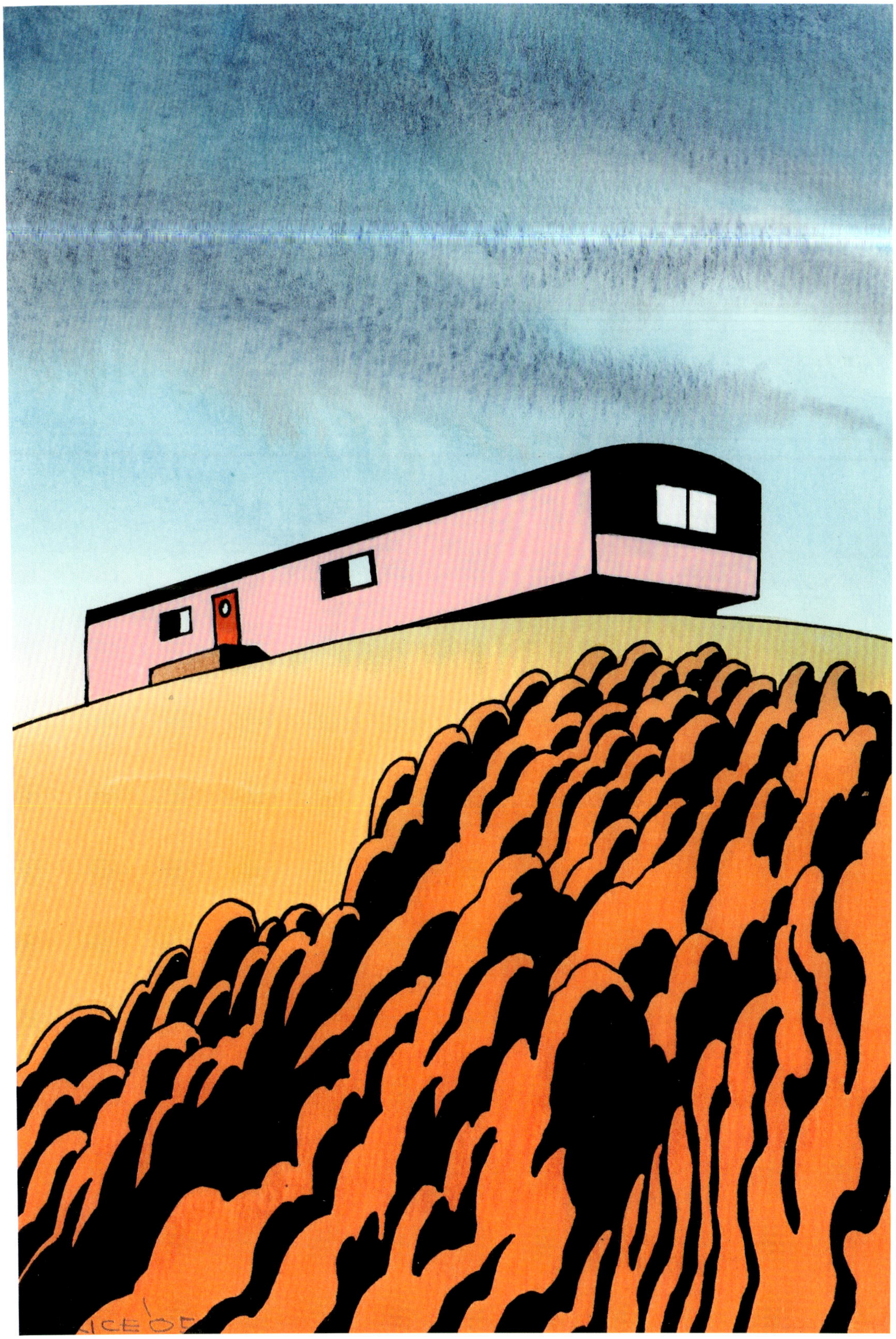

Raul's Trailer, 2005

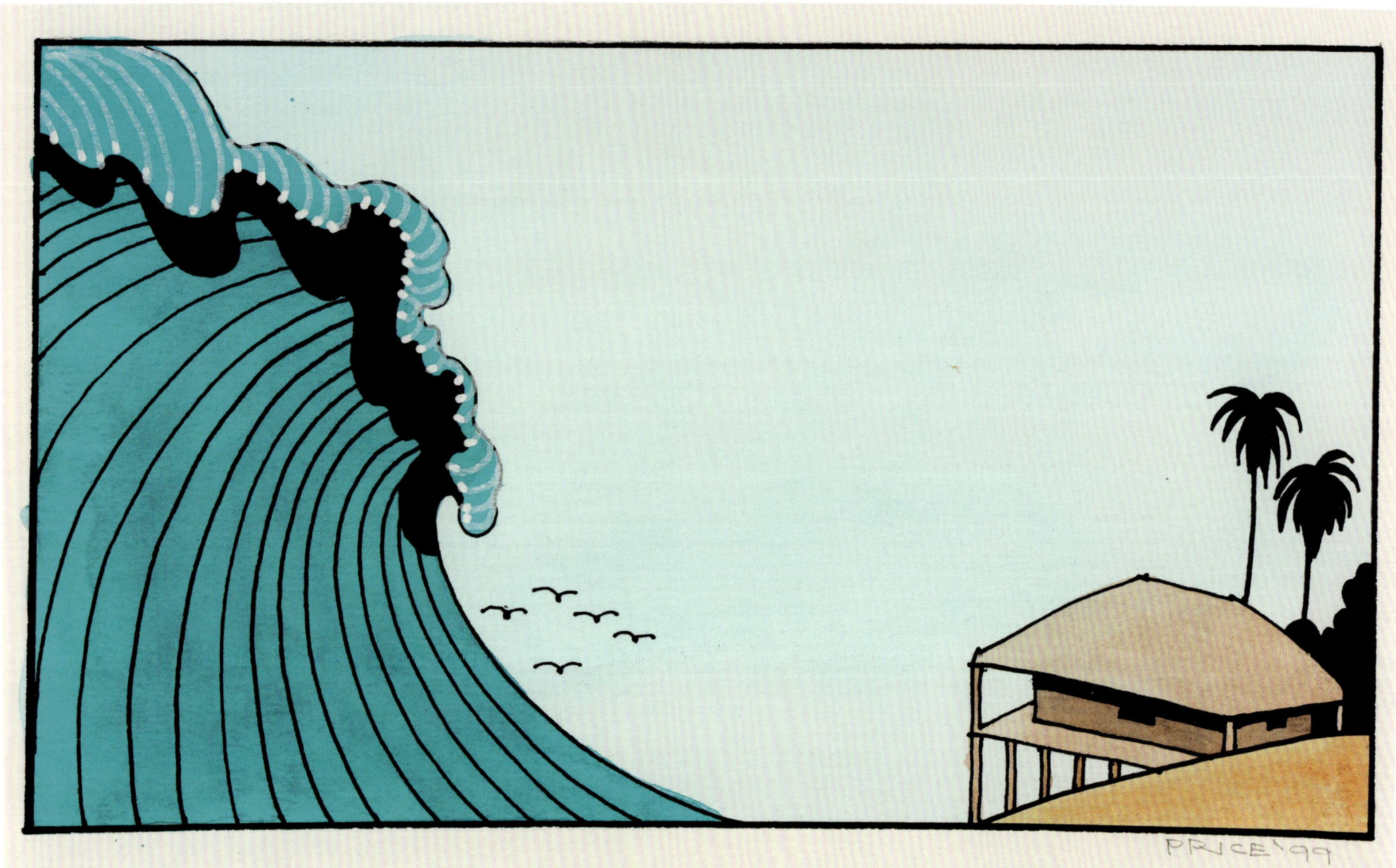

Untitled, 1999

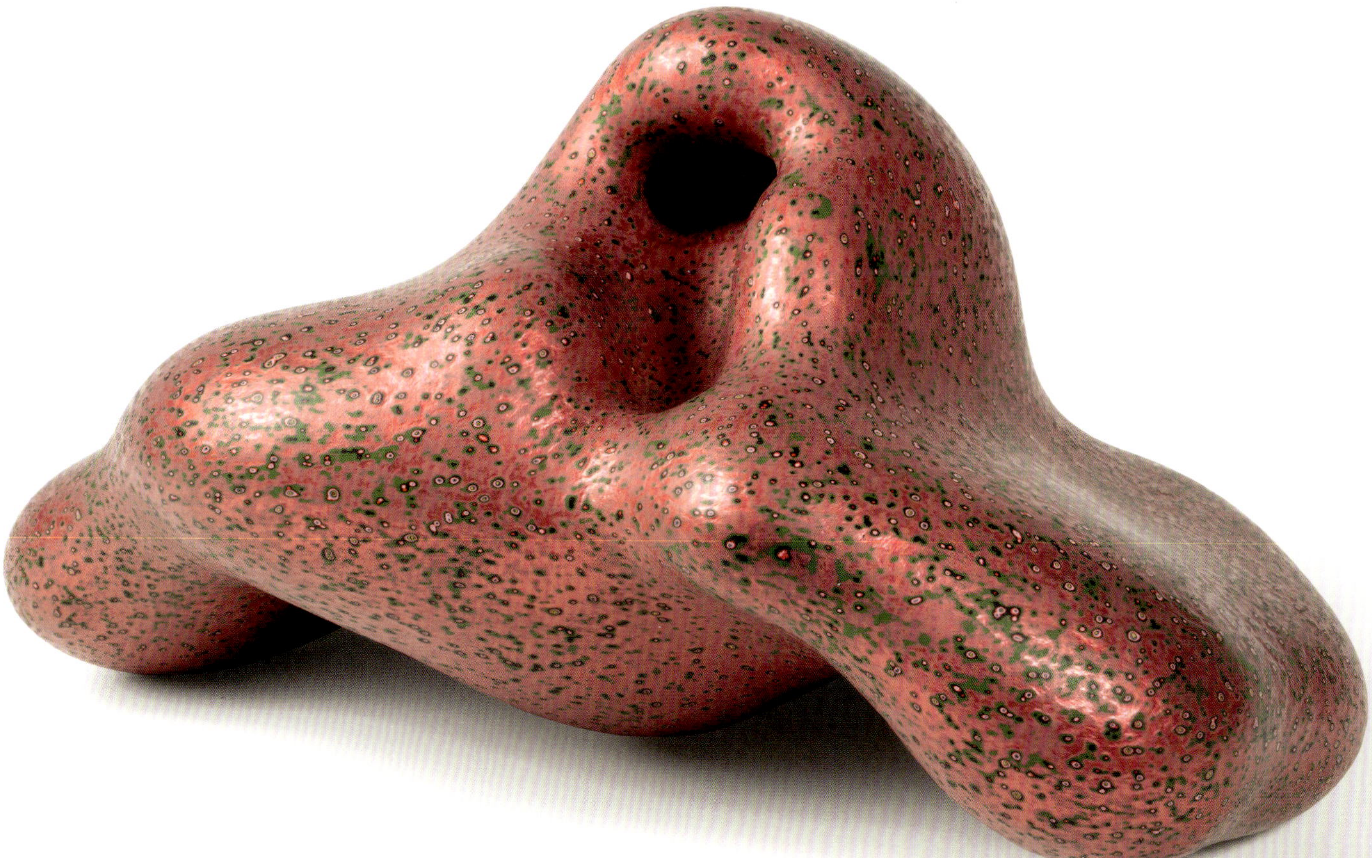

Humpback, 1998

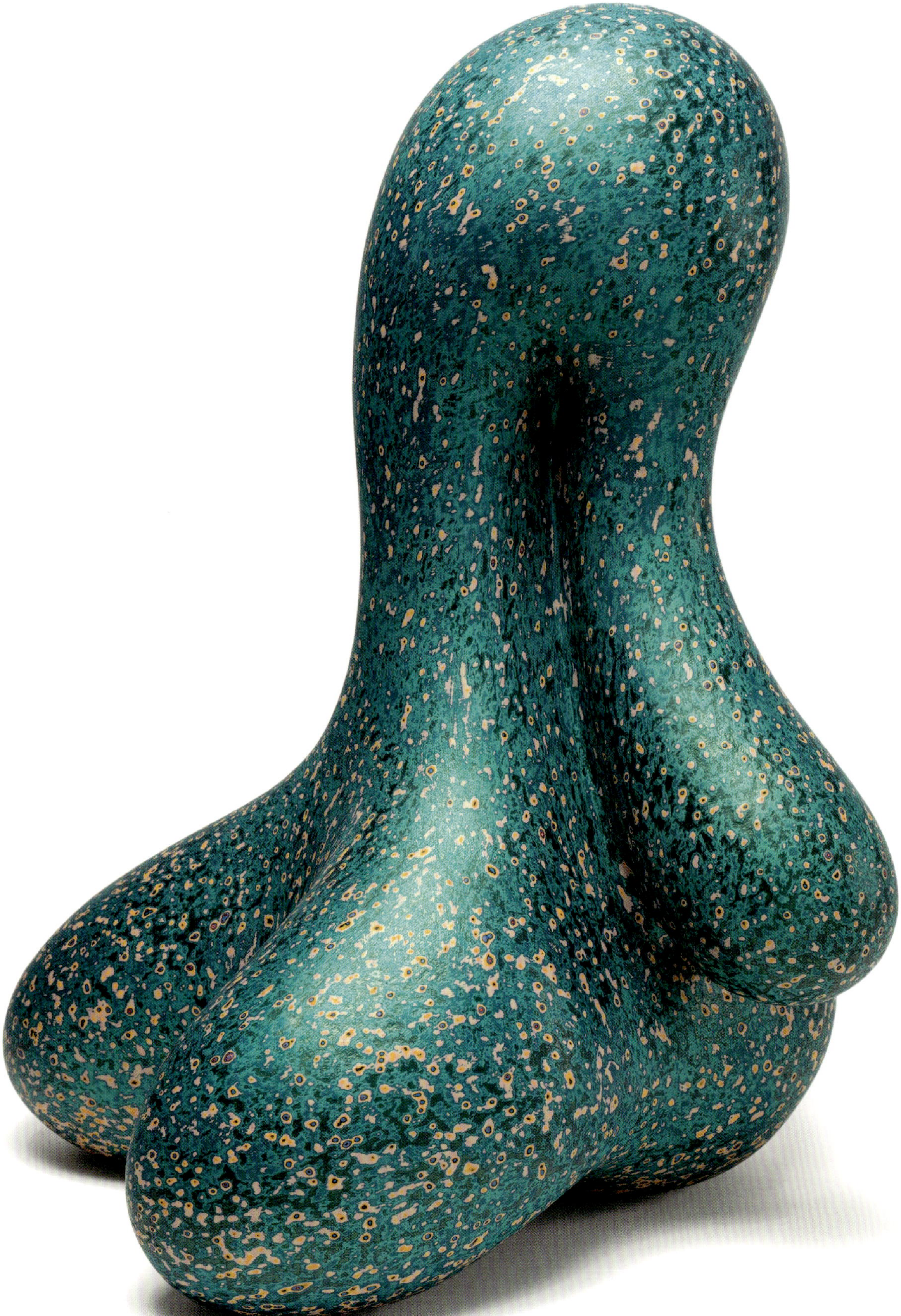

Kiki, 2003

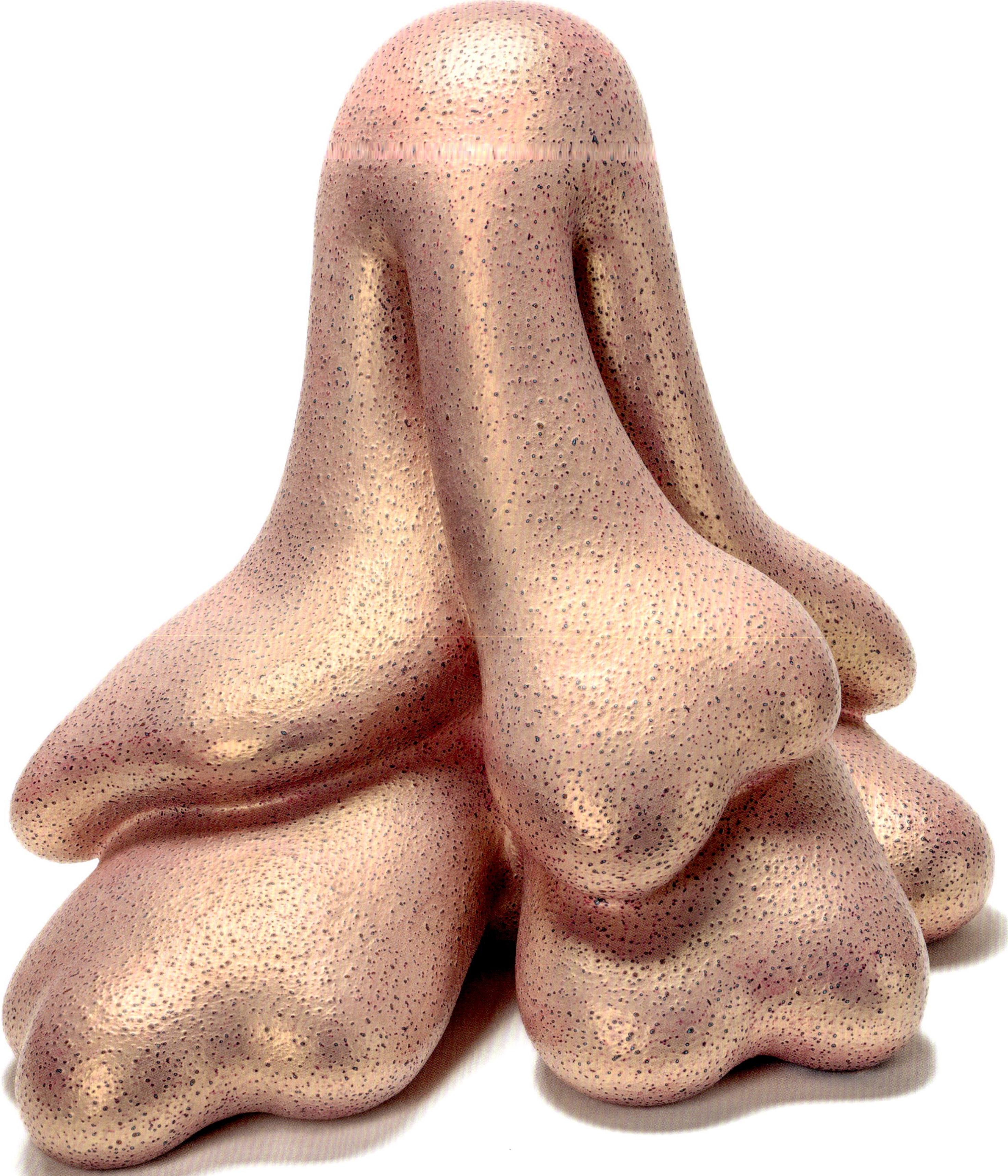

McLean, 2004

APPENDICES

LIST OF WORKS ILLUSTRATED

Dimensions are given in centimeters and inches, with height preceding width (and width preceding depth, if applicable). Works on paper with no dates ascribed to them were drawn after the depicted sculptures were made, and the inscribed dates refer to the dates of the sculptures.

Page 2
The Capri Apartments, 1994
Acrylic and ink on paper
38.4 × 31.1 cm (15⅛ × 12¼ in.)

Page 4
Downtown, 1994
Acrylic and ink on paper
38.1 × 27.9 cm (15 × 11 in.)

Page 5
TOP: *Before the Earthquake*, 1994
Acrylic and ink on paper
33 × 38.6 cm (13 × 15¼ in.)

BOTTOM: *L.A. Sky*, 1994
Acrylic and ink on paper
27.3 × 31.1 cm (10¾ × 12¼ in.)

Page 6
Looking East, 1994
Acrylic and ink on paper
38.1 × 31.1 cm (15 × 12¼ in.)

Page 7
Made in L.A., 1994
Acrylic and ink on paper
34.9 × 26.7 cm (13¾ × 10½ in.)

Page 8
Picture Window, 1994
Acrylic and ink on paper
38.4 × 31 cm (15⅛ × 12¼ in.)

Page 9
Room 308, 1994
Acrylic and ink on paper
36.7 × 26.7 cm (14½ × 10½ in.)

Page 10
Security, Domesticity, Leisure, 1994
Acrylic and ink on paper
35.9 × 29.2 cm (14⅛ × 11½ in.)

Page 11
With Everything Turned Off, 1994
Acrylic and ink on paper
38.1 × 30.8 cm (15 × 12⅛ in.)

Pages 25, 12 (detail)
Avocado Mountain, 1959
Glazed ceramic
61 × 53.3 × 53.3 cm
(24 × 21 × 21 in.)

Page 27
TOP LEFT: *Chevrolet Brothers*, 1960
Fired and painted clay, enclosed in wood box construction
Box 17.8 × 25.4 × 13.3 cm
(7 × 10 × 5¼ in.),
cup 7.5 × 12.7 × 7.5 cm
(3 × 5 × 3 in.)
Collection of Joan and Jack Quinn, Beverly Hills

BOTTOM LEFT: *Specimen*, 1963
Glazed clay, acrylic paint, wood, velvet, and string
Pedestal 20.3 × 35 × 35 cm
(8 × 13¾ × 10¾ in.),
ceramic 8.3 × 4.5 × 5 cm
(3¼ × 1¾ × 2 in.)
Smithsonian American Art Museum, Washington, D.C., Gift of an anonymous donor and museum purchase through the MCI Fund (1997.48)

RIGHT: *Astronauts in the Ocean*, 1960–61
Fired and painted clay, enclosed in wood box construction
Box 27.3 × 14 × 10 cm
(10¾ × 5½ × 4 in.),
ceramic 12.7 × 9.5 × 9.5 cm
(5 × 3¾ × 3¾ in.)
Laura-Lee W. Woods

Page 30
LEFT: *Untitled*, 1972–77
Glazed ceramic
27.9 × 16.5 × 16.5 cm
(11 × 6½ × 6½ in.)

RIGHT: *Untitled*, 1972–77
Glazed ceramic
29.2 × 15.2 × 15.2 cm
(11½ × 6 × 6 in.)

Page 32
Wart Nose, 1969
Ink on paper
15.2 × 11.4 cm (6 × 4½ in.)

Page 33
Sea Turtle Cup, 1969
Graphite on paper
34.9 × 27.3 cm (13¾ × 10¾ in.)

Page 34
Von Bayros Snail Cups, 1968
Graphite on paper
40.6 × 31.8 cm (16 × 12½ in.)

Page 36
From Happy's Curios, 1973
Poster paint on paper
83.8 × 71.1 cm (33 × 28 in.)

Page 37
Unit 6, from *Happy's Curios*, 1972–78
Ceramic with acrylic paint (6 vases); height of vases 19.1–24.1 cm (7½–9½ in.),
cabinet 254 × 243.8 × 71.1 cm
(100 × 96 × 28 in.)
Kayne Griffin Corcoran

Page 38
Untitled, 1972–77
Tempera on paper
31.8 × 24.1 cm (12½ × 9½ in.)

Page 39
Untitled, 1980
Watercolor and ink on paper
24.1 × 15.2 cm (9½ × 6 in.)

Page 40
Untitled, 1993
Watercolor and ink on paper
20.3 × 20.3 cm (8 × 8 in.)

Page 41
1914, 1983
Fired and painted clay
42 × 43.2 × 20.3 cm
(16½ × 17½ × 8 in.)
Collection of Emily Fisher Landau, New York

Page 42
TOP: *Chinese Block*, 1984
Fired and painted clay
11.4 × 11.4 × 12.7 cm
(4½ × 4½ × 5 in.)
Happy Price

BOTTOM: *Mungor*, 1985
Fired and painted clay
Two parts: 19.8 × 19 × 18 cm
(7¾ × 7½ × 7 in.), 18.2 × 16 × 13.5 cm (7¼ × 6¼ × 5¼ in.)
Stedelijk Museum 's-Hertogenbosch

Page 43
Ultra-Purple, 1987
Fired and painted clay
58.4 × 27.9 × 38.1 cm
(23 × 11 × 15 in.)

Page 44
Phobia, 1995
Fired and painted clay
43.2 × 58.4 × 47 cm
(17 × 23 × 18½ in.)
The Museum of Modern Art, New York, Gift of Edward R. Broida (756.2005)

Page 45
Not from Yesterday, 2006
Fired and painted clay
14 × 21.6 × 17.8 cm
(5½ × 8½ × 7 in.)

Page 50
LEFT: *Untitled*, 1960
Glazed ceramic
29.2 × 25.4 × 25.4 cm
(11½ × 10 × 10 in.)

RIGHT: *Untitled Jar*, no date
Ink on paper
30.5 × 22.9 cm (12 × 9 in.)

Page 51
TOP LEFT: *Untitled Cup*, no date
Ink on paper
30.5 × 22.9 cm (12 × 9 in.)

TOP CENTER: *Lizard Cup*, no date
Ink on paper
30.5 × 22.9 cm (12 × 9 in.)

TOP RIGHT: *Pressed Cup*, no date
Ink on paper
30.5 × 22.9 cm (12 × 9 in.)

BOTTOM: *Frog Cup*, 1967
Colored pencil on paper
34.3 × 26.7 cm (13½ × 10½ in.)

Page 52
TOP LEFT: *Lid Tips to the Left*, no date
Ink on paper
30.5 × 22.9 cm (12 × 9 in.)

TOP RIGHT: *Upside Down "V" Jar*, no date
Ink on paper
30.5 × 22.9 cm (12 × 9 in.)

BOTTOM: *Upside Down "V" Cup*, no date
Ink on paper
30.5 × 22.9 cm (12 × 9 in.)

Page 53
Untitled, c. 1962
Glazed and painted ceramic
15.2 × 12.1 × 12.1 cm
(6 × 4¾ × 4¾ in.)

Page 54
Untitled, 1967
Graphite on paper, mounted on board
35.6 × 27.9 cm (14 × 11 in.)

Page 55
TOP LEFT: *Electric Cup*, c. 1966
Glazed ceramic
7.8 × 15.2 × 8.3 cm
(3⅛ × 6 × 3¼ in.)

TOP RIGHT: *Untitled*, 1968
Glazed ceramic
7.9 × 11.4 × 8.3 cm
(3⅛ × 4½ × 3¼ in.)

BOTTOM: *Twisted Twig Cup*, 1966
Glazed ceramic
8.3 × 13.3 × 8.3 cm
(3¼ × 5¼ × 3¼ in.)

Page 56
LEFT: *Untitled*, 1965
Glazed ceramic
7.6 × 8.9 × 10.8 cm
(3 × 3½ × 4¼ in.)

RIGHT: *Untitled*, 1976
Glazed ceramic
7 × 6.4 × 6.4 cm
(2¾ × 2½ × 2½ in.)

Page 57
TOP LEFT: *Untitled*, c. 1966
Glazed ceramic
7.3 × 12.7 × 7 cm
(2⅞ × 5 × 2¾ in.)

TOP RIGHT: *Untitled*, 1960
Glazed ceramic
7.3 × 10.8 × 7.9 cm
(2⅞ × 4¼ × 3⅛ in.)

BOTTOM LEFT: *Untitled*, 1964
Glazed ceramic
7.6 × 10.2 × 12.1 cm
(3 × 4 × 4¾ in.)

BOTTOM RIGHT: *Untitled*, 1976
Glazed ceramic
8.3 × 6.4 × 6.4 cm
(3½ × 2½ × 2½ in.)

Page 58
TOP: *Reflecting Bump*, 1967
Watercolor, colored pencil, and ink on paper
37.1 × 35.6 cm (14⅝ × 14 in.)

BOTTOM: *Reflecting Bump*, 1967
Watercolor, colored pencil, and ink on paper
34.9 × 31.8 cm (13¾ × 12½ in.)

Page 59
TOP: *Untitled*, 1967
Colored pencil on paper
22.2 × 27.9 cm (8¾ × 11 in.)

BOTTOM: *Untitled*, 1970
Ink on paper
27.9 × 35.6 cm (11 × 14 in.)

Page 60
TOP: *Two-Frog Cup*, 1968
Graphite on paper
40.6 × 30.5 cm (16 × 12 in.)

BOTTOM: *Round Snail Cup*, 1968
Glazed ceramic
8.3 × 12.7 × 8.9 cm
(3¼ × 5 × 3½ in.)

Page 61
Specimen, 1968
Colored pencil and crayon on paper
40.3 × 47.9 cm
(15⅞ × 18⅞ in.)

Page 62
Slab Handle, 1976
Graphite on paper
12.7 × 17.8 cm (5 × 7 in.)

Page 63
TOP: *Nose Cup—Late '30s*, 1969
Glazed ceramic
8.4 × 12.7 × 7.9 cm
(3¼ × 5 × 3⅛ in.)

BOTTOM: *Untitled*, 1968–69
Glazed ceramic
8.3 × 15.2 × 8.9 cm
(3¼ × 6 × 3½ in.)

Page 64
Study for Chinese Figurine Cup, 1969
Ink, acrylic, and colored pencil over screenprint and lithograph
55.9 × 45.7 cm (22 × 18 in.)

Page 65
Specimen G5228, 1971
Acrylic and ink on board
55.9 × 45.7 cm
(22 × 18 in.)

Page 66
TOP ROW, LEFT: *Untitled*, 1972–77
Glazed ceramic
8.3 × 9.5 × 9.5 cm
(3¼ × 3¾ × 3¾ in.)

TOP ROW, RIGHT: *Untitled*, 1972–77
Glazed ceramic
6.4 × 5.1 × 5.1 cm
(2½ × 2 × 2 in.)

SECOND ROW, LEFT: *Untitled*, 1976
Glazed ceramic
8.9 × 7 cm × 7 cm
(3½ × 2¾ × 2¾ in.)

SECOND ROW, RIGHT: *Untitled*, 1972–77
Glazed ceramic
5.7 × 7.6 × 7.6 cm
(2¼ × 3 × 3 in.)

THIRD ROW, LEFT: *Untitled*, 1972–77
Glazed ceramic
8.3 × 9.5 × 9.5 cm
(3¼ × 3¾ × 3¾ in.)

THIRD ROW, RIGHT: *Untitled*, 1972–77
Glazed ceramic
7 × 5.1 × 5.1 cm (2¾ × 2 × 2 in.)

BOTTOM ROW, LEFT: *Untitled*, 1976
Glazed ceramic
6.4 × 7 × 7 cm
(2½ × 2¾ × 2¾ in.)

BOTTOM ROW, RIGHT: *Untitled*, 1982
Glazed ceramic
7.6 × 6.4 × 6.4 cm
(3 × 2½ × 2½ in.)

Page 67
Untitled No. 312, 1972–77
Glazed ceramic
50.8 × 48.3 × 27.9 cm
(20 × 19 × 11 in.)

Page 68
Kemper Clay Bun, 1972
Acrylic, watercolor, graphite, and colored pencil on paper, mounted on board
35.6 × 27.9 cm (14 × 11 in.)

Page 69
Untitled #7, 1974
Glazed ceramic
Two parts: 10.2 × 16.5 × 14 cm (4 × 6½ × 5½ in.), 12.7 × 7.9 × 8.9 cm (5 × 3⅛ × 3½ in.)

Page 70
LEFT: *Untitled*, c. 1980
Glazed ceramic
29.8 × 18.4 × 2.5 cm
(11¾ × 7¼ × 1 in.)

RIGHT: *Untitled*, c. 1980
Glazed ceramic
29.8 × 18.4 × 2.5 cm
(11¾ × 7¼ × 1 in.)

Page 71
Untitled, 1972–77
Glazed ceramic
29.2 × 18.4 × 2.5 cm
(11½ × 7¼ × 1 in.)

Page 72
Carmen, 1974
Gouache, watercolor, and graphite on paper
27.9 × 21.6 cm (11 × 8½ in.)

Page 73
Untitled, 1974
Gouache and graphite on paper
18.4 × 26.7 cm (7¼ × 10½ in.)

Page 74
LEFT: *Untitled*, 1978
Watercolor, colored pencil, and graphite on paper, mounted on board
35.6 × 27.9 cm (14 × 11 in.)

RIGHT: *Untitled*, 1978
Graphite on paper, mounted on board
39.4 × 31.8 cm (15½ × 12½ in.)

Page 75
Untitled, 1978
Graphite on paper
45.7 × 35.6 cm (18 × 14 in.)

Page 76
Untitled, 1978
Watercolor, colored pencil, and graphite on paper
15.2 × 20.3 cm (6 × 8 in.)

Page 77
TOP LEFT: *Untitled*, 1972–77
Glazed ceramic
13.3 × 9.5 × 9.5 cm
(5¼ × 3¾ × 3¾ in.)

BOTTOM LEFT: *Untitled*, 1978
Glazed ceramic
6.4 × 5.1 × 5.1 cm
(2½ × 2 × 2 in.)

RIGHT: *Untitled*, 1972–77
Glazed ceramic
13 × 7.6 × 0.6 cm
(5⅛ × 3 × ¼ in.)

Page 78
Untitled, 1979
Watercolor and colored pencil on paper, mounted on board
27.9 × 21.6 cm (11 × 8½ in.)

Page 79
Untitled, 1980
Watercolor, colored pencil, and ink on paper
27.9 × 21.6 cm (11 × 8½ in.)

Page 80
TOP: *Untitled*, 1980
Watercolor, ink, and graphite on paper
10.2 × 21.6 cm (4 × 8½ in.)

BOTTOM: *Untitled*, 1979
Graphite on paper
27.9 × 35.6 cm (11 × 14 in.)

Page 81
LEFT: *Untitled*, 1980
Watercolor and ink on paper
24.1 × 15.2 cm (9½ × 6 in.)

RIGHT: *Untitled*, 1980
Watercolor, colored pencil, and ink on paper
24.1 × 15.2 cm (9½ × 6 in.)

Page 82
Untitled, 1981
Watercolor, ink, and graphite on paper
27.9 × 21.6 cm (11 × 8½ in.)

Page 83
TOP: *Nonquitt Cove/Nonquitt Rocks*, 1981
Graphite on paper
25.4 × 40.6 cm (10 × 16 in.)

BOTTOM LEFT: *Rock at Nonquitt*, 1981
Gouache, colored pencil, and graphite on paper
21.6 × 17.8 cm (8½ × 7 in.)

BOTTOM RIGHT: *Untitled*, 1980
Ink on paper, mounted on board
20.6 × 14.6 cm (8⅛ × 5¾ in.)

Page 84
Untitled, 1981
Colored pencil, graphite, and ink on paper
20.3 × 25.4 cm (8 × 10 in.)

Page 85
TOP: *Saucers Fighting*, 1981
Watercolor, colored pencil, and ink on paper
33 × 45.7 cm (13 × 18 in.)

BOTTOM: *Unreported Sighting*, 1981
Watercolor, colored pencil, and ink on paper
33 × 45.7 cm (13 × 18 in.)

Page 86
LEFT: *Untitled*, 1986
Ink on paper
35.6 × 27.9 cm (14 × 11 in.)

TOP RIGHT: *Untitled*, 1989
Ink on paper
21 × 24.1 cm (8¼ × 9½ in.)

CENTER RIGHT: *Untitled*, 1989
Ink on paper
13.7 × 17.8 cm (5⅜ × 7 in.)

BOTTOM RIGHT: *Decor for Vase*, 1984
Ink on paper
12.7 × 17.1 cm (5 × 6¾ in.)

Page 87
TOP: *Lorna Stunned*, 1981
Watercolor, colored pencil, and ink on paper
35.6 × 27.9 cm (14 × 11 in.)

BOTTOM: *Lorna Diving*, 1981
Watercolor, colored pencil, and ink on paper
27.9 × 35.6 cm (11 × 14 in.)

Page 88
TOP LEFT: *Untitled*, 1982
Glazed ceramic
8.3 × 6.7 × 6.7 cm
(3¼ × 2⅝ × 2⅝ in.)

TOP RIGHT: *Untitled*, 1982
Glazed ceramic
7.6 × 6.4 × 6.4 cm
(3 × 2½ × 2½ in.)

BOTTOM LEFT: *Untitled*, 1982
Glazed ceramic
7.6 × 6.4 × 6.4 cm (3 × 2½ × 2½ in.)

BOTTOM RIGHT: *Untitled*, 1982
Glazed ceramic
7.6 × 6.4 × 5.7 cm
(3 × 2½ × 2¼ in.)

Page 89
TOP LEFT: *Untitled*, 1972–77
Glazed ceramic
7.6 × 7 × 7 cm
(3 × 2¾ × 2¾ in.)

TOP RIGHT: *Untitled*, 1972–77
Glazed ceramic
8.9 × 6.4 × 6.4 cm
(3½ × 2½ × 2½ in.)

BOTTOM LEFT: *Untitled*, 1972–77
Glazed ceramic
7 × 7 × 7 cm
(2¾ × 2¾ × 2¾ in.)

BOTTOM RIGHT: *Untitled*, 1972–77
Glazed ceramic
7 × 7 × 7 cm
(2¾ × 2¾ × 2¾ in.)

Page 90
Untitled, 1983
Ink on paper
27.9 × 21.6 cm (11 × 8½ in.)

Page 91
TOP: *Padanaram*, 1983
Fired and painted clay
9 × 14 × 8 cm
(3½ × 5½ × 3⅛ in.)

BOTTOM: *Untitled*, 1983
Fired and painted clay
8.9 × 12.7 × 7.6 cm
(3½ × 5 × 3 in.)

Page 92
Untitled, 1980
Watercolor and ink on paper
17.1 × 14.6 cm (6¾ × 5¾ in.)

Page 93
Untitled, 1986
Ink on paper
21.6 × 27.9 cm (8½ × 11 in.)

Page 94
LEFT: *Untitled*, 1986
Ink on paper
21.6 × 16.8 cm (8½ × 6⅝ in.)

Page 94
RIGHT: *Untitled*, 1986
Watercolor, graphite, and colored pencil on paper, mounted on board
15.9 × 14.6 cm (6¼ × 5¾ in.)

Page 95
Untitled, 1986
Watercolor and ink on paper
17.8 × 21.6 cm (7 × 8½ in.)

Page 96
TOP: *Untitled*, 1987
Watercolor, colored pencil, ink, and pastel on paper
22.9 × 30.5 cm (9 × 12 in.)

BOTTOM: *Untitled*, 1986
Watercolor, graphite, and ink on paper
15.2 × 19.1 cm (6 × 7½ in.)

Page 97
TOP LEFT: *Variant*, no date
Ink on paper
30.5 × 22.9 cm (12 × 9 in.)

TOP RIGHT: *Minos*, no date
Ink on paper
30.5 × 22.9 cm (12 × 9 in.)

BOTTOM: *Breech*, no date
Ink on paper
30.5 × 22.9 cm (12 × 9 in.)

Page 98
TOP: *Untitled*, 1987
Watercolor, colored pencil, and ink on paper
21.6 × 27.9 cm (8½ × 11 in.)

BOTTOM: *Untitled*, 1987
Watercolor, colored pencil, and ink on paper
11.7 × 19.7 cm (4⅝ × 7¾ in.)

Page 99
Untitled, 1987
Watercolor, colored pencil, and ink on paper
30.5 × 22.9 cm (12 × 9 in.)

Page 100
Untitled, 1987
Watercolor, colored pencil, and ink on paper
27.9 × 21.6 cm (11 × 8½ in.)

Page 101
Untitled, 1987
Watercolor and ink on paper
22.9 × 30.5 cm (9 × 12 in.)

Page 102
TOP: *Untitled*, 1988
Watercolor, colored pencil, graphite, and ink on paper
21.6 × 27.9 cm (8½ × 11 in.)

BOTTOM: *Untitled*, 1988
Ink on paper
15.2 × 21.6 cm (6 × 8½ in.)

Page 103
Untitled, 1988
Watercolor, colored pencil, and ink on paper
27.9 × 21.6 cm (11 × 8½ in.)

Page 104
TOP: *Untitled*, 1988
Watercolor and ink on paper
21.6 × 27.9 cm (8½ × 11 in.)

BOTTOM: *Untitled*, 1988
Watercolor, colored pencil, and ink on paper
27.9 × 21.6 cm (11 × 8½ in.)

Page 105
LEFT: *Untitled*, 1988
Watercolor and ink on paper
27.9 × 21.6 cm (11 × 8½ in.)

RIGHT: *Untitled*, 1988
Watercolor and ink on paper
27.9 × 20.3 cm (11 × 8 in.)

Page 106
The Lug, 1988
Fired and painted clay
22.9 × 30.5 × 21.6 cm
(9 × 12 × 8½ in.)

Pages 107, 16 (detail)
Ghosted, 1998
Fired and painted clay
44.5 × 41.9 × 25.4 cm
(17½ × 16½ × 10 in.)

Page 108
TOP: *Untitled*, 1989
Watercolor, colored pencil, and ink on paper
27.9 × 21.6 cm (11 × 8½ in.)

BOTTOM: *Untitled*, 1989
Watercolor, colored pencil, and ink on paper
19.1 × 24.1 cm (7½ × 9½ in.)

Page 109
Color Sample, 1989
Fired and painted clay
22.9 × 33 × 21.6 cm
(9 × 13 × 8½ in.)

Page 110
Untitled, c. 1990
Fired and painted clay
7 × 8.3 × 7.6 cm
(2¾ × 3¼ × 3 in.)

Page 111
TOP: *Untitled*, 1990
Watercolor and ink on paper
57.2 × 76.2 cm (22½ × 30 in.)

BOTTOM: *Untitled*, 1990
Watercolor and ink on paper
57.2 × 71.1 cm (22½ × 28 in.)

Page 112
TOP LEFT: *Untitled*, 1993
Glazed ceramic
8.9 × 8.3 × 8.3 cm
(3½ × 3¼ × 3¼ in.)

TOP RIGHT: *Untitled*, 1993
Glazed ceramic
7.6 × 10.2 × 10.2 cm
(3 × 4 × 4 in.)

BOTTOM: *Untitled*, 1990
Watercolor and ink on paper
38.4 × 57.2 cm (15⅛ × 22½ in.)

Page 113
TOP: *Untitled*, 1990
Watercolor and ink on paper
31.4 × 40.6 cm (12 3/8 × 16 in.)

BOTTOM: *Untitled*, 1990
Ink on paper
29.2 × 38.7 cm (11½ × 15¼ in.)

Page 114
TOP: *Untitled*, 1990
Watercolor and ink on paper
12.7 × 21.6 cm (5 × 8½ in.)

BOTTOM: *Untitled*, 1991
Watercolor and ink on paper
52.1 × 66 cm (20½ × 26 in.)

Page 115
Untitled, 1991
Watercolor, colored pencil, and ink on paper
64.8 × 93.3 cm (25½ × 36¾ in.)

Page 116
TOP LEFT: *Untitled*, 1972–77
Glazed ceramic
4.6 × 4.4 × 6.5 cm
(1⅞ × 1¾ × 2½ in.)

TOP CENTER: *Untitled*, 1972–77
Glazed ceramic
5.1 × 4.4 × 6.7 cm
(2 × 1¾ × 2⅝ in.)

TOP RIGHT: *Untitled*, 1992
Glazed ceramic
4.8 × 4.4 × 4.4 cm
(1⅞ × 1¾ × 1¾ in.)

BOTTOM LEFT: *Untitled*, c. 1982
Glazed ceramic
7 × 5.1 × 5.1 cm (2¾ × 2 × 2 in.)

BOTTOM CENTER: *Untitled*, c. 1982
Glazed ceramic
7 × 5.1 × 5.1 cm
(2¾ × 2 × 2 in.)

BOTTOM RIGHT: *Untitled*, c. 1982
Glazed ceramic
7 × 5.7 × 5.7 cm
(2¾ × 2¼ × 2¼ in.)

Page 117
Untitled, c. 1993
Glazed ceramic, enclosed in wood box construction
Box 24.1 × 25.4 × 12.7 cm
(9½ × 10 × 5 in.)

Page 118
Untitled, 1993
Watercolor and ink on paper
29.2 × 37.8 cm
(11½ × 14⅞ in.)

Page 119
Untitled, 1993
Glazed ceramic
3.7 × 7.8 × 7.8 cm
(1½ × 3⅛ × 3⅛ in.)

Page 120
Untitled, 1993
Watercolor and ink on paper
28.6 × 38.7 cm (11¼ × 15¼ in.)

Page 121
TOP LEFT: *Untitled*, 1993
Glazed ceramic
3.5 × 7.3 × 7.3 cm
(1⅜ × 2⅞ × 2⅞ in.)

TOP RIGHT: *Untitled*, 1993
Glazed ceramic
5.1 × 14 × 14 cm
(2 × 5½ × 5½ in.)

BOTTOM LEFT: *Untitled*, 1993
Glazed ceramic
3.5 × 7 × 7 cm
(1⅜ × 2¾ × 2¾ in.)

BOTTOM RIGHT: *Untitled*, 1993
Glazed ceramic
3.8 × 7 × 7 cm
(1½ × 2¾ × 2¾ in.)

Page 122
TOP LEFT: *Untitled*, 1993
Glazed ceramic
3.8 × 12.7 × 12.7 cm
(1½ × 5 × 5 in.)

TOP RIGHT: *Untitled*, 1993
Glazed ceramic
5.4 × 14 × 14 cm
(2⅛ × 5½ × 5½ in.)

BOTTOM LEFT: *Untitled*, 1993
Glazed ceramic
5.1 × 12.1 × 12.1 cm
(2 × 4¾ × 4¾ in.)

BOTTOM RIGHT: *Untitled*, 1993
Glazed ceramic
5.4 × 16.2 × 16.2 cm
(2⅛ × 6⅜ × 6⅜ in.)

Page 123
TOP LEFT: *Untitled*, 1993
Glazed ceramic
3.2 × 9.8 × 9.8 cm
(1¼ × 3⅞ × 3⅞ in.)

TOP RIGHT: *Untitled*, 1993
Glazed ceramic
5.1 × 15.2 × 15.2 cm
(2 × 6 × 6 in.)

BOTTOM: *Untitled*, 1991
Glazed ceramic
5.4 × 23.2 × 23.2 cm
(2⅛ × 9⅛ × 9⅛ in.)

Page 124
Untitled, 1993
Watercolor and ink on paper
28.6 × 39.1 cm (11¼ × 15⅜ in.)

Page 125
Untitled, 1993
Watercolor and ink on paper
27.3 × 27.9 cm (10¾ × 11 in.)

Page 126
Untitled, 1993
Watercolor and ink on paper
27.9 × 30.5 cm (11 × 12 in.)

Page 127
Untitled, 1993
Watercolor and ink on paper
29.2 × 27.9 cm (11½ × 11 in.)

Page 128
Bubbles, 1995
Fired and painted clay
55.9 × 74.9 × 55.9 cm
(22 × 29½ × 22 in.)
Kayne Griffin Corcoran

Page 129
Pastel, 1995
Fired and painted clay
36.8 × 38.1 × 35.6 cm
(14½ × 15 × 14 in.)

Page 130
Untitled, 1997
Watercolor and ink on paper
17.1 × 10.2 cm (6¾ × 4 in.)

Page 131
Raul's Trailer, 2005
Watercolor and ink on paper
22.9 × 15.2 cm (9 × 6 in.)

Page 132
Untitled, 1999
Watercolor and ink on paper
15.2 × 22.9 cm (6 × 9 in.)

Page 133
Humpback, 1998
Fired and painted clay
30.5 × 37.5 × 19.7 cm
(12 × 14¾ × 7¾ in.)
Kayne Griffin Corcoran

Page 134
Kiki, 2003
Fired and painted clay
40 × 31.1 × 31.8 cm
(15¾ × 12¼ × 12½ in.)

Page 135
McLean, 2004
Fired and painted clay
49.5 × 58.4 × 48.3 cm
(19½ × 23 × 19 in.)

ABOUT THE ARTIST

KEN PRICE was born in Los Angeles, California, in 1935 and died in 2012 in Taos, New Mexico. He had his first solo exhibition at Ferus Gallery, Los Angeles, in 1960, and his work was included in the 1979 and 1981 Whitney Biennials in New York. The Walker Art Center, Minneapolis, and the Menil Collection, Houston, mounted his first retrospective exhibition in 1992. In 2012, the Los Angeles County Museum of Art (LACMA) presented the major exhibition *Ken Price Sculpture: A Retrospective*, which traveled to the Nasher Sculpture Center, Dallas, and the Metropolitan Museum of Art, New York. A survey exhibition of Price's works on paper was organized in 2013 by the Drawing Center, New York, and traveled to the Albright-Knox Art Gallery, Buffalo, and the Harwood Museum of Art, Taos. A comprehensive bibliography on Ken Price is included in LACMA's catalogue *Ken Price Sculpture: A Retrospective* (2012).

ABOUT THE AUTHORS

PAUL SCHIMMEL is a Vice President and Partner of Hauser & Wirth and a co-founder of Hauser Wirth & Schimmel in Los Angeles. From 1990 to 2012, he was Chief Curator of The Museum of Contemporary Art, Los Angeles (MOCA), and from 1981 to 1989, he was Chief Curator of the Orange County Museum of Art in Newport Beach, California. Exhibitions he has organized for Hauser & Wirth include *Re-View: Onnasch Collection*, *Revolution in the Making: Abstract Sculpture by Women, 1947–2016*, and *Philip Guston: Painter, 1957–1967*. He has also organized significant thematic exhibitions, including *Hand-Painted Pop: American Art in Transition, 1955–62*, *Out of Actions: Between Performance and the Object, 1949–1979*, and *Destroy the Picture: Painting the Void, 1949–1962*, as well as major one-person monographic exhibitions devoted to Chris Burden, Charles Ray, Sigmar Polke, Robert Gober, Willem de Kooning, Laura Owens, and Robert Rauschenberg.

SAM THORNE is the director of Nottingham Contemporary, a contributing editor of *frieze*, and a co-founder of Open School East in Hackney, London. His book *School: A Recent History of Self-Organised Art Education* (2016) is published by Sternberg Press.

Published to accompany the exhibition
Ken Price: A Survey of Sculptures and Drawings, 1959–2006
December 8, 2016–February 4, 2017
Hauser & Wirth London

Editor: Paul Schimmel
Editorial Coordination: Michaela Unterdörfer
Project Coordination: Melissa MacRobert
Assistance: Francis Till, Patricia Nam
Editing and Proofreading: Jennifer Bernstein, Tenacious Editorial
Design and Typography: Catherine Lorenz, booklab LA
Production Director: Karen Farquhar, DelMonico Books • Prestel

With thanks to Linda Lee Bukowski; Romy Colonius; Mary DelMonico; Elizabeth Hamilton; Kayne Griffin Corcoran; Tracy Lew, James Corcoran Gallery; Matthew Marks Gallery; and Happy Price

Published in 2017 by Hauser & Wirth Publishers and DelMonico Books • Prestel

PHOTOGRAPH CREDITS
All photography of works by Ken Price is by Fredrik Nilsen unless otherwise indicated.
p. 21: Happy Price; courtesy of the Ken Price Studio
p. 23: © Seymour Rosen SPACES—Saving and Preserving Arts and Cultural Environments
pp. 24, 29: 2016 © Museum Associates / LACMA. Licensed by Art Resource, NY
p. 42, bottom: © Peer van der Kruis

ISBN: 978-3-7913-5613-6
Printed and bound in Italy by Graphicom

Hauser & Wirth Publishers
Limmatstrasse 270
8005 Zurich

548 West 22nd Street
New York, NY 10011

www.hauserwirth.com

DelMonico Books, an imprint of Prestel Publishing, a member of Verlagsgruppe Random House GmbH

Prestel Verlag
Neumarkter Strasse 28
81673 Munich

Prestel Publishing Ltd.
14-17 Wells Street
London W1T 3PD

Prestel Publishing
900 Broadway, Suite 603
New York, NY 10003

www.prestel.com

Library of Congress Cataloging-in-Publication Data

Names: Schimmel, Paul, editor. | Hauser & Wirth London, organizer, host institution.
Title: Ken Price : a survey of sculptures and drawings / edited by Paul Schimmel.
Description: New York : DelMonico Books/Prestel, 2017. | "Published to accompany the exhibition Ken Price: A Survey of Sculptures and Drawings, 1959–2006, December 8, 2016–February 4, 2017, Hauser & Wirth London." |
Includes bibliographical references.
Identifiers: LCCN 2016045024 | ISBN 9783791356136 (hardcover)
Subjects: LCSH: Price, Kenneth, 1935–2012—Exhibitions.
Classification: LCC N6537.P685 A4 2017 | DDC 700.92—dc23
LC record available at https://lccn.loc.gov/2016045024

A CIP catalogue record for this book is available from the British Library.